D1499969

CRIME AND MARKETS
Essays in Anti-criminology

CLARENDON STUDIES IN CRIMINOLOGY

Published under the auspices of the Institute of Criminology,
University of Cambridge, the Mannheim Centre, London School of
Economics, and the Centre for Criminological Research, University
of Oxford.

Crime and Markets

Essays in Anti-criminology

VINCENZO RUGGIERO

OXFORD
UNIVERSITY PRESS

OXFORD

UNIVERSITY PRESS

Great Clarendon Street, Oxford OX2 6DP

Oxford University Press is a department of the University of Oxford.
It furthers the University's objective of excellence in research, scholarship,
and education by publishing worldwide in

Oxford New York

Athens Auckland Bangkok Bogotá Buenos Aires Calcutta
Cape Town Chennai Dar es Salaam Delhi Florence Hong Kong Istanbul
Karachi Kuala Lumpur Madrid Melbourne Mexico City Mumbai
Nairobi Paris São Paulo Singapore Taipei Tokyo Toronto Warsaw

and associated companies in Berlin Ibadan

Oxford is a registered trade mark of Oxford University Press
in the UK and in certain other countries

Published in the United States
by Oxford University Press Inc., New York

© V. Ruggiero 2000

The moral rights of the author have been asserted

Database right Oxford University Press (maker)

First published 2000

British Library Cataloguing in Publication Data

Data available

Library of Congress Cataloging in Publication Data

Data available

ISBN 0–19–826838–6

1 3 5 7 9 10 8 6 4 2

Typeset in Sabon
by Hope Services (Abingdon) Ltd.
Printed in Great Britain
on acid-free paper by
T. J. International Ltd.,
Padstow, Cornwall

Contents

1

Introduction

There are imaginary geographies which place imperfect minorities in marginalized locations: in a social *elsewhere*. These locations consist of protected zones which ensure the reproduction of those who inhabit them, who are separated from the majorities living outside. These geographies of exclusion associate *elsewhere* with that which is contaminated, filthy, offensive to morality and olfaction. Nineteenth-century reformers used a chromatic topography to identify such zones, colouring them in black, a colour which in their view was suggestive of a mixture of sewage and dirt, an undefinable debris of a compounded nature. Those who lived *elsewhere* were immediately recognizable for the halo of sludge surrounding them, and for the subhuman features which they had slowly acquired during a long residence in hell.

The distinction between pure and impure, clean and excremental, informs the symbolic order of many traditional and contemporary societies, and engenders rites of separation which pursue the constant dream of purification by warding off contagion (Douglas, 1966; Sibley, 1995). In the cities of the industrial revolution, to purify morality was tantamount to clearing the sewer system, healing the poor from diseases, inculcating the control of passions, and instilling temperance and continence.

Traditional criminology thrives on these notions, and makes filth, sewers, and excrement, in brief that 'inferno' delimited by imaginary geographies, its main terrain of analysis and development. This book, to paraphrase a contemporary theologian, tries to suggest that if hell exists, it might well be empty. Are we faced with the decline of the house of the damned? Surely, its perimeter escapes measurement, and its boundaries are not now, nor perhaps have ever been, precisely identifiable. And yet, we cannot claim that there is today a diffuse infernality, a ubiquitous and slimy zone, a sort of protozoic sewage which penetrates everywhere; in sum we are not faced with a universal, sticky, and sordid dunghill (Camporesi, 1995). Such a claim would amount to the argument that all behaviour is criminal, determined as it is by self-ish, aggressive, and at times destructive urges. This book, which will not make such general claims, contents itself with occupying a critical observation point from which conceptual revisions are suggested, ideas are overturned, and aspects of received wisdom are contested. This is a collection of essays in anti-criminology, not a treatise on the universal-ity of crime and its inevitable corruptive effect on humanity. A similar general formulation would make redundant not only criminology, per-haps a negligible loss after all, but also all other academic production. It would be sufficient to reproduce the great classics of religious faith and political thought, which, from a theological or secular vantage point, hinge on a notion of original sin corrupting either the soul or the social system.

The Criminological Artifice

I would now like to provide a brief overview of the approaches to which anti-criminological analysis is indebted.

The study of white collar and corporate crime determined a focal shift from that social *elsewhere* and the imperfect minorities inhabiting it onto individuals and groups inhabiting markets or private and pub-lic organizations. Criminology finally came out of the sewers. This study unravelled some of the mechanisms underlying the illegal con-duct of entrepreneurs, politicians, and administrators. It also permitted students of deviance to include, among the causes of crime, the avail-ability of excessive resources rather than the lack of them, the ability to forge acceptable models of behaviour and to reject deviant imputations by others. In my opinion, the short and controversial history of anti-criminology starts with the study of the crimes of the powerful, before, as canonical chronologies would suggest, labelling theories appeared on the scene. Offences committed by powerful actors show how crim-inal behaviour may be determined by a series of causes, but also by their contrary. This is one of the possible readings of E. Sutherland's (1949) suggestion that criminal conduct is learned within social groups, be they socially vulnerable or powerful, which provide individuals with the techniques to commit crime and the rationalizations necessary to make it ethically acceptable.

The interaction approach also contains an anti-criminological ele-ment, because of its caution in identifying ontologically deviant behav-iours. In this approach, it is not the intrinsic nature of an act, but the rhetorical processes, the social reactions, the institutional ceremonies and professional typification which lead to its identification as deviant. Professionals employed in the criminological enterprise, for example, offer criminal typologies to clients, who choose the one they find more suitable to describe their behaviour and personality, and end up with time adapting to it. There is no causality, in this perspective, which is not exempt from artificial injunctions: deviance is therefore the outcome of an interaction which shapes and accelerates a criminal career. Consequently, the study of the causes of crime should coincide with the study of the interactive processes between agencies and their clients, the latter being unworthy of specific attention *per se*.

Similarly, in the contribution of labelling theorists, criminal behaviour is a behaviour so designated by official and social reaction. Responsibility for the causation of crime is thus attributed to the institutions and their activity, along with public perceptions, which classify certain conducts as unacceptable. The analysis of labelling theorists is consequently addressed to the ways in which labels are constructed and how moral entrepreneurs promote them, while their practice is devoted to the reduction of state intervention with a view to causing a corresponding decline in criminal labelling.

It is interesting to note that interactionists and labelling theorists, while criticizing positivism for its focus on the individual criminal, bring the debate back to its origin, namely to classical criminology. Classicism too, in fact, was less concerned with specific criminal acts than with institutional responses preventing those acts from recurring.

In successive developments, with the well-known variants of critical, new, Marxist, and radical criminologies, little space is left for the causes of crime, as these are imputed to the social system and linked with the conflictual interests characterizing it (Cohen, 1988; Walton and Young, 1998). Again, it is argued that criminology should focus on the social conflicts causing criminal behaviour, rather than on that behaviour in isolation. Echoing aspects of labelling theory, institutional agencies are anatomized and their role in manufacturing criminal careers is scrutinized. Campaigns are launched for their reform or abolition, while the clients of such institutions, who are identified as the casualties of social conflicts, are encouraged to join, at times even to lead, the fight against social injustice. Mechanisms building consensus are deconstructed, as are devices which amplify deviance and generate moral panic. On occasions, the crimes of the powerful are also focused upon, and abuses are unveiled which are said to intensify and perpetuate class structure and power. In some cases, criminologists abandon criminology, criticizing the concepts and the identity imposed by tradition and seeking inspiration from other disciplines. They borrow notions from politics and political economy; some become campaigners, activists, reformers: in brief, they take sides, and in doing so they implicitly discard any claim to scientific neutrality. Official criminology is seen as the repository of a set of biased analytical tools resulting from, and simultaneously reinforcing, the power against which they are fighting.

With abolitionism, the rejection of official conceptualizations is complete: the real problem is the criminal justice system, not the acts which this system tries to tackle. Crime is a social construction which should be unmasked through, among other tools, a radical linguistic revision. Among abolitionists, some advocate lexical reform of the official jargon, a jargon whose repetitious use of signifiers such as 'crime' grants unwarranted scientific value to the concept behind it. Other abolitionists highlight the dysfunctional character of penal institutions, or suggest that social conflicts, including conflicts commonly described as crime, are a precious asset. Even when they appear to be unmanageable, the solution of such conflicts should be entrusted to the community in which they arise. In an exemplary episode, a distinguished abolitionist was invited to deliver a speech by the members of a newly established centre for criminology, and amid the academic pomp and the excitement of those who expected an authoritative seal on their work, he remarked that such centres should never be opened but shut down.

Against a criminology which produces, along with its own activism, the object of its own study, only the exercise of self-reflection may free the discipline from social and institutional constraints. Feminist critique identifies in the absence of self-reflectivity a mechanism which reproduces crime and criminologists. The latter are said to be unaware of how their profession, socialization, gender, prejudices, and personal interests determine the knowledge that they so hastily present as scientifically neutral (Naffine, 1997).

The Sociology of Misery

I cannot claim affiliation to each of these schools of thought: I would otherwise be claiming an improbable group maternity. The brief review I have sketched above is meant to describe a critical climate surrounding the study of crime and identify a tentative anti-criminological discourse which constantly accompanies it. This book locates itself in such a path, though two final specifications may help define its position more precisely.

The critical approaches summarized above include, in varying measures, a particular sensibility, a set of specific research tools, a distinctive rhetorical vocabulary, and a predictable object of enquiry, which characterize what I would call a *sociology of misery*. I am alluding to a sociology which is always prepared to focus on other people's predicaments, while regularly ignoring its own; a sociology which believes itself to be needed by its objects of study more than it needs them. In criminology this is exemplified by the propensity of some researchers to study marginalized communities with a missionary zeal and a honeyed paternalism which derive from traditional philanthropy. This propensity, which in Britain is prevalent even among critical and radical criminologists, is akin to that guiding eighteenth-century reformers, religious militants, sewer-cleaners, and the Salvation Army. The sociology of misery appears to be the expression of sociologists' sense of guilt, of scholars who can only face the underprivileged if their redemptive role is acknowledged. However, by seeking to affirm this role, sociologists may unwittingly reproduce the injustices they seem to combat. For example, the assumption that criminals have elected criminologists as their spokespersons, or even as their political representatives, implies that the latter can offer the former an attractive alternative to their routine, such as a conventional life-style, an income, or a job. This offer, in fact, even when realistic, may be turned down by individuals who have already found an alternative life-style and income through participation in illegal economies. Moreover, in most cases the alternatives offered by sociologists of misery (poorly paid, dull, and humiliating jobs) would only perpetuate the very misery which makes their objects of study an inexhaustible human source. Finally, though most sociologists of misery are inspired by Mertonian analytical categories, they appear to endorse such categories very selectively. Merton's deviant adaptation described as 'rebellion', for example, is excluded by such sociologists, who therefore rule out the possibility that their objects of study may, through collective action, modify their social condition. This would deplete the human resource which acts as their object of study. In brief, a sociology which tries to redress social injustice, when inspired by such an ambiguous philanthropy, may end up re-inforcing it. Personal experience may provide an indication of how widespread the sociology of misery is: while I know many colleagues who study marginalized communities in, say, Hackney, Tower Hamlets, or Hull, I know only one who studies the illicit transfer of arms, but he is not a criminologist.

Causality of Contraries

The 'essays in anti-criminology' which compose this book do not sit comfortably with this type of sociology. Moreover, they try to keep at some distance from what Cohen (1985: 20) sees as 'a major distortion compounding the already distorting tendency in sociology to overgeneralize'. In his view: 'By concentrating on systems, structures, patterns and trends, by talking glibly of societies, systems and epochs, sociological analysis is often quite insensitive to variations, differences and exceptions.' This book rejects generalizations, and embraces variations and differences in a particular way, namely by focusing on the interpretative oscillations which may always occur when we are faced with criminal activity. This implies that each time we subscribe to one cause of crime we may realize that the opposite cause also possesses some reasonable validity. It is what I would like to term the *causality of contraries*.

There is a sort of foundational curse, mixed with an unconfessed inferiority complex, which compels social scientists constantly to search for universal causations of phenomena. Giving up this search, many believe, would exclude them from the scientific community (Dal Lago, 1995). Amongst sociologists of deviance and criminologists, this compulsion manifests itself in the attempt to identify a unified theory of crime. Often, the more limited and selective the observation of phenomena, the more vigorous the formulation of theories. Here is a paradox: it is usually those who observe partial, circumscribed sets of behaviour who seem convinced that they have reached a unified theory explaining all behaviour. I am thinking of scholars who focus exclusively on vulnerable sectors of the population, who may find that crime is a result of vulnerability or marginalization, and end up establishing an automatic association between illegitimate behaviour and low social status.

The study of offending behaviour adopted by powerful individuals shows that this automatic association can easily be refuted. As I have already remarked, 'learning theories' of crime possess an embryonic element of the *causality of contraries* that I would like to endorse. Let us provide some examples.

A small company may adopt illegitimate procedures because it operates in a competitive business environment. In its case, criminal practices may grant a supplementary strength to be utilized in the market, and translate into a competing edge on competitors. On the contrary, a large company may adopt criminal practices because it operates in a monopolistic business sector: by virtue of its position in such a sector of the economy this company may escape control by competitors and evade institutional monitoring. In the former case the putative cause of criminal conduct is the competitive environment in which the company operates, while in the latter it is the opposite, namely the absence of a competitive environment. Similarly, companies engaged in long-term investments, which are forced to delay the enjoyment of profits, may be tempted to seek immediate returns through illegitimate practices. Conversely, one may suggest that companies engaged in the acquisition of rapid returns 'learn' profit-making techniques so well that they are induced to apply such techniques in the illicit domain. This causality of contraries, in a sense, throws doubt on the adequacy of a criminology devoted to the search for universal causes of crime.

In the following chapters the search for omnipresent social conditions, for an 'original sin', though sociologically cloaked, in brief, for a primary, universal cause of criminal behaviour, will be carefully avoided. How could we do otherwise? If we, for example, identify variables such as financial success, the pursuit of status, or the accumulation of resources as the primary causes of crime, we end up expanding the criminal label to cover all behaviour. Success and financial gain, in fact, are also the main motivations of legitimate behaviour. On the contrary, if we focus on variables such as lack, deficiency, deficit (of opportunities, socialization, or resources), we end up excluding from the criminal rubric all those illegitimate practices caused by abundance, wealth, and excess.[1]

The causality of contraries to which I am referring is not related to what Young (1988) describes as an aetiological crisis in criminology. According to Young's formulation, the volume of criminal activity grows in all parts of the world, especially in countries where economic development is more vigorous. How can we explain the persistence and

---

[1] I have dealt with the 'aetiology of deficit' on a number of occasions (Ruggiero, 1993a; 1996a; 1999), questioning a criminology which bases its explanations on notions such as 'deficiency' and 'inadequacy'. These notions, I have argued, tend to associate all antisocial behaviour with a condition of disadvantage, be it economic, cultural, or psychological. For a subsequent discussion of the 'deficit' see Young (1999).

growth of crime even when the general production of wealth simultaneously increases? The answer commonly given to this question hinges around the notion of inequality, which includes variables such as social disadvantage and relative poverty. The argument is therefore put forward that the distance between the elite and the socially disadvantaged determines the 'strain' which leads to illegitimate behaviour: relative deprivation is located at the centre of crime causation. This explanation reintroduces surreptitiously an aetiology of deficit, though the notion of absolute deprivation, or indeed deficit, is replaced with that of relative deficit. The greater the relative deprivation, it is argued, the more intense the pressure to resort to crime for those who lack the legitimate means for the acquisition of wealth and success. The perplexity which such analysis raises is due to the exclusive attention it devotes to conventional crime, to which the variable relative deprivation is particularly suitable.[2] How can such a variable explain corporate criminality? This type of criminality, perhaps, may be aptly explained through 'relative affluence', which is the contrary of relative deprivation.

Essays in Anti-criminology

What is termed 'aetiological crisis' should not be regarded as the effect of recent developments, but seen as an intimate dilemma ingrained in criminology itself. This academic discipline has always encountered difficulties in combining nomographic analysis, namely the search for general causes of crime, with ideographic analysis, namely the search for its individual causes. Let us see some examples.

Some murders are committed in abysmal familial conditions and marginalized economic contexts. The absence of a family structure, which might provide primary socialization, is usually invoked to explain the causes of such murders. On the other hand, there are cases in which the 'immoderate' presence of a family, which feeds its members with authoritarianism, excludes them from responsibility, and even paralyses them with infantilism, may be the cause triggering mur-

---

[2] Attempts have been made to apply the notion of relative deprivation to the crimes of the powerful. The outcome of such attempts may be unwittingly clumsy, if not comical. For example, how can we claim that, say, Berlusconi commits crime because he is relatively deprived when compared with Murdoch? Or that Giovanni Agnelli (the owner of Fiat) indulges in illegitimate practices because he is strained by the success of Bill Gates? Merton (1968: 198), in fact, is adamant on this point: the notion of relative deprivation is mainly to be applied to disadvantaged individuals: 'the greatest pressures toward deviation are exerted upon the lower strata'.

der within the household. In many cases known to the public, matricide and patricide are the consequence of the excessive social advantages enjoyed by parents; in other words, of offspring pursuing the immediate enjoyment of the patrimonial resources of parents by speeding up their definitive departure.

A similar causality of contraries emerges when, for example, organized crime is observed. The activities conducted by organized groups can also find some plausible explanatory variables as well as their opposite. It could be argued that the lack of resources and legitimate employment opportunities, or even want of a sense of the collectivity, may be among the causes leading to involvement in organized crime at the low levels of its hierarchical structure. However, a similar aetiology based on *deficit* may explain only conventional criminal activity conducted by 'soldiers' of the organization, not the criminal entrepreneurial logic of the activities conducted by the organization as a whole. These activities may, rather, be explained through the availability of resources, access to markets and to political mediators. As for the idea that the absence of the state encourages the development of enterprise-type criminality, this deficit aetiology too, if we consider the examples of Italy and the USA, can be easily overturned. Access to the political, business, and financial elite has determined, rather than discouraged, the development of organized crime in those countries. Again, we are faced with a causality of crime which constantly nullifies itself.

Let us now repeat this simple exercise with respect to the economy of illicit drugs. Do people become habitual drug users because they are deprived, marginalized, unemployed, or do they become all these things because they are habitual drug users? Similarly, are people attracted to the drugs economy because they want to 'retreat' from social life, as classical sociology of deviance would suggest, or because they intend to participate in the competitive 'hustle and bustle' of social life? In effect, many participants in drugs markets lead a highly participative life-style, made up of hectic, unpredictable tasks, exciting exploits, in what at times may be a succession of fulfilling acts. By the same token, is involvement in such markets determined by a lack or an excess of individual resources? How can we explain the general causes of drug-related offences, if for some these offences amount to the search for a basic income, while for others they are part of strategies for the valorization of an income they already have?

So far I have considered only instrumental offences, namely offences the main motivation of which is the pursuit of material benefit. But let us try to expand this exercise to other types of offending behaviour. Is racially motivated violence caused by social disadvantage, or by its opposite, namely the relative social advantage enjoyed by offenders over their victims? Similarly, can we attribute to violent football fans a deficit of socialization? Not always. In many cases, in fact, theirs is a form of 'excessive' socialization, which takes the form of an intense attachment to their locality, city, or country. Some English fans, for example, while clashing with their European rivals, draw their nationalistic chants from the political rhetoric and the insular culture in which they have been socialized. Their violent behaviour may signal a perfectly acquired, if 'excessive', national identity. This identity is so consistent with 'normality' that it is almost impossible for the England team to encounter its Irish counterpart. In Glasgow, the fans of the two city teams have clashed for decades, and in the affirmation of their respective identities as Catholic and Protestant have shown perfect signs of assimilation to the general climate in which they have been brought up. Analogously, it is difficult to establish whether sexual violence results from the failed internalization of the rules governing interactions between sexes, or whether it is the effect of an 'excessive', obsessive internalization of such rules. Finally, could child abuse be interpreted as a 'normal' extension of a generational pecking order, whereby the only possible relationship between adults and young ones is one characterized by animosity and resentment?

As the emergence of criminal conduct may be imputed to one cause and, at the same time, to its contrary, students of crime are faced with few analytical options. They may totally abandon the search for general explanatory theories. In this respect, see the contribution of Jack Katz (1988), who attributes to crime a repertory of motivations which explain both illegitimate and legitimate behaviour (Van Hoorebeek, 1997). They may, in the capacity of ethnographers, limit themselves to the description of events, dynamics, and acts, while leaving to others the evaluation of their illegitimacy, the causes underlying them, and the procedures which allow their definition as criminal. Or they may observe phenomena individually, seek their causes within the specific context of observation, only to nullify what they find when observing other phenomena in other contexts. They may, in brief, accept a specific aetiology with the awareness that this can always turn into its exact reverse. Each of these routes, I believe, entails the rejection of official criminology, the main objective of which remains the identification of the conditions that are always present when crime takes place and always absent when crime does not take place (E. Sutherland, 1983). Each of these routes, which are taken in the present book, offers some scope for anti-criminological analysis.

Markets and Opportunities

The chapters forming this volume describe a series of criminal activities conducted in different European contexts. The use of some, elementary, economic categories adds to their anti-criminological character. These activities should be located against the backdrop provided by the economic changes which have occurred in Europe over recent decades. I am thinking of the increase in the volume of production and profits, and the simultaneous decline in employment, job security, union and welfare rights. I am also thinking of the large discrepancy between official employment data and the reality of the labour market. In other words, of the sensational growth of occupational opportunities in hidden, parallel, and semi-legal economies. Finally, I am alluding to the growth of flexibility and casualization of work, which for many amounts to a pendulum-like movement between underemployment and unemployment.

This apparent mobility, which seems to promise ascent and promotion, in reality ties many individuals in stagnant positions, forcing them to very predictable forms of flexibility, to horizontal motion without vertical movement. The parallel or hidden labour market, which hosts what I would term a 'stagnant mobility', possesses numerous points of contact with activities conventionally defined as criminal. The growing emphasis on market forces may have contributed to the blurring of differences, thus favouring the periodical journey of both labour and entrepreneurs between the two. Those who are active in the parallel, hidden economy, in sum, given their proximity to the criminal economy proper, are encouraged to find occupation, or investment opportunities, in both. Areas of 'dirty economy' are therefore created, in which overlaps, exchanges, alliances, and various forms of consortia take shape.

Market Europe, therefore, promotes two symmetrical types of criminality: on the one hand, it generates new forms of conventional crime while, on the other, it offers business new ambits of investment which are increasingly bereft of rules, thus favouring the proliferation of new forms of crime of the powerful (Ruggiero *et al.*, 1998; I. Taylor, 1999).

In the first part of this book a conventional criminal activity *par excellence* is examined, namely activity related to the economy of illicit drugs. Chapter 2 provides an analysis of the way in which 'criminal labour' linked to drug use and distribution took on a particular configuration during most of the 1980s. The suggestion is made that the development of a complex economy such as the drugs economy determined the partial decline of professional forms of criminality and the formation of an unskilled criminal workforce. The description of this Fordist phase of criminal activity is carried out against the backdrop of a crucial distinction regarding the structure of criminal economies. Professional crime is embedded in a *technical* division of labour, where roles are allocated on the basis of individual capacity and skills. This type of crime is carried out by relatively small groups which plan and execute tasks, and then plan successive tasks within a horizontal structure. This structure, which is devoid of strong hierarchical connotations, grants a relatively equitable distribution of profits after each task is performed. On the contrary, the development of the drugs economy produces an increasing *social* division of labour, whereby benefits are dependent upon roles, within a structure where planning and execution are rigidly separated (Ruggiero, 1992*a*; 1996*a*). As with other forms of conventional organized crime, the division of roles, in this case, echoes the typical configuration of industrial work.

This distinction also underlies the argument put forward in Chapter 3, where the attempt is made to identify a continuum between irregular, hidden, semi-legal, and overtly illegal economies. This continuum is given the name of *bazaar*, which captures the notion of a constant movement, a form of occupational commuting, as it were, between legitimate and illegitimate activity characterizing many urban contexts. Here the 'scandalous normality' of criminal markets will be noted, in that such markets reproduce the most repulsive aspects of legitimate ones. Chapter 4 examines one of these aspects, namely the perpetuation of racial barriers in criminal economies. The analysis in this case will reach the tentative conclusion that ethnic minorities have reduced opportunities not only in the official economy, but also in the criminal one. Chapter 5, in its turn, tries to update the analysis of the characteristics of criminal labour in light of the growing variety of the demand and supply of illegal goods and services. It will be hypothesized that the criminal labour force, as a consequence of this growth, is required to adapt its skills, to become flexible and respond 'just in time' to customers' needs. In this respect, it will be argued that a

Toyota-model criminality is taking shape, which parallels a similar trend emerging in the legitimate economy. This chapter links in logical combination some of the arguments around 'crimes in the street' with those around 'crimes of the elite'. Both types of crimes will be examined against the processes of informalization characterizing contemporary economies.

By analysing the interface between the formal and the informal, Chapter 6 (the First Intermezzo) prepares the terrain for the second part of the book, which is devoted to the 'crimes of the elite'. However, as if taking a breath, the second part of the book is preceded by the First Intermezzo, which allows this author, and hopefully also readers, to step back from the arguments put forward and to pose more general questions. Centred on the debate around drug prohibition and legalization, the First Intermezzo does not enquire why illicit drugs are produced, distributed, and consumed. Rather, it asks what 'drug' means, and to what extent its use should be regarded as part of individual rights. Ironically, the First Intermezzo testifies to the artificial nature of official criminology and to the utility of anti-criminological exercises: if drugs were legalized, the first part of this very book would become irretrievably redundant.

The second part is composed of a series of specific cases of criminality of the elite. Chapter 7 examines the dynamics underlying trafficking in human beings and the illicit transfer of arms. Here, I hypothesize that conventional organized crime and the official economy exchange services and establish mechanisms of mutual entrepreneurial promotion. This hypothesis, which I have put forward in previous work (Ruggiero, 1996a), is here updated. It will be noted, for example, that on some occasions the official economy may forgo the services offered by organized crime and establish its own 'in-house' sector for the provision of illicit services. In other words, the official economy may make organized crime redundant, and in doing so monopolize the benefits of both licit and illicit practices. In this part of the book also, as will become apparent, little sympathy is displayed for aetiological approaches, particularly those hingeing on notions of *deficit*, such as underdevelopment, lack of entrepreneurial spirit, absence of the state, and deficiencies of various nature.

Chapters 8 and 9 discuss political and administrative corruption in Italy and France respectively. The Italian case will show how the evolution of corrupt practices is simultaneous with economic development, rather than the outcome of underdevelopment. It will also be argued that corruption, in that context, is congruent with the establishment of democracy, though not the type of democracy described by official texts, but that experienced by citizens. Also in the analysis of the French case, variables such as development and underdevelopment will be ignored because they can provide little help. The existence of corruption will be taken as a given, and the attempt will be made to understand why and under what circumstances it comes to light and is perceived as such. Chapter 10 examines cases of crimes of the elite in the British context. As a confirmation that variables centred on deficit are unhelpful, this chapter tries to analyse how a strong sense of the state, both artificially imposed and genuinely felt, may impact on the emergence of economic-administrative crime and its perception.

The second part of the book also has its own Intermezzo, in which general questions are posed. For example: is it true that the elite itself sees with clarity the distinction between acceptable and unacceptable business and administrative practices? Where are the boundaries between legitimate and illegitimate economic behaviour located, and according to what criteria are they drawn? The Second Intermezzo discusses how the elite of eighteenth-century England were haunted by similar dilemmas. Through the study of some of the writings of Daniel Defoe we shall see how the definition of what constitutes business crime was as problematic then as it is now. A brief conclusion will reiterate the utility of anti-criminology which, in deconstructing the definitional processes of crime, expresses scepticism for the received ideas on the causes generating it.*

* Chapters 6 and 11 are reprinted by permission of Sage Publications Ltd—Chapter 6 is my contribution to South, N. (ed.) (1999), *Drugs: Cultures, Controls & Everyday Life*, while Chapter 11 appeared in *Social & Legal Studies*, 6(3): 323–42 (1997). Finally, Chapter 9 was first published, though in a different version, in Levi, M. and Nelken, D. (eds.) (1996), *The Corruption of Politics and the Politics of Corruption*, Oxford: Blackwell.

2

A Fordist Model of Criminal Activity

In the late 1980s some long-term heroin users came to act as my key informants and guided me in my research into illicit drugs markets. One of them saw himself as a member of the elitist cohort of initiators, the original, unique, politically aware pioneers of heroin use in Italy (Ruggiero, 1992*b*; Ruggiero and South, 1995). There was a cultural gulf, he claimed, between old and new users, the latter being mere 'perpetuators of conformity'. He lamented:

Many users today live like industrial workers: go out in the morning, hustle without knowing who they are working for; buy a substance of which they know nothing; use it without knowing why. They get up early in the morning, go to *work*, hustle, score: everything at precise times of the day, the times accepted by the productive rhythm of the town. The last shot is at ten in the evening, when normal people watch their last programme on TV.

A friend of his suggested that many of the new users lacked any motivation and could not spell out or identify the reasons underlying their choices:

If you ask any youths why they use heroin, they don't know what to say. It's like asking them why they watch TV. They use heroin because it's there, it's part of the scene. They don't even grasp how heroin is by now part of the local economy in which they themselves play a very important role.

Another user, who liked moaning about the indolence of some of his colleagues, expressed his work ethic in the following terms:

Some are real wrecks and lack imagination. They just don't want to understand that they have to take their situation seriously, as if they had a real job. They have to dress properly, go out in the morning, and find the way of getting hold of some money. My point is: Do you like smack? Well, get up, shave, get dressed, and go to *work* like everybody else.

The description of crime as work need not sound too provocative. Many of those who engage in crime on a regular basis regard theirs as an occupational role. Concepts such as specialization, professionalism, apprenticeship, and job satisfaction may help one to understand the dynamics of illegal behaviour (Letkenman, 1973). The work perspective takes into account the skills required in different criminal activities and may offer important elements to help identify the organization of these activities.

In a pioneering study of this type, for example, the relationship between criminal organization and the wider social organization is analysed against the background of a pivotal variable: criminal technology (McIntosh, 1975). In this study an important variety of urban crime is described as *project* crime, a definition which refers to large-scale thefts and frauds. These activities are said to be technically sophisticated and less routinized, and are usually performed by individuals endowed with long illegal apprenticeship. 'Each of these crimes, or short series of crimes, is a *project* in itself, involving separate advance planning and organisation' (ibid.: 42).

In this chapter I will adopt a similar line of analysis, though I would clarify from the outset that 'project crime' mirrors some aspects of artisan work, where skills are slowly learned through apprenticeship, and are often transmitted within the social networks and groups to which one belongs. I would also like to stretch the parallel further. It is widely known that industrial work inherited many characteristics of craftsmanship, namely the knowledge of the work process in its entirety and a degree of pride related to it. In 1914, with the installation of the first assembly line at Ford, a different type of labour became necessary. Briefly, the Fordist model of work implied the segmentation of tasks, the displacement of knowledge from labour to management, repetitive and alienating acts, and consequently a high degree of job disaffection (Braverman, 1974).

This simplified definition may be of help when illicit drugs markets are examined. In these markets assembly-line delinquents seem to operate who are devoid of training, specific skills, and a detailed knowledge of the economy which employs them. Are we faced with the tendential deskilling of criminal labour and the simultaneous development of a Fordist model of illegal activity?

In the following pages an attempt is made to assess the validity of this hypothesis. The analysis will focus on the configuration of criminal networks engaged in drug distribution and drug-related crime. Broadly, the time span considered will be between the 1970s and the early 1990s, while geographically the Italian and the British context will be observed.

Bureaucracy and Enterprise

The spread of illicit drug consumption between the 1970s and the early 1990s significantly altered the profile of criminal business in most European countries. New characteristics emerged within the criminal economies which developed varying forms and degrees of organization and which would warrant a re-examination of classical definitions. Let us, for example, concentrate on one particular aspect of what is defined as organized crime.

There are recurrent features in the definition of organized crime, among which is the notion that its members are endowed with criminal skills acquired by means of long-term apprenticeship. The well-known polemic between Donald Cressey and Joseph Albini hides the fact that the above-mentioned notion belongs to both authors and many after them. Cressey's description of organized crime is based on a so-called bureaucratic model, whereby different groups or families are said to co-ordinate and direct, within a commission formed by representatives of all groups, all activities carried out on the national territory (Cressey, 1969). Albini suggests instead that organized crime is not to be viewed as a nationwide conspiracy, but should be described as a series of local, relatively independent entities which are loosely structured and only informally co-ordinated (Albini, 1971). Now, these interpretations describe networks and relationships which, if differently structured, nevertheless involve similar actors, namely professional criminals or 'men of honour'. These actors are given a central location in many definitions of organized crime, thus conveying the idea that activities are performed only by criminals who are extremely skilled, have undertaken an exclusive career, and are often related by either familial or ethnic bonds. As Kelly (1997: 50) has argued, there is a sort of empirical equivalence between the formulation of Cressey and that of Albini, despite the differences in approach:

Then we should recognize the two as equally well warranted. We might even, as I think it may be prudent to do, oscillate between them for the sake of a more powerful and fertile perspective on organised crime.

However, other definitions, which do not focus on professionalism, can help develop a more fruitful perspective when organized crime is analysed *vis-à-vis* the drug economy.

According to Haller (1992: 2), families involved in organized crime are not to be regarded as centrally controlled business enterprises. Rather, members independently conduct their activity: 'A family, then, is a group which is separate from a member's economic ventures and to which members belong roughly in the same way that legal businessmen might join a Rotary Club' (ibid.). The author also argues that many members are not involved in permanent structures nor engaged in long-term partnerships. They may undertake one-off operations, make temporary alliances with legal or illegal entrepreneurs, and often recruit part-timers. We will see how these characteristics aptly describe the drug economies in the two countries considered.

Employees of criminal organizations pose a serious threat to their employers:

> The entrepreneur aims then to structure his relationship with employees so as to reduce the amount of information available to them concerning his own participation and to ensure that they have minimal incentive to inform against him (Reuter, 1983: 115).

This threat can be reduced if employees are recruited from among family members and close associates who guarantee a degree of loyalty. However, this is not possible for all illegal businesses, especially those presenting with large and ramified distribution structures. The drugs economy, for instance, does not lend itself to centralized control by entrepreneurs, whose capacity to monitor the suitability and skills of dealers is very limited. The fact that many dealers are also users, the precariousness of their 'jobs', and the high turnover in the economy in which they participate are indications of this. In other words, the involvement of organized crime in the drug economy may lead to its relative *disorganization*. It may also entail a shift in the way in which profits are made and in the occupational characteristics of those who contribute to their creation. Individuals with no previous criminal record may constitute the majority of employees in the drug economy, but paradoxically their non-professional and disorganized illegal acts end up benefiting their professional and organized employers. Moreover, it is often the case that drug selling is a complement to, rather than a substitute for, legitimate employment, which explains the rudimentary skills of many users and small distributors (Reuter *et al.*, 1990). Surely, the notion that organized crime is a monolithic structure formed exclusively by professional affiliates loses pertinence when its involvement in the drug economy is observed. Here, organized groups are forced to renounce the traditional regulatory function commonly attributed to them. Petty, disorganized, and opportunistic offences can no longer be controlled or regulated, as they become an important component of organized crime itself.

This seems to have occurred in both Italy and England, the specific drug economies of which I will now briefly describe.

Italian Narco-entrepreneurs

The involvement of Italian organized crime in the drug economy dates back to the 1950s. One of the first large seizures occurred in 1952, when 6 kg of heroin was found in the area between Palermo and Trapani (Santino and La Fiura, 1993). Among those arrested were distributors residing in both Sicily and the USA. Other traffickers and wholesale distributors operated in the North of Italy, where some industrialists managed to divert quantities of heroin from the legal to the illegal market. According to the Antimafia Commission set up by the Italian parliament, for a period Lucky Luciano obtained drugs from these 'licit' dealers in pharmaceuticals (Commissione Antimafia, 1976; Pantaleone, 1976). When a laboratory for the processing of heroin was discovered near Milan, it was clear that Italian criminal groups also purchased the substance in the producing countries and, after refining it in Italy, exported it to the USA. This pattern of activity was destined to remain unaltered until a proper heroin market developed in Italy around the early 1970s.

It was during the course of the 1970s and the 1980s that the participation of organized crime in the drug economy assumed new characteristics. Judge Falcone's investigation proved that decisions regarding involvement in illegal drugs were never taken centrally, but were the result of personal initiative (Falcone, 1991). In other words, the drug business gave the old mafia families the opportunity to claim independence from so-called consortia, commissions, or domes (the organs where members of the different traditional mafia families allegedly plan and co-ordinate their exploits). All supergrasses of the mafia confirmed that finances invested in drugs came neither from the common assets of the organization nor from the collective proceeds accumulated by members of a specific family. The money invested was individually owned finance. Members who resolved to enter the drug business, therefore, had the opportunity to build partnerships with other investors who were not members of their family or, for that matter, members of the mafia (Arlacchi, 1992; Gambetta, 1992). The informant Antonino Calderone tells of the way in which some men of honour could sometimes become independent from their very families if their attempt to build up a remunerative drug business was successful. Among these was Pippo Bono, who 'never took side with any precise group within the organization, and would always be absent at critical moments' (Arlacchi, 1992: 136). Pippo Bono was perhaps the first example of a member of the mafia being able to abstain from the war between families, while becoming a partner with other legal or illegal entrepreneurs.

In some cases the members of traditional organized crime syndicates in Italy performed the role of mediators, as they invested somebody else's money in the drug economy. In other cases, both imported drugs and drugs refined in Italian laboratories were sold to wholesale distributors who did not belong to traditional groups of families. In brief, due to the typical hierarchical structure which distinguishes drug distribution, 'men of honour' were forced to deal with 'ordinary men'. Among middle-range distributors individuals emerged who had acquired skills and funds in previous criminal activities on the one hand, and entrepreneurs without those skills on the other. In turn, small-scale distribution was also taken on by individuals who had never been associated with organized crime (Ruggiero, 1993a). None of the prevailing groups managed to establish a monopoly in the distribution of illegal drugs. Rather, they shared an oligopoly with regard to both the national territory and the specific local market which they supplied.

Turning to small-scale distribution, in many Italian cities some common traits could be observed. In Naples, for example, small dealers had previously been involved in sectors of the hidden economy or, specifically, in illegal cigarette markets and smuggling networks. Among the user-dealers many had no previous involvement in crime (Feo, 1989). Similarly in Rome many small distributors were neophytes who were employed by local professional criminals. In Milan, official statistics suggest the cursory apprenticeship undergone by small dealers and users: among those arrested only a small minority had previously been charged with any offence. Finally, in Turin small distributors and users seemed unable to develop a real career in the economy of drugs, as they were intermittently arrested either after committing the same type of offence or while possessing the same quantity of drugs (ISTAT, 1992). In other word, their careers were 'blocked', for they proved incapable

of ascending the distribution hierarchy and acquiring the professionalism needed to do so.

The argument presented so far can be summarized as follows. The
drug business in Italy both remodelled traditional organized crime and
shaped new organized groups which occupied, along with the former,
the leading positions in it. None of the old or new groups appeared to
acquire a monopolistic position in the market. Meanwhile, the drug
business fostered a process whereby the creation of a number of
'expendable labourers' servicing the market ran parallel with a drive
towards more structured and professionalized operations. These developments were not oppositional. On the contrary, it was the employment of one which allowed for the promotion of the other. Let us see
whether similar characteristics are encountered in the second country
under investigation.

England: Indigenous Entrepreneurs and their Partners

The existence of a heroin market in England can be traced back to the
mid-1960s. Until 1968 this market offered 100 per cent pure heroin,
which was legally bought with a medical prescription but partly ended
up feeding a grey market. Legislation introduced between the late
1960s and the early 1970s is said to have modified this situation and
indirectly caused the development of a black market, where illegally
imported heroin became available (Whynes and Bean, 1991). This
legislation limited doctors' power to prescribe and marked the slow
decline of the maintenance model, a model allegedly abused by over-
generous practitioners.

In England, many commentators point to the early 1980s as a turning point for drug distribution. Supply, which was locally centred and
poorly structured, became increasingly organized and regularized
(Stimson, 1987). The explosion of the heroin phenomenon is said to
have favoured this shift, which is commonly also described in relation
to the variety of the substances available on the market and the respective producing countries. Chinese, Iranian, and Pakistani illicit drugs
successively predominated in the markets of English cities, a circumstance which leads many observers to investigate the trafficking routes
and the criminal enterprises connected to the respective countries.
England's position on the traditional trade routes of the main source
countries of heroin and other opium-based products, along with its
historical, both imperial and post-imperial, relationships with these

countries, should be borne in mind. Here, however, a point of clarification is necessary.

While charting the development of drug trafficking, especially in England, one may become entangled in the vexed questions surrounding the relationship between ethnicity and crime. In particular, there is a danger that the notion of drugs as an alien conspiracy is unwittingly endorsed. This notion has been adequately demythologized on a number of occasions (Kohn, 1987; McCoy, 1991; Labrousse, 1991; Murji, 1998). In Chapter 4 of this book the issue will receive more detailed analysis. However, it is important to add a number of initial observations which are frequently lacking in the existing literature. The drug economy seems to mirror licit economies, particularly with respect to its division of labour. Often, the most remunerative positions within criminal economies are occupied by indigenous groups, whereas the most poorly paid and dangerous tasks are entrusted to minorities (Padilla, 1992). In England, for example, some groups or individuals engaged in the importation of drugs may well belong to ethnic minorities, but the 'added value' involved in their task may be much lower than that involved in wholesale distribution. In turn, wholesale and middle-range distribution are frequently controlled by indigenous groups which have easier access to the market and to smaller distributors who service it. In London, for instance, it is rare that black people climb the distribution echelon, due to their visibility and the lack of trust with which they are regarded by both partners and consumers. In other words, in the criminal economy they find the same obstacles they meet in the official one. These aspects, which will be further discussed later, need to be borne in mind when looking at the drug business in England.

In the first phase, groups of immigrant traders purchased heroin in the Golden Triangle, routed the substance through Hong Kong, and imported it into England concealed among other products destined for the Chinese community. The trade conduits utilized for licit goods also acted as conveyors of illicit goods. Due to their ancient custom of reciprocity and their system of payment entirely based on trust, the Chinese illegal enterprises are said to have carried out business undisturbed for years. At the same time, their sophisticated money-laundering system allowed for operations to be virtually undetected. Underground banking would then guarantee the invisibility of profits (Nove, 1991).

Iranian groups are singled out as the major heroin importers during the 1982–4 period. Illicit drugs constituted a currency for middle-class migrants who escaped the Ayatollah regime and brought their assets to London, where they found refuge (Burr, 1984). The new settlers continued to feed limited sectors of the market for about two years after the collapse of the old Iranian regime. They availed themselves of well-established connections with wholesale distributors in their country of origin. The fact that they never developed a highly remunerative economy is perhaps due to their lack of contacts with locally established figures. Moreover, English drug distributors preferred to establish partnerships with other importers and to deal with higher-quality drugs than the Iranian 'brown' variety.

It is finally with the 'Pakistani phase' that the tasks performed within the drug economy became increasingly polarized. After the mid-1980s the characteristics of individuals charged with drug offences showed that users and small distributors performed repetitive activities within a career which was virtually stagnant. Their hyperactivity, as revealed by the number of arrests, did not translate into ascendant mobility, but into pendulum-like movement: from the street to prison and back. Jarvis and Parker (1989) attempted an economic evaluation of the illicit activities carried out by users, who were found to receive only a small fraction of the value of the commodities handled. While they moved considerable wealth from one place to another and from one person to another, what they retained consisted primarily of drug doses. Moreover, 'despite the glamour of the setting and the considerable sums of money involved, many subjects described repetitive life-styles of dull uniformity' (ibid.: 125).

In this respect, the following hypothesis can be formulated. Wholesale operations were increasingly conducted by well-organized groups which had access to large quantities of drugs and were in a position to invest large quantities of money. In order to minimize risk, but also thanks to the increasing finances at their disposal, these groups undertook a reduced number of operations involving larger amounts of drugs. Wholesalers, in other words, experienced a selective process whereby only those endowed with effectiveness, professionalism, and larger funds were left in operation. On the other hand, the number of people stopped and searched for drugs by the police rose in the proportion of one to three. This threefold increase in drug seizure opportunities at street level did not result in more drugs being found. Street dealers and user-distributors, in other words, did not show an increased level of participation in the drug economy. The age composition of drug offenders may also yield interesting information. In 1990 well over half of drug offenders were aged 17–24, and very few had a criminal record prior to involvement in drug use and petty distribution. Young and clumsy, many did not have the time to acquire criminal skills, a circumstance which exposed them to great danger in their day-to-day activity.

In England too we therefore witness the creation of an inexperienced 'army' of users and small dealers who serviced the drug market. This army, with its rudimentary professionalism, contributed to the professionalization of the higher strata of the distribution hierarchy.

A Criminal Reserve Army

In both countries considered, an important role in the forging of a Fordist-type criminal labour force was performed by the prison system. In this respect, let us bear in mind the historical function of custody in imposing a work routine and ethic. In Italy, the period between the mid-1970s and the early 1990s was characterized by a 'great internment' of illicit drug users. This process intensified after 1982, when a new piece of legislation was introduced which no longer encouraged, but obliged, users to undergo therapeutic treatment if they intended to avoid custodial punishment. Then in 1986 the therapeutic choice was dramatically reduced for 'recidivists', in the sense that users convicted for the third time could no longer opt for therapy but would incur imprisonment (Pepino, 1991; Solivetti, 1994). The harsher statutes of 1982 and 1986 reflected the international war on drugs, but were also the result of increasing public alarm over the involvement of organized crime in the production of and trafficking in illicit substances. However, the social panic fed by traffickers resulted in more users and small dealers being incarcerated (Ruggiero, 1998). In England and Wales, a more integrated and less informal penal system resulted from the ascendancy of the New Right and the concomitant development of state and social authoritarianism. 'This system was increasingly responding to problems of crime and public disorder in a manner which was rational, professional and ruthless' (Ryan and Sim, 1995: 121). Demonized groups, including illicit drug users, also experienced a process of internment, favoured by the massive prison building programme drafted and implemented since 1979. In both countries users and small dealers became part of a carceral social zone also inhabited by the marginalized, the underemployed, occasional workers, petty criminals, and all others whose life-styles and economic activities straddle legality and illegality. These sections of the population were trained to remain and survive in the carceral social zone just as their counterparts in the past were trained to the discipline of industrialism. Prison discipline lowered their social expectations, turning the majority of them into routine criminal workers. Drug users, in other words, were treated as a 'criminal reserve army', as their predecessors, the poor of the era of forced industrialization, were redefined as the reserve army of labour.

Conclusion

Between the 1970s and the early 1990s the drug business modelled the organization of crime to the point where patterns of illegal activity in diverse contexts became increasingly uniform. In the lower ranks, drug-related activities assumed a Fordist-type model, whereby the skills required to perform tasks visibly declined. Skills, one might suggest, tended to be concentrated at the managerial level of the drug economy, and became slowly ingrained in the organization of labour and in market mechanisms, irrespective of those who played a part in it. In this organization, criminal labour became increasingly 'abstract', as it was fragmented in a number of repetitive operations whose purpose was lost. Gramsci's (1951) formulation of Fordism here comes in very useful. This model of work, he explains, includes both technical and social aspects, thus 'colonizing' both the productive and the reproductive spheres of labour. Many who worked in the drug economy were similarly trapped in a highly productive system, the profits of which they never shared, and in a social self-reproduction also dictated by that system.

As we have seen, in Italy the involvement in the drug business of traditional organized crime led to its partial 'disorganization'. 'Men of honour' were forced to form alliances and set up partnerships with ordinary men, sometimes even with neophytes. The recruitment of an army of unskilled criminal labour, inexperienced and vulnerable, contributed to this process of disorganization. Similarly, in England the development of the drug economy was accompanied by the partial decline of independent groups and their subjection to more organized structures. Simultaneously, 'delinquent workers' without criminal expertise were recruited. We shall discuss later how, during the course of the 1990s, the features of criminal labour were altered by the growing segmentation of illegal markets. We shall see, in sum, how the demand for illicit drugs, which became increasingly differentiated, determined a consequent flexibilization of the criminal labour force. In the phase examined so far, however, what is striking is the degree of conformity, rather than of deviancy, displayed by drug economies. One could legitimately question why such 'conformism' is so vehemently penalized.

Traits that one would associate with the official society are para-doxically reproduced in the non-official one. Like many licit industries, the drug industry is characterized by a vertical structure, a low degree of co-operation among its members, or rather an abstract, 'Fordist' kind of co-operation among them. Planning and execution are strictly separated. Moreover, as in licit industries and society at large, the division of roles and tasks is frequently based on ethnicity and gender. While I shall return to ethnicity and drugs, with respect to gender divisions within the criminal labour force one has to think of the exploitation of women by the sex industry and of their consequent capacity to provide drugs both for themselves and their partners. 'Some partners exploit the women's ability to earn money through prostitution, giving up their own earnings to live off those of their female partners' (A. Taylor, 1993: 156). But also consider how they are used, due to their alleged inconspicuousness, in activities such as shoplifting, and how they are often employed as couriers, so that the worst-paid and most dangerous task of importing is left to women. Finally, it has to be noted that those women involved in the drug economy who do manage to acquire skills and status are met with a higher degree of stigmatization than their male counterparts (Rosenbaum and Murphy, 1990; Connor, 1990). They are looked down upon, not because they are dealers, but because they are female dealers.

Final consideration should be given to the type of Fordism operating in the drug economy. When Ford introduced the first assembly line into his car factory, a substantial incentive was given to the workforce in terms of salary. This pay rise was defined with hindsight as the best cost-cutting measure ever devised by the car industry (Braverman, 1974). The Fordist model in the licit economy established itself within the sphere of what is termed the 'monopoly sector' (O'Connor, 1973). Here, a relative work stability made up for the brutal rhythm of work and exploitation. Those employed in the monopoly sector could, at least temporarily, avoid the fear of unemployment, as production seemed assured for ever. Conversely, the drug economy seemed to adopt a Fordist model of labour within the sphere of the 'competitive sector', where markets are irregular and unstable, and work is often seasonal. Working conditions in competitive industries tend to be poor and unemployment and underemployment high. Normally, as O'Connor (ibid.: 15) remarks:

workers do not earn enough to save for times of unemployment, indebtedness, sickness, or death. Weak and corrupt labour organisations do not secure adequate company-paid health, retirement, and other fringe benefits.

In Chapter 5 this analysis will be updated in light of the extraordinary diversification of the demand for illicit drugs which occurred during the course of the 1990s. If a predominantly mono-drug market, long fostered by the demand for heroin, shaped a relative specialization of roles, how did these roles evolve *vis-à-vis* the increasing demand for other types of drugs? As we shall see, a redefinition of criminal labour in post-Fordist terms can be attempted. Such redefinition is prompted by the flexibility which the growing multi-drug markets require. But before attempting this analysis it may be useful to specify further some characteristics of criminal work, and try to identify the way in which licit and illicit activities intermingle in irregular markets. These markets, which display new social divisions, will be described with the help of the metaphor of the *urban bazaar*, while the new social divisions will be depicted by recurring to the metaphor of the *barricades*.

3
Illegal Enterprise and Occupational Barriers

A London restaurant that I visit regularly is not only a place where one gets good food and wine, but also a sort of multi-service agency where contacts with plumbers, carpenters, or mechanics are provided.[1] They perform good work at low prices and, being unregistered, share the financial benefits of tax evasion with their customers. Other regulars are less attracted by meals and wines than by a crucial resource that the place offers: information. Whether this relates to the quality of specific products, the ongoing prices of goods, or market possibilities and developments, information is the untold item on the menu which binds customers together. The restaurant, in brief, is informally organized in a way that reduces the ignorance of frequenters on important aspects of their life in the city. There, the search for information is laborious, complex, and irregular, but it may be rewarding, because individuals are given the opportunity, not only to balance options, but also to find out what the options are.

The place offers a small variety of workers and entrepreneurs who oscillate between legal and illegal activities, a repertory of human types who adapt to the city as a market-place. Two men make no secret of their activity: they sell plastic jackets to gullible fashion enthusiasts who love wearing leather. A team distributes smuggled wine and spirits and tips off smokers about where to find cheap smuggled cigarettes. Some limit their work to the provision of information services, as they direct customers to traders and dealers who handle a variety of licit and illicit goods. The range of the information service they provide covers cocaine as well as TV aerials, mobile phones as well as designer-labelled clothes.

---

[1] The empirical work for this chapter started in this restaurant, but developed thanks to snowballing contacts made throughout central London. All names mentioned are, of course, fictitious.

This chapter describes some of these activities, which are conducted in the occupational arena incorporating sections of both the official and the hidden labour market. The analysis focuses on the constant movement of individuals who simultaneously inhabit licit and illicit markets and find in both opportunities and income.

Bazaars and Barricades

In many European cities criminal work intermingles with regular economic activity in what can be termed a contemporary *urban bazaar* (Ruggiero, 1987; Ruggiero and South, 1997). The bazaar is constituted by a network of retailers, ambulatory vendors, distributors, wholesalers, seasonal workers, casual assistants, and apprentices, who are all required to possess flexibility and versatile skills. This network offers partnership arrangements as well as employer–employee contracts. In effect the bazaar performs the crucial role of an employment agency, where people hear of potential job opportunities and emerging economic sectors: there they meet, establish bonds, exchange information, and at times undergo informal training. Moreover, in the bazaar they identify demands, try to create new ones, and establish supply channels. Finally, a mixture of official and illegal activities, and a constant flow of commodities, whose nature may be legal or otherwise, are frequent features of many European city bazaars.

The metaphor of the bazaar intends to convey an image of the city as a market-place, a notion of urban economic activity servicing a diffuse general store, where licit consumables, regular pleasures, and illegitimate services are made available within the same context. Unlike the Middle Eastern bazaar, which is physically formed, precisely laid out, and sectioned into parts, the Western urban bazaar is diffuse and connects sellers and buyers who are spatially and socially scattered. The bazaar in North African countries hosts forms of petty illegality. For example, it is the scene for 'buyer and seller, producer and consumer, master and apprentice, transporter, auctioneer, moneylender, and market official', but it also

includes the man who squats on a carpet and tells sad stories of the death of kings, the man who wanders through the crowds . . . collecting pious contributions, the man who sits behind a small table and writes whorled grandiloquent letters to order; and it includes the gambler, the pickpocket, the snake charmer, the prostitute, even the idler just hanging around (Geertz *et al.*, 1979: 173).

In the Western urban bazaar, instead, the diverse commodities and services are located in a continuum where, most significantly, the distinction between legally acceptable practices and criminal behaviour is blurred, both practices being adopted by the entrepreneurs and workers involved. Criminal activity as work, a formula already suggested in the previous chapter, also informs the multi-commodity provision found in the urban bazaar. However, in this case 'crime as work' not only alludes to the utility of categories such as specialization, professionalism, or apprenticeship for the understanding of illegal behaviour, but it also implies that often official, regular work, and its opposite, that is irregular and hidden, illegal work, are not part of a definitive employment choice. Bargaining, multiplicity, movement, and manœuvre inspire the choices of those involved in the bazaar, as regards both the occupational route followed and the degree of illegality required by tasks.

However, the Western city bazaar contains occupational barriers which delimit job opportunities for some and bar access to wealth for them. It possesses a conventional grid of occupational differentiation. While in the Moroccan bazaar 'communalism in the home' is counterbalanced by 'cosmopolitanism in the streets' (ibid.: 141), in the contemporary Western bazaar communalism, in the form of parochialism, prevails in both practices. In this respect, it may be useful to utilize the metaphor of the *barricades*, which remain an important feature of the city in both literary and sociological accounts. The possibilities opened up by the city as a market-place clash with the limitations imposed by its internal occupational barriers. While being characterized by mobility and flexibility, and despite its apparent function as status provider for all, the bazaar reveals a degree of rigidity in its internal role division. In brief, illegal economies are not homogeneous 'equal opportunity' environments. Let us see some examples of European city bazaars and their in-built occupational barriers.

Magliari and Others

Paul is a regular customer of the London restaurant I have mentioned. A low-paid, underemployed carpenter, he met people who sell clothes on the street. He started to sell forged Ralph Lauren shirts, in partnership with his new acquaintances, who would give him 30 per cent of the money earned. After three years as a street vendor, he realized that his supplier was making more money than he was, and tried to become self-employed.

The London bazaar offers a wide range of counterfeit clothes, but also well-known brands of perfume bottles, watches, and leather goods. France's luxury goods industry is particularly hard hit: seven out of ten fakes are of French products, causing the textile industry alone to lose up to FF30 billion a year. Companies vulnerable to the 'competition' of fakes also include the record, motoring, and medicine industries. Fake car components are widely available and difficult to detect by vendors, who may at times even be aware of the forged goods they are buying, but be prepared to purchase them because of lower prices. Gucci T-shirts on sale in the streets of London are in fact bought in Turkey.

Once allegedly the preserve of illegal entrepreneurs based in the Far East, the production of counterfeit goods have moved to European countries. The shirts sold by Paul were made in Britain, where competition between counterfeit firms is said to be turning increasingly violent. When trying to set up his own business, Paul was 'persuaded' by his employer that he could only buy his stock of goods from one specific supplier, and that approaching other suppliers would be 'dangerous'. He eventually met a colleague who buys from non-British producers and started to sell his imported merchandise in weekend street markets. However, because costs at purchase points allowed him to establish competitive retail prices, he was reprimanded by other pedlars and asked to move elsewhere. He now retains his job as carpenter while 'moonlighting' by selling forged goods.

Similar urban bazaars are in operation in many European cities, where official and hidden labour markets intermingle. Take the case of Marseille, a city which prospers on the semi-legal marketing of cars, textiles, and electrical appliances. The car market developed as a consequence of legislation introduced in France in 1982, whereby immigrants who had been resident in the country for a certain period of time could benefit from discounts when purchasing French cars. Small enterprises were soon set up with mediators purchasing cars on behalf of more recent immigrants who were not entitled to discounts, and shortly the business spread internationally. Commissions came from other migrant communities in Germany and Belgium, and even compatriots resident in the Maghrib now benefit from this semi-legal market. The development of car parts was an obvious consequence of the expansion of this market. Marseille produces forged car parts for French and Italian customers, selling these parts both in the local market and abroad. Some of these parts are sold to Italian contractors of car manufacturers, who import them illegally, thus benefiting simultaneously from low production costs and tax evasion (Tarrius, 1995, 1996).

In the Marseille bazaar clothes retail at less than half the price of their legally manufactured counterparts. Counterfeit labelled items come from the Far East, with importers establishing staging posts in the ports of the south of the country. Electrical and electronic appliances follow the same route.

Part of the urban bazaar in Marseille, as elsewhere, is characterized by networks of entrepreneurs, workers, and customers establishing business bonds without sharing precise geographical spaces. However, other sectors of this bazaar are spatially located, between the old port and Marignane airport. This visible bazaar offers food, second-hand clothes, antiques, and up-market fashion items; it is

an almost indescribable scene, with its complex commercial structure, joining different disjointed elements in space, time, and sociability. It is a universe which, resembles a hypermarket or a commercial centre in its dimensions, *souk* in its environment and colours, and a fleamarket in the social mix that operates in it (Péraldi *et al.*, 1995: 78).

Despite the fixity of the location, this bazaar requires a high degree of mobility of entrepreneurs and labour, as well as innovative marketing techniques. New demands are met irrespective of their licit or illicit nature, and new supply sources are accessed regardless of distance.

Marseille and Naples share more than a resemblance based on their being large Mediterranean ports. They share the entrepreneurial characteristics shaping their respective urban bazaars and the wide availability of labour prepared to be employed in them (Monzini, 1999). The hidden economy of Naples embraces activities as varied as the smuggling of cigarettes, the selling of untaxed household commodities, the marketing of electrical goods, and the production and wholesaling of counterfeit clothes. Some of the clothes manufactured in Naples are exported to other European bazaars, while labour is provided by the huge pool of the unemployed, underemployed, and casual workers. This labour force shifts from one activity to another, depending on contingent demand and the constant change in illicit entrepreneurial strategy. Many cigarette vendors, for example, moved to illicit drug distribution when investments were heavily directed towards illicit substances. Working in the Naples bazaar requires that any opportunity be taken, be it legal, semi-legal, or overtly illegal. In Naples, the difficulty in establishing precise boundaries between illegality and licit activity is also due to an opportunistic, institutionalized consideration: the hidden and the illegal economies constitute a safe haven, a surrogate source of income to supplement or replace the non-existent or inadequate social and economic provisions afforded by the welfare state.

Perhaps the most characteristic illustration of the Neapolitan bazaar, with its labour force commuting between legality and illegality, is provided by the old profession of the *magliari*. The *magliari* are street, or door to door, pedlars of clothes, bedlinen, and household furnishings. Their name comes from the items they originally supplied, the *maglie*, namely woollen vests which contained anything but wool. In the 1960s, when demand for clothing became more sophisticated, they started to sell pieces of cloth, for the tailoring of dresses or suits, with forged logos of famous and fashionable companies. The Ermenegildo Zegna brand, still on display in London shops, was among the most widely forged, with producers offering both the cloth and the decalcomanias. With the development of ready-made suits and dresses, the business of the *magliari* moved on to top-market designer clothes. Today, many do the job only on a part-time basis, while retaining a position in the official labour market. Some housewives are also occasionally involved in the business, and their success is attributed to their gender, which staves off suspicion. Success in this business may also be achieved by taking elocution lessons in order to lose one's Neapolitan accent. The *magliari* are perhaps the precursors, as well as the contemporary spearheads, of the counterfeit industry which now prospers in many European city bazaars. Among the rationalizations of their illegal activity is the argument that customers are punished for their greed: how do they expect to pay so little for, say, a Pierre Cardin?

Theft, Strip, and Drugs

Returning to my London restaurant, Paul introduced me to Deb, who defines herself as an acrobatic dancer. A professional, she worked for years in a circus before running dance classes. She then started managing a 'strip dancing' club, owned by her partner. At my enquiry whether employees of the club were only women, she said that they had tried to include men in the show, but their customers started dangerously to deplete. She added:

Our strategy is to create a good clientele for the club, people like yourself, for example, professionals, educated people. Then slowly try and introduce artistic innovation. Our club employs classical dancers and trained acrobatic dancers. In this sense it is completely different from traditional, mainstream clubs, where girls open up their legs on stage, and that's it. Also, we don't do 'table or lap dancing', where the girls all move in the same way, and are unable to actually dance. In the club we have a dance-floor dancer, a professional south American dancer, a classical ballet dancer, and so on. Our customers have to appreciate the female body, but they also have to appreciate the show. We don't want to excite them to the point that they lose control; we want them to come back because what they see is artistic, nice.

Deb places a professional barrier between herself and her 'vulgar' colleagues who do not understand art. Her tolerance for foreigners stops somewhere in the vicinity of the former Iron Curtain. Romanian, Yugoslavian, Polish, and particularly Albanian girls need not apply for jobs in her club: they are too different from us and would equivocate about what is expected of them. These girls 'seem to believe that the only work available to them in European cities is prostitution'. For this reason, they would turn the club into a brothel. On Mondays, when the club is shut, Deb sells cannabis to acquaintances and friends, and wishes she could extend her clientele to the audience of her shows, who instead 'are intoxicated with alcohol'.

Casual plumbers and part-time unregistered electricians selling illicit drugs are not unusual in the London bazaar. They also establish ethical barriers beyond which their disapproval begins. They claim that they sell illicit substances only to those they know very well, and particularly to those who badly need them. They oppose the prevailing 'supermarket model' of drug distribution, whereby anonymous retailers sell to anonymous customers.

Prostitutes also erect similar barriers, which separate the 'straight' service they provide from the unnatural performances offered by others, usually from distant countries.

The moral and occupational barriers established by Henry, another customer of the restaurant, are located somewhere between Rome and Eboli, where, according to Carlo Levi's novel, Christ decided to stop. An amateur singer, occasional cook, a bohemian, self-confessed right winger, he fled Italy in the mid-1970s, 'when the political left was getting too strong'. With a wealthy family background, he claims he does not need to work. In his view 90 per cent of Neapolitans are born criminals and, because their social background is poor, their criminality, even when successful, retains the typically unsavoury characteristics of the *parvenus*. His motto is: 'Be wary of swelling fleas', namely of the poor who become rich. For this reason he selects his business partners only from among white English people, to whom he sells cocaine.

Among Henry's friends and customers are groups devoted to theft of, or from, heavy goods vehicles. They mainly target small-sized companies, and act preferably during the weekends, so that only on Monday mornings do their victims realize they have been victimized. It would be plausible to suggest that some of these thefts are organized by, or in complicity with, employees of the victimized companies, and that the goods, instead of being legitimately delivered, are sold to fences and distributors within the 'black' market. Some owners may also arrange for the theft of their own vehicles, especially when these are ageing, with a view to claiming insurance money. Research conducted by Brown (1995: p. vi) showed that most stolen vehicles are never found, and that 'from the regional point of view, the South East has the highest number of thefts, followed by Yorkshire and Humberside and the North West'.

As customers' tastes become increasingly sophisticated, thefts of designer clothes consequently grow in the city bazaar. Clothes are either sold in the bazaar itself or shipped to the Far East, where they are copied and put on the market. They return to the West as counterfeits. Tobacco smugglers also service the London bazaar, and many shops appoint 'runners' who cross the Channel to buy untaxed goods. Dutch-made Drum tobacco is among the best-selling brands, despite the fact that it is not officially available in London shops. Alcohol is among the other goods smuggled, due to the wide disparities in duty in Britain compared to Continental Europe: French beer duty, for example, is one-sixth of the British level (Customs & Excise, 1998).

Moonlighting and Mobility

In Åkerström's (1993) research, which compares the lifestyles of criminals with those of non-criminals—'square johns'—the former are found to have a condescending attitude towards the latter. Criminals are said to see their own lives as exciting and special and the lives of non-criminals as dull, boring, and insipid (Cromwell, 1996). In my own observation of the city bazaar I found that a condescending attitude was held simply towards those whose income was deemed insufficient, be it of licit or illicit origin. Straddling legality and illegality, my informants did not derive a specific identity or adopt distinctive sets of values from either activity, or perhaps they derived these from both. In brief, 'square johns' were disapproved of only when poor, in such a way that goals had absolute priority over means. Their evaluation of other people's behaviour, including mine, did not consider 'how', but 'how much' they earned.

In this sense, those who are active in the bazaar remind us of some of Dostoyevsky's characters who inhabit the underground, where identities are not 'unitary and compact', but are constituted by an anarchy of atoms, a multiplicity of pulsations which 'cannot be imprisoned in a distinct individuality' (Magris, 1999). The bazaar is also the quintessence of Simmel's city (1971, 1990), where the decolouring of things, the disappearance of peculiarities, and the indifferent quality assumed by events require an emotional 'distantiation' from any specific, accomplished, identity. The blasé attitude in the bazaar entails a constant negotiation of practices and boundaries. Mobility, across legality and back, mirrors flexibility of work.

The following statement of a heroin user conveys a physical notion of mobility which illustrates a common pattern in many European cities:

The dealer I bought from for about two years moved at least five times. He came from East London, and then moved south of the river, where initially nobody knew him. Every three or four months, when I went to score, he would tell me that next time he would be at another address. His customers remained the same, and it was on us to follow him around to his new addresses (Ruggiero and South, 1995: 120–1).

This physical mobility is compounded by the constant shifting between different sectors of the irregular economy. As already clarified in the previous chapter, such movement does not imply upward social mobility, but rather a type of sideways mobility, an intermittent skipping from badly paid jobs to property offences, from forms of unemployment benefit to small-scale street dealing in a variety of commodities. This type of mobility characterizes many of those who are active in the urban bazaar, few of whom could be described as 'full-time miscreants' (Mack, 1964) or career delinquents. In brief, careers in crime do not exclude participation in the official, legal economy. Polsky's (1971: 102) classic study of 'hustlers, beats and others', including this important point, argued that most criminals

are employed in and identify with perfectly lower-class jobs, get way behind in their bills, and see temporary or 'one shot' criminal activity as a way to get solvent without giving up their regular jobs.

In this respect, the author coined the term 'crime as moonlighting'. The bazaar offers numerous versions of moonlighting, as it provides a supplement to regular employment. Here, 'crime as work' is not just a metaphor but an apt description of the activities being conducted in parts of the contemporary city, where individuals seize legal and illegal opportunities alike. In other words, the individuals involved in illegal economies adopt a model of legitimate behaviour, but in doing so they also commute from the official to the underground economy, and back again. In this process, they constantly negotiate the moral acceptability of their behaviour.

In this respect, the activities conducted by the last informant I would like to mention are exemplary. Bill is a regular heroin user who inhales the substance rather than injecting or 'chasing' it. He works part-time in a company importing olive oil from Greece and buys one or two £20 doses per day. His second activity consists of distributing pornographic tapes that he himself reproduces from private TV channels. This artisan activity, which is performed thanks to a good satellite dish, avails itself of publicity channels through advertisement magazines. He sells four tapes at £25, six at £40, and ten at £60, and uses a 'pay-as-you-talk' portable telephone, which he changes regularly. Paedophiles are excluded from his clientele. He delivers the tapes with a car provided for him by the local social services department, as he is registered as disabled. Confirming somehow the dull uniformity described in the previous chapter in relation to heroin use, his complaints revolve around the lack of excitement he finds in the bazaar, where he feels isolated. He sees individualistic behaviour prevailing and genuine communication and co-operation wanting. Besides unemployment benefit, his income also comprises revenues from the sale of paintings, which he buys from mediocre artists and sells at £100–£140 each. When one of his customers, in exchange for four videos, offered him some cocaine, for his own use or to 'sell on', he refused the offer, because he did not trust him: he was black.

Occupational Barriers as Barricades

As we have seen so far the boundaries surrounding illegal markets and activities within them are uncertain. Yet, in most cases examined, occupational barriers are in place which delimit their moral and economic confines. Albanians, Neapolitans, East Europeans, and at times the blacks are kept at a distance by those who operate in the bazaar, as if physical or imaginary barricades stopped them from playing a part there. Let us expand on this.*

Among the features which characterize literary, but also early sociological, descriptions of cities is the notion of *barricades*, both physical and metaphorical. In his writings, Victor Hugo gave an impressive picture of barricades in the city of Paris at the time of the Revolution, describing them as towering shadows revealing broken, irregular outlines, profiles of strange constructions. The ambiguous beauty of these irregular forms was praised by Baudelaire, who admired the magic cobblestones erected as makeshift fortresses (Benjamin, 1983). On the one hand, such admiration conveyed a sense of pity for the doomed dispossessed manning the barricades. On the other hand, it was inspired by their very symbolism, as the erecting of barricades and the setting of boundaries were assumed to signal revolt, but also protection of one's otherness. Marx located barricades at the centre of conspiratorial movements, but at the same time he recognized their metaphorical meaning as marking the perimeters of a cocooned urban space to which the dispossessed could retreat. When, in 1871, the Commune of Paris came to its tragic end, the rioters grouped behind the barricades, 'as a mortally injured animal withdraws to its lair' (Benjamin, 1983: 16). The Communards preferred to fight in their own territory rather than face the open battle, and their choice proved fatal.

Invisible barricades are in place which outline the contours of irregular economies and moral otherness. This otherness has long been the focus of attention of both poets and sociologists. It was the illegitimate and irregular, rather than officially celebrated, subjects who featured in Baudelaire's description of modern heroism. Thus the poet was attracted to 'the thousands of irregular existences led in the basements of a big city by criminals and kept women' (Benjamin, 1983: 78). Again, he conveyed the notion of a protected territory, one surrounded by imaginary barricades which delimited a social space, its moral values and economy. However, the *flâneur*, a character with whom Baudelaire identified, not only held an aesthetic perception of the underworld, he also admired it as a locus of economic reproduction, of hectic exchange of commodities and services. The underworld was a bazaar.

In the analysis of the late-modern city provided by Sennett (1976), the barricades make a return, though they are not erected by rebellious

---

* The concluding pages of this chapter draw on work I have carried out with Nigel South, whom I warmly thank.

communities. Rather, they are built around communities by official planners, who devise new districts of a single class; the rich and the poor have to be isolated from one another. Here, barricades constitute a tangible demarcation between legally acquired wealth and legal, semi-legal, or illegal survival. The delimited territory has also been studied as an example of how the poor can be sequestered, as in the dystopian analysis of Davis (1992, 1998).

During the 1920s and 1930s US sociologists focused on the moral and material economy of the districts of the poor, and (often sympathetically) described the alternative social order within them. Studies conducted in marginalized urban areas unveiled microsocieties of immigrants which were perfectly organized (Whyte, 1943). The high degree of their organization contrasted with the absence of meaningful relationships that such microsocieties established with society at large (Thrasher, 1927; Shaw, 1930). One could say that the barricades separating poor districts from wealthy society, in this perspective, appeared to be functional to the reproduction of both. These barricades, in other words, allowed for the dispossessed to set up their own economy, be it legal or illegal.

It has been noted that various theories of delinquency and deviance that were derived from the study of Chicago and a handful of other US cities have always been limited in their applicability to other contexts. Furthermore, these theories focused almost exclusively on a specific class. As Downes and Rock (1988: 164) put it, this 'may be termed differential magnification, the tuning of the analytical lens to an almost exclusive degree on the "subordinate" cultures, with a corresponding neglect of the "dominant" cultures'. Two further points should be added here. First, these theories fail to consider in any thorough fashion the mixture of legality and illegality within urban territories, and, secondly, they treat city areas as both morally and physically isolated. The type of barricades that the sociologists of Chicago alluded to— zonal barriers, transition zones, and so on—consisted of imaginary perimeters circumscribing communities of the dispossessed and their illegalities. Their definition of 'delinquent areas' left no doubt about the notion endorsed: there are behaviours adopted in the ghetto which are precisely and unproblematically identified as being delinquent. Moreover, their notion of barricades excluded the likelihood that these may be erected from within the ghetto itself. It should be noted that subsequent descriptions and analyses provided by Merton also appear to exclude such likelihood. In his suggestion that the 'gangster' is a

popular individual in his own environment, and that Al Capone represents the triumph of amoral intelligence over morally prescribed
failure, Merton (1968) posits the existence of a coherent set of values
and, consequently, a specific group of interconnected individuals supporting and performing illegal acts. This group, which reacts to prescribed failure, appears to operate in isolation from the official
law-abiding society.

The description I have provided above questions the simplicity of an
image of precisely identifiable delinquent areas, both in moral and
physical terms. The suggestive value of the idea of the bazaar is that it
alludes to a variety of individuals interacting in a market where commodities and services are bought and sold irrespective of their being
legal or illegal. The notion of the bazaar, as applied to contemporary
cities, entails the coexistence of legality and illegality and the permanent shifting of the boundaries between the two. In a sense, my intention is to convey an idea of the city that 'can turn people outward, not
inward; rather than wholeness, the city can give experience of otherness' (Sennett, 1993: 123). The bazaar is an urban space in which open-
ness to strangers and acceptance of differences are essential in
establishing communal life. It offers incessant opportunities to experience otherness; it is not a tightly knit universe offering stable roles to its
members. Rather, it offers a variety of segmented roles and grants
membership in widely different groups interacting within it. It is not
surprising that in such urban bazaars, and, for that matter, in contemporary cities in general, labour market statisticians find the defining of
occupational categories and activities to be no simple task. Part-time
work, temporary jobs, self-employment, semi-legal occupations, and
the hidden activities conducted within the parallel economies combine
to blur conventional distinctions between employment and unemployment. The bazaar includes all of this socio-economic activity; it is the
place where legality and illegality meet, overlap, and mix. The moral
universe of the bazaar gives individuals that sense of tentativeness
about their own beliefs which every civilized person should have
(Sennett, 1976).

It is arguable that from this perspective, the *barricades*—whether
born of resistance or imposed by control—metaphorically vanish, as
otherness, difference, and a multiplicity of moral orders characterize
what I describe as the contemporary bazaar. However, we have seen
how the barricades are, none the less, always likely to appear—if not
imposed from without, then built from within. These barricades are

represented in the division of labour which characterizes the bazaar, and consist of occupational barriers which limit career opportunities for some while enhancing them for others. Contrary to the notion of delinquent areas whose boundaries delimit legality and illegality, I convey a notion of the barricades separating individuals within illegality. We have seen examples of such barricades being erected on the basis of moral repulsion expressed by some inhabitants of the bazaar against others. Often such repulsion results in a competitive edge allowing those who express it to exclude from the benefits of illegal activity those whom they target. The next chapter will deal entirely with one specific form of such barricades built from within, namely with the occupational barriers which characterize the ethnic division of labour in illicit economies. The remarks below are aimed at providing a brief general introduction to the arguments presented later.

Barricades Built from Within

The association of ethnic groups with illicit drugs is still a strong constant in public and private rhetoric, and encapsulates the widespread suspicion directed towards the 'alien' and the 'other' since at least the late nineteenth century (Helmer, 1975; Kohn, 1992). However, whether because of difficulties with research access, or sociological timidity, or some kind of 'political correctness', the literature on the urban drug scene in Britain generally shows a strange neglect of the experience of black and other minority communities (Ruggiero and South, 1997). Only recently has this changed, as shown by research conducted in Nottingham (Bean and Pearson, 1992), in the London areas of Lewisham (Mirza et al., 1991) and Brixton (Ruggiero, 1993b), and on the media perception of black youth and drugs (Murji, 1998). However, all of this amounts to very little when compared to the US literature on the subject (for a review of such literature see Trimble et al., 1992; Gunst, 1995; Bourgois, 1996). Perhaps the only significant exception to this point is the study carried out by Pryce (1986), who links the inequalities observed in Bristol to the illicit economies operating in that city. Some observations made by Pryce may provide indirect support for the argument developed here. For example, the author describes the evolution of 'alternative economies' in relation to the official economy and, while revealing the division of labour within the drug market, he analyses the circumstances which lead to changes in the street supply scene along with the dynamics which trigger criminal careers.

In more recent work it has been argued that the riskiest and most stigmatized tasks in domestic and international drug markets are left to unskilled criminal labourers who are almost inevitably poorly paid (Ruggiero and South, 1995). At the level of international smuggling and importation these are, with some exceptions, non-European nationals whose roles are limited, who are regarded as 'expendable mules' and are frequently unaware of the exemplary sentences they may receive if detected (Green, 1991). Large-scale importers, of whatever background, are not usually *directly* involved in the smuggling itself, but limit themselves to the organization of transit between point of departure and arrival. Thereafter they are likely to 'sell on'. Established indigenous groups tend to keep at some distance from international trafficking and importation, and in doing so they both minimize risk and maximize profits. Indigenous wholesalers are often in a position of some strength when negotiating prices with importers. In terms of added value, this link in the distribution chain can often be more financially rewarding than other segments of the drug economy. Wholesalers, in other words, exploit their advantageous position in domestic markets and, through access to middle-range suppliers, master the most remunerative segments of distribution. As we shall see in the examples provided in the next chapter, the division of roles and profits in criminal economies often takes on a distinctive ethnic character.

It would be unwarranted to romanticize the bazaar: it is a site which, while favouring acquaintance with otherness and difference, reproduces prejudices characterizing the official economy. These prejudices design occupational barriers which predetermine roles and careers. The internal barricades constitute the other face of the bazaar, which otherwise appears to offer both horizontal and vertical mobility. In reality, a 'principal and agent' model prevails in the bazaar, with the former commanding the latter to take actions on his/her behalf in exchange for monetary reward (Strong and Waterson, 1987). In other words, barricades are in place which prevent many agents from eventually becoming principals, or employees from becoming employers (what seems to be a notable exception to this rule will be described in the next chapter). Even customers may contribute to the creation of these internal barricades, as for example in the case of drug users who prefer to buy from white dealers rather than from black ones, the former, in their view, possessing more business ethics than the latter (Ruggiero, 1993*b*). Similarly, in a study carried out by Bean and Pearson (1992), dealers operating in Nottingham claim that the real work, namely the hard and risky tasks, is mainly undertaken by 'black guys'.

Such observations are neither new nor unique. Lindesmith's (1965) classic work points to the exclusion of blacks from managerial positions in the illicit economy of various cities in the USA. Redlinger (1975) provides a similar account in his study of the heroin market in San Antonio, Texas, and competing involvements of blacks, Mexicans, and whites. He notes that illicit markets may offer upward social mobility to Mexican-Americans and Europeans but not to blacks.

Conclusion

I have tried to argue that illicit economies mirror characteristics of the legal economy. Wider social disadvantages based on ethnicity are reflected in the less favourable trading positions occupied by non-indigenous participants in illegal economies.

In this chapter, I have attempted to locate these economies in the contemporary urban bazaar, a site of electrifying movement, diversity, and exhilarating temporariness. Those who inhabit the bazaar, as I have suggested, undertake unstable careers and commute from illegality to legality and back again, with both spheres contributing income and shaping life-styles. In the bazaar, opportunistic merchants, and 'Jacks-of-all-trades', who are constantly on the look-out for every opportunity and jump from one sector to the other, are common (Hobbs, 1988; Åkerström, 1993). 'There is blessing in movement,' says a Moroccan proverb: 'move and you will confound your enemies, sit and they will confound you' (Geertz et al., 1979). The Western urban bazaar also appears to reward talents and versatility. Yet, in this exciting environment, with its incessant stimulations, the independence of some translates into the dependence of others, the work of many is determined by strategies designed by a few. In brief, the bazaar contains internal barricades which delineate discrimination and inequality. The economy of the bazaar reproduces some of the worst aspects of the official economy. In other words, one of the problems with illegal economies is that in so many ways they are, sadly, similar to legal ones.

4
Illegal Activities Without Criminal Economies

Among the occupational barriers which are in place in illegal economies, those based on race and ethnicity are the most sharply drawn. Let us examine how the metaphorical barricades discussed in the previous chapter shape illegal activities in a specific context. This chapter is the result of ethnographic work conducted in a London inner-city area inhabited by large ethnic minority groups. The analysis of drug use and distribution in this area permits the formulation of some hypotheses around the relationship between illicit drugs, crime, and ethnicity. Although such analysis does not lend itself to generalization, in the second part of the chapter an attempt will be made to draw a broad comparison with other European contexts. A discussion of the convergences and anomalies shown by a second case study, which focuses on the involvement of Albanian immigrants in the drug economy in Italy, will conclude this chapter.[1]

Deprivation and Drug Abuse

Lambeth has the second largest population in inner London, with some 240,000 people officially living in the borough. It is a multi-cultural community with over 30 per cent of the population coming from black or other ethnic minorities. The borough displays all indicators commonly associated with social and economic deprivation: low average income, high unemployment rate, a high proportion of single-parent families, and mortality rates well above the national average.

All of these data may lead one to think that an area such as Lambeth, particularly its central part, Brixton, is more likely than other areas to

---

[1] The empirical material for this chapter includes information collected in Lambeth in two different periods, namely the early 1990s and the 1998–9 period. As for the second case study, the findings pertain to ongoing research funded by the European Commission.

be affected by drug abuse. However, the association of drugs with deprivation is far from clear or unequivocal. Drug use affects both deprived and affluent areas, and social conditions seem to determine, at most, the motivation pattern, the effects, and the degree of risk related to drug use, rather than drug use prevalence in itself. It is true that some unemployed youths may find in the drug scene a vicarious occupational arena providing them with income, sociability, and life structure. Nevertheless, it is also true that unemployment may be an outcome rather than a cause of drug use, and that in some social groups it is the availability of money rather than the lack of it which may lure some into the drugs business.

If drug use involves diverse social groups and classes, its impact varies. The conditions under which drugs are used, their quality, the individual expectations of users, along with their life-styles, determine the degree of severity of what is termed a 'drug problem'. Disadvantaged individuals may find in drug use a supplementary source of disadvantage, thus adding to their social vulnerability. Others may find in drug use an additional vehicle of group sociability and integration. Yet others may discover in the commercial use of drugs a parallel source of economic advantage.

In brief, *there are drug economies virtually devoid of a drug culture*. Here, a well-structured drug business may be in operation which does not foster distinctive, visible attitudes among both suppliers and customers. In some areas, for instance, the supply of drugs occurs in a protected environment, and use takes place in safe conditions. Here, discretion keeps the official agencies at bay. By contrast, some areas present themselves with *a drug culture which is virtually devoid of a drug economy*, in the sense that suppliers and customers do not participate in a lively, prosperous illegal economy. Here, both users and dealers may be conspicuous enough to contribute to the shaping of stereotypes attached to them and the area where they reside. These areas, where well-structured, highly remunerative, illegal transactions rarely take place, often become a high-profile target for the intervention of official agencies.

These hypotheses formed the premiss to the research whose findings are summarized below. The research availed itself of a variety of informants, including key observers, groups, and individuals who in different capacities were or had been participants in the drug scene: users, ex-users, and distributors, but also social workers, doctors, and psychologists.

Self-victimization

The perception of the drug phenomenon as a problem depends upon the distance, both geographical and moral, from which one observes that phenomenon. Typically, many Brixton residents did not perceive the signs of what could be termed a drug emergency, nor were those who did see the marks of a drug problem in the area inclined to regard that problem as more severe than in other inner-city areas. Drug-related deaths, they noted, were fewer in Lambeth than in more affluent areas.

Similarly, the day-to-day experience of many social workers was at odds with official concern about a drug problem in Lambeth. Members of the local Youth Justice Team, for example, claimed that 'there are drugs in Brixton, but this does not necessarily mean that there is a drug problem'. Rather, problems associated with legal drugs such as pharmaceuticals and alcohol were said to be prevailing. Moreover, social workers said that the problem affected the parents of their young clients, rather than the clients themselves, because

many of our young people have parents who are drug users or dealers, and even when it is the young ones who use drugs it is the parents who pay, anyway, in economic, social, and psychological terms.

The notion that the local community was submerged in a drug culture fostered by unscrupulous large distributors was also contested by journalists working in the press whose readership is mainly of ethnic minority background. Some of them highlighted that major police operations against 'barons' and large dealers invariably translated into the arrest of 'foot soldiers' and 'pathetic users'.

On the contrary, the drug problem was said to affect mainly those who inhabited a social circle close to the drug scene itself. The workers for a local drug project, for instance, could hardly avoid the perception that in central Lambeth the drug problem was serious. Their day-to-day experience was based on the provision of support for users; drugs constituted the pivot of their professional life and their effort to improve the quality of life in the community. The manager of one such project explained:

It is difficult to say if there is a drug problem in Lambeth. People who come through this door, to our project, have certainly got a drug problem. But I don't know to what extent drugs affect the social fabric of Lambeth. All I know is that there are people who individually are using drugs in a very dangerous way.

The drug scene seemed to be characterized by forms of what I would call 'internal victimization' or 'self-victimization', as in the following examples provided by a doctor:

Wives are affected if husbands are drug abusers. I think that the rate of separations in Lambeth is so high also because of drug use. The problem regards family members, including children of users. We will see the consequences of this in a few years, when children of users will be teenagers.

Many literary classics have explored the magic properties of drugs and pondered the spiritual phenomena engendered by their use. The 'mediocre' human condition was explored through mood-altering substances, and exploration showed that humans are not mediocre creatures after all (Paz, 1990). This seemed to apply to everyone. Drugs were deemed 'democratic'. However, as suggested so far, in disadvantaged urban areas the effects of drug use and retail distribution may be felt mainly within the limited enclave of individuals who are active in the market and among those (relatives, friends, and acquaintances) who are close to them. In some cases, in sum, we are faced with self-victimizing behaviour which is adopted amid the relative unawareness of the surrounding members of the community. Let us see whether the other illegal activities related to drug use and distribution also display similar forms of self-victimization.

A Drug Economy?

A group of social workers suggested that drugs are tolerated in Lambeth because they provide an alternative economy where deprived people may find a surreptitious source of income. However, a very frequent comment made by my informants was that the reputation of central Lambeth, in particular Brixton, produced an imaginary magnification of the actual dimension of the drugs economy in the area. It was felt, for example, that due to the notorious poverty of the borough, 'people tend to believe that there are a lot of drugs around'. The poverty/drugs association, it was suggested, leads the authorities to step up action, so that a process is triggered whereby more police activity in the area leads to more arrests being made and higher quantities of drugs found.

The reputation of Brixton as a prosperous drug market also caused bizarre incidents. Buyers were attracted by the fame of the area but were often disappointed by the quantities and variety of the drugs they

found there. Hence the appearance on the scene of improvised suppliers who 'did their best' to meet such high demand. These 'amateurs'
were deemed incapable of 'doing the job properly'. In the words of a
user:

Here, the chances of getting oregano instead of 'grass' are very high. For this
reason it's always best to have personal contacts, or to cultivate particular dealers. If you know somebody, a serious supplier, you'd better stick to him.

It also happened that bogus drugs were sold in certain periods
because suppliers were holding on to the 'good-quality stuff' for a
while, with the intention of bringing it back, eventually, at higher
prices. Consequently:

Those who come from other areas to buy cannabis make us laugh. We call the
stuff they get 'Brixton bush'. Young people know that customers come from all
over London, and of course they don't always have the good-quality stuff to
sell, so they just offer what comes handy.

In effect, some cannabis dealers stocked two different qualities—one
for their clients and friends, and the other for occasional customers
allured by the reputation surrounding the area. Some of the local users
argued that the incompetence and dishonesty of some dealers made the
whole drug trade unreliable. Many resident users, consequently, went
elsewhere to buy, in order both to find better deals and to escape what
they saw as a heavily policed environment.

Users who resorted to drug agencies complained that prescriptions
were ungenerous, and found it difficult to keep up their habit with only
legally obtained drugs. Intermittent recourse to property crime and
involvement in the grey market of pharmaceuticals were the most common ways of supporting habitual use. In turn, some users who were
unknown to official agencies also resorted to predatory offences in
order to obtain money for their doses. However, what kind of offences
and what type of economy they generated deserve brief discussion.

In the view of most informants, the drug economy in central
Lambeth was a domestic, petty, hand-to-mouth economy. In a sense,
this informal economy mirrored the regular exchange of things and
small amounts of money occurring in some housing estates. Small
quantities of drugs were sometimes exchanged, borrowed, or sold, just
as sums as low as £10 were sometimes lent to neighbours. A solicitor
noted that when drug users turned to burglary, they revealed how
hopelessly unskilled they were:

The number of burglars arrested while holding stolen goods at home is perhaps an indication of their professional inadequacy and their little knowledge of networks where the goods can be circulated.

In this respect, it is legitimate to wonder whether the success claimed by the police in fighting local burglaries was to be imputed to their new strategies and increasing efficiency or to the increasing number of professionally inadequate burglars operating on the scene.

The heroin economy was particularly limited in scope; its consumption was felt to be as steady as the money circulation connected with it. Other circumstances also seemed to indicate that the development of a prosperous heroin economy in the area was unlikely. According to a drug worker:

Heroin still requires users to adopt a set, albeit vague, of 'counter-values'. Heroin users often feel they have something in common, and in the name of their tacit complicity, social, racial, and sometimes even gender differences among them may blur.

In contrast, the cocaine market was seen as more conducive to commercial individualism and therefore more prone to possessive attitudes and harsh competition. Because the substance suits diverse life-styles and attracts a variety of social groups, conflicts emerging in the cocaine milieu resonated with or mimicked the conflicts taking place in law-abiding circles. Race differences were strongly felt, and hierarchies identified and respected.

According to the prevailing feeling among informants, little money was accumulated, and remained, in the area through drug selling. The poverty of the drug economy, *vis-à-vis* the number of estimated users, was interpreted as a sign that profits went to other city areas where police control was not as strict. In other words, investors and large distributors were said to keep at a considerable distance from the market they supplied. If large distributors operated in central Lambeth, it was noted, this would result in more visible availability of finances, and would be apparent in more licit businesses being set up with the proceeds of drug selling.

Some small dealers were also engaged in other activities with a view to supplementing their income from drugs. Claiming state benefits, selling stolen goods, and petty theft were among those activities. Although periodically apprehended, such dealers intermittently returned to operate in the same petty economy, especially if they were users as well as suppliers. In the view of a social worker, 'their role is to be arrested, they are there to feed the criminal justice system'. Some of them had started a career with the desire of escaping the boredom of a regular low-paid job. In this sense, most of the users I talked to thought that a residual 'glamour' was attached to the drug scene, and that it appeared to be a 'free' and exciting world. But, as they soon realized, 'in fact it also involves a lot of work'.

Speaking from personal experience, a crack dealer described the drug economy in central Lambeth in the following terms:

There are about twelve middle-range distributors who never go on the street in this area. They take between fifty and seventy per cent of the street value of the substances sold. In turn, they buy in other areas. It is very rare that distributors here are in direct contact with importers, or are importers themselves. These middle-range distributors are in contact with street sellers, and it is here that problems start. Those who operate at street level are unreliable, and what is happening now is that many users go somewhere else to choose their own supplier. It is also happening that users prefer to buy from white dealers, who are seen as more serious traders. Among dealers you now find ordinary people who just get up promptly in the morning to do their job. They have a mortgage to pay, children to support.

The majority of my informants felt that the community in which they lived benefited very little from the drug economy. The proceeds of drug distribution, they argued, could at most feed individual 'flashy' consumption.

There is prosperity in a criminal economy, at least potentially, when parts of the illegal proceeds are converted into legal enterprises. In the area under examination, the degree to which this conversion took place was negligible. In some cases, in fact, it was not success in crime which led to ventures into the official business world but, on the contrary, failure in business which prompted forays into crime. Most of my informants suggested that disadvantaged people in central Lambeth were doomed, as they lacked opportunities and infrastructures to change their condition. Often, when trying to venture into some sort of business, they were denied bank loans. This lack of infrastructure and finance reverberated in the illegal economy, which remained sloppy, amateurish.

In views expressed by official commentators, the increase in the use of firearms indicates that drug markets are well structured and that territorial conflicts are under way for their control. These conflicts, it is assumed, tend to the establishment of monopolistic conditions. The reality in central Lambeth seemed to invalidate such assumptions. The use of firearms was either independent of the drug market or marked a phase which preceded the involvement of organized groups in it. Some armed robberies, for instance, were carried out with a view to generating a preliminary accumulation of funds, which eventually would or would not have been invested in drugs. In sum, the market was far from being rigidly structured, nor did it display monopolistic features or tendencies. It was as chaotic as drug use, and allowed for the exploits of diverse individuals, often improvised dealers, and unlikely firms.

Violent episodes occurring in the drug economy were not perceived as symptoms of the increasing stakes involved in it. It was felt that no rational relationship between risks and benefits could be observed, and that the degree of violence deployed by those involved in the market was not proportionally related to the profits pursued. This also characterized other illegal activities carried out in the area. Even armed robberies, for example, did not necessarily bring large amounts of money. The local press described, in thorough detail, armed robberies which yielded average sums of £50. Mugging, given the modest amounts of money involved, appeared rather as a form of 'violent begging'. A drug worker argued that the degree of violence in the drug business was just a reflection of the increasing level of violence in society as a whole. He also argued that this produced self-images and mutual perceptions, among users and small dealers, which often magnified their actual calibre:

Among my clients I don't see any Dillinger or Al Capone, but they all think they are gangsters. Somebody made them think they are—perhaps the media or the police. In fact they delude themselves: they think they are making a career, but they are just setting up the scene for themselves. They are vulnerable and obvious, they'll never make it to the top.

Among my informants, violence was more associated with alcohol than with illicit drug use.

A cocaine dealer suggested that even so-called Yardies (alleged professional criminals and illegal immigrants from Jamaica) would find it hard to put some kind of order in what seemed to them to be a very low-profile and confused economy. He also hypothesized:

The Yardies don't have a chance to develop their business because other gangs of white professional criminals would not allow them to. I also suspect that the white gangs themselves fuelled the panic about the Yardies, because they saw them as dangerous competitors. They must have informed the police, who in fact got information about the Yardies that they would never have picked up by themselves.

Incidentally, the depiction of the Yardies as the most threatening symbol of social disorganization, with the inevitable emphasis on their volatility and random violence, not only reinforces notions of 'the dangerous Other, those without law who threaten us' (Murji, 1999: 59), but also affects the career prospects of minorities. This depiction, in sum, provides hurdles making upward mobility difficult. As already mentioned, in my own research many users regarded black dealers as 'cheats', a circumstance which, along with their visibility, made their ascent to the higher echelons of the criminal economy somewhat problematic. Those who had 'made it' were highly stigmatized, not so much for being drug dealers as for being black entrepreneurs. The moral disapproval of relatively prosperous black suppliers hid a resentment of those who overturned the 'natural' order of society, rather than of drug suppliers.

A dealer claimed that, even in the crack business, allegedly controlled by black entrepreneurs, the position of black dealers was in fact confined to the lower strata of the distribution chain. They would buy cocaine from white large suppliers, and then 'wash it' before selling on the street. The good stuff, he said, was kept outside Lambeth.

The disorganization of the drug market in central Lambeth was confirmed by a number of episodes. People without any previous experience were approached and asked if they wanted to be involved in drug selling even before they were asked to buy drugs for themselves. This job offer did not take into account the low commercial efficiency that neophytes can offer.

Users who felt incapable of committing remunerative offences resorted to stealing from people who were closest to them. Their victims included other users, small dealers, but also relatives and friends. Few admitted to resorting to this specific practice, though many attributed it to others. However, most of the users claimed their 'honourableness' in the choice of targets. Attacking a person on the street, for example, was said to be a taboo, whereas shoplifting was presented as the favourite activity. Moral principles mixed with a vague political 'awareness' underlay this claim: stealing from large companies (big stores and the like) was not regarded as being as socially damaging as stealing from vulnerable passers-by.

Many users did not like the drug scene; they just liked drugs. Therefore, the choice of which illegal activity, if any, they engaged in was prompted by their reluctance to be 'bogged down' in the drug market. Their dislike included images and stereotypes harboured by outsiders, particularly those describing them as callous and indiscriminate predators. Was this one of the reasons they kept a low criminal profile? In a drug agency this point was endorsed as follows:

Here, drug-related crimes are not as many as people think. In this area we didn't have a real hard drugs epidemic, one which would be visible through the dramatic increase in property offences. Property crime is relatively independent of drugs. In this sense, the ordinary residents in Lambeth may not perceive the existence of a drug problem in their own area.

Immigrants and Self-inflicted Crime

Let us summarize briefly. In the urban area I have examined, all drugs were available, though this does not mean that the area as such had a 'drug problem'. The drug problem, increasingly, seemed to be confined to the most vulnerable section of the drug scene itself, and affected mainly users, small dealers, their acquaintances, friends, and relatives. In other words, the shorter the distance from which one observed that problem the greater the perception of its magnitude. I have hinted, in this respect, at forms of self-victimization, characterized by property offences committed by users and small dealers within their own enclave, their own community, often against peers, friends, and colleagues.

The drug suppliers operating in the area, in their turn, were supplied by large distributors residing outside the borough. This geo-economic configuration of the drug market may have been the result of former institutional intervention during the mid-1980s, which presumably displaced large distribution and the most remunerative segments of the drugs economy to less suspect areas. A tentative, general point could be highlighted: deprived urban areas are not only denied the opportunity to set up successful legitimate enterprises, they are also impeded in the establishment of prosperous criminal economies.

In the drug market I have described, tasks requiring a limited set of skills were left to ethnic minorities, which therefore operated in risky conditions, were underpaid, and had poor prospects of career advancement. This was due, among other things, to the particular attention to which they were subjected by law enforcement agencies. Figures released in 1999 suggest that this pattern continues to be repeated: the Afro-Caribbean population in Britain is five to seven times more likely to be targeted by police stop-and-search strategies; black people form over one-quarter of all stops and searches in the London Metropolitan

Police area (*Statewatch*, 1999). In Brixton, a new car or a suit just above mediocrity may be enough to raise police suspicion. What criminal career can persons who are met with hurdles at the embryonic stages of their illegal initiative undertake?

But to what extent do the criminal enterprises operating in other European contexts present with similar ethnic patterns?

There are visible elements of self-victimization in illegal activities carried out by ethnic and immigrant communities in a number of European countries. For example, trafficking in human beings, when undertaken by minorities, victimizes members of minority groups who are also the customers of such services. Germany, Italy, France, Portugal, and Spain are cases in point. In turn, organized prostitution, and therefore pimping, mainly victimizes African, East European, and Albanian women. It is extremely rare that immigrant criminal entrepreneurs manage to recruit West European sex workers, who are instead more likely to be self-employed or employed in the protected luxury sectors of the sex economy. Protection rackets operating in many European cities, when involving immigrant groups, usually target members of the very same groups, nor would indigenous criminal groups tolerate their compatriots being victimized by foreigners. Finally, violent crimes against immigrants, which are frequently perpetrated by indigenous people against minorities, may also occur within the very enclaves of ethnic minorities themselves.

In the face of self-victimization, one may be drawn to a cynical observation. Among the dreams of many 'reformers', there is little space for utopian islands which free themselves of crime once and for all. Rather, there is the desire to circumscribe crime and delimit it within precise social boundaries: by making crime more easily identifiable, processes of stigmatization encounter fewer obstacles, collective resentment is more easily mobilized, and crime itself becomes, after all, more manageable. This not only permits society to generate Durkheimian reassurance for righteous and honest citizens, but also allows for the concentration of the social costs of crime within delimited communities. In brief: let the offenders also be the victims.

In the *barrios*, the ghettoes, and the slums of most 'advanced' countries it is not easy to distinguish offenders from victims, while it is extremely easy to observe the price that both pay for their involvement in, or proximity to, criminal economies. Participation in the New York crack economy, for instance, produces a dramatic reduction in life expectancy for ethnic minorities, high risk of physical and psychological maiming, and alternatively offers a future of incarceration (Bourgois, 1996). On the contrary, the benefits of criminal activity are hard to identify, as normally these flow elsewhere, namely where the managerial and entrepreneurial tasks of illegal economies are performed. This relates to current developments in the relationship between ethnicity, immigration, and crime in Europe. Let us analyse the broad contours of such developments with the help of some examples.

In France, arrests for drug trafficking show a sensational over-representation of ethnic minorities. Import operations carried out in the north of the country, across the border with Belgium, feed the markets of Lille and surrounding areas as well as the French market as a whole. The area is also a transit zone from where illicit drugs are sent to markets in Spain and Portugal. In terms of arrests, this northern area shows the highest figures in France, with the majority of individuals charged with drug trafficking having an ethnic minority background (OFDT, 1996). The social composition of those arrested shows a predominance of poorly qualified individuals, unemployed and often unregistered immigrants, most of whom are first-time offenders (Duprez and Kokoreff, 1997). Similarly, in the Paris *banlieue*, arrests for street supply show an incidence of ethnic minorities which far exceeds the proportion of foreign residents. New immigration laws introduced in France since the early 1990s have made street supply an increasingly hazardous task for minorities, which are targeted by race-related police activity, as shown by their over-representation in statistics of prisoners on remand (Gallo, 1995).

In Barcelona, the least remunerative sectors of the drug economy are run by immigrant groups: in the Place Real and surrounding area drugs are sold amid vendors of smuggled cigarettes, prostitutes, and transvestites who 'bear the marks of AIDS', while the syringe-exchange van and a couple of police cars complete the scene (Tarrius, 1999). Similarly circumscribed and exposed to formal control is the area of La Mina, where Maghribi expelled from France, Senegalese, and gypsies who commute from Perpignan mingle in a 'market for the poor', servicing the most desperate segments of the drug-using population. The police presence in the area seems to guarantee that dealers, periodically arrested, do not climb the distribution echelon and do not delude themselves about their career prospects. Migrants, especially gypsies, find it extremely hard to gain access to large-scale distribution, and 'although capable of crossing international borders, they are incapable of selling the products outside their own milieu' (ibid.: 52). In brief, migrants are confined to open-space markets, to poor 'psychotrope territories' which have little possibility of dissembling.

In Hamburg, the open drug scene has long been characterized by the visibility of ethnic minority suppliers. In the St Georg area, which is rendered easily accessible by the railway and underground stations, cheap hotels and boarding houses attract unemployed people on social benefit, and 'ex-offenders and refugees who are placed there because it is not possible to find accommodation elsewhere for them' (Alpheis, 1996: 60). Until 1990 St Georg offered job opportunities for freelance drug dealers and prostitutes. When the fight against the open drug scene started, as a result of public demand for order and security, it became apparent that the outcome of police operations would restructure the drugs market and substantially alter the cost-benefit balance for the ethnic minorities involved. The vulnerability of ethnic minorities in the drug business became manifest when a Commission appointed by the Department of Justice found that excessive force and racially motivated violence were used by the police in tackling a phenomenon which, in the official view, was strongly associated with minority groups rather than with drug demand.

In Belgium, two out of five drug charges are brought against people of ethnic minorities, while in Spain the immigrant community, which represents 2 per cent of the population as a whole, constitutes around 20 per cent of the prison population charged with drug offences (Marshall, 1997). In the Netherlands the illicit drugs trade is tackled both at international trafficking level and at the local level. At the former level, organized crime represents the main target, the term 'organized crime' alluding to 'foreign' criminal groups operating transnationally. At the local level police intervention against street suppliers and 'foreigners' is exemplified by Operation Victor, carried out in Rotterdam in the mid-1990s. The open drug scene in Rotterdam, confined around the area of the central station, came under attack after complaints by local residents. The dispersal of the market which followed the operation resulted in yet more complaints from residents in residential areas, where users and suppliers were displaced. The operation also targeted frontier runners operating on the highway between the Belgian border and Rotterdam. Law enforcers targeted groups and individuals, approaching potential buyers and bringing them to dealers in Rotterdam (Lap, 1995). Runners were all from ethnic minority backgrounds, while dealers employing them were mainly white distributors. This pattern still persists because police operations failed to halt hard-drug tourism: immigrants are still in demand for visible, hazardous tasks such as running and promoting, looking for new customers who come from abroad, and if possible contacting them on motorways (Tuteleers and Hebberecht, 1997).

Drug users from visible minorities are exposed to higher risks for a number of discriminatory factors. In most European countries their drug use is more likely to be dealt with by the criminal justice system, rather than the health service. Moreover, it frequently happens that, even when they are only drug users, they are more likely to be regarded as dealers or traffickers (Khan, 1997). For this reason, freelance drug selling by ethnic minorities is becoming increasingly difficult. In most European urban contexts, particularly those characterized by more recent immigration, drug running is still one of the limited job opportunities available to ethnic minorities. In France, runners are also described as 'kamikazes' for the self-destructive nature of their occupation (Devinat, 1996). Heroin markets, for example, employ illegal immigrants at the lowest level of distribution. Whether the new street suppliers have replaced indigenous dealers or whether they have just joined them in the job is difficult to establish; nor are official statistics of any help in this respect (Barbagli, 1998). However, what is to be noted is the position of immigrants in drug markets. While indigenous dealers service an increasingly stable and reliable clientele, immigrants trying to escape detection are forced to rely on a clientele with similar characteristics. In order to do so, they are forced to accept employment from established suppliers, and become their personal 'kamikazes'. Home delivery and street running are among the tasks undertaken by them. In this sense, immigrants do not replace indigenous suppliers; they become their employees. In this way, European cities appear to develop characteristics which prevail in US cities, where, despite a superficial multi-ethnic interaction in street drug scenes, the market displays a quasi-apartheid organization shaped by bitter ethnic divides (Bourgois *et al.*, 1997). Moreover:

The positioning of drug addiction in the Maastricht Treaty, alongside asylum and immigration is a way of keeping the drug addict in the category of the others, among them, and not among us (Kaminski, 1997: 125).

However, in the final case study which makes up this chapter, some new elements seem to emerge which both confirm and slightly modify the pattern presented so far. The case study focuses on Albanian drug suppliers operating in Italy.

Immigrants as Job Providers

The involvement of Albanians in drug trafficking across Europe has been explained by their ability to exploit access to suppliers in Turkey and the Caucasian republics, their simultaneous access to the Adriatic, and their own established presence in Switzerland, Italy, and Germany. Drugs refineries have been discovered in Macedonia, Kosovo, and Albania. The Albanian port of Durrës is the destination for hundreds of vehicles for the transportation and bartering of heroin and other products through the Balkans and via the ferry to Italy. Protected warehousing is provided in Albania itself, with consignments earmarked for Italy, Switzerland, and Germany (Lewis, 1998).

Investigators suggest that Albania could become the Colombia of Europe. In the testimony of an officer of the Servizio Antidroga of the Ministero dell'Interno:

Turkish heroin passes through Albania, and is destined for western European markets. Marijuana is cropped in Albania, particularly on the hills surrounding Saranda. The large plantations are well visible in that area. Marijuana cropping was the result of conversion, in the sense that it is grown in the same greenhouses set up by skilled floriculturists from Terlizzi, in the southern region of Puglia. The new plantations, of course, are more remunerative. In 1996, more than 7 tons of Albanian marijuana were seized by Italian customs police.

In Italy, between 1992 and 1998, the quantities of heroin and cocaine intercepted by the police declined, those of hashish remained stable, while quantities of marijuana underwent a tenfold increase (EMCDDA, 1998).

Interviews with marijuana suppliers in Rome revealed that drugs may be transported to Italy as a form of fee due to traffickers. Each migrant may be given between four and five kilograms. Large bags carrying around thirty kilograms are entrusted to families leaving Albania together. In the words of one informant:

Sometimes, the Albanians do not bring the drugs all the way to the Italian coasts, as other boats from Italy meet them a few miles from shore and take the consignments.

Regarded by investigators as physically 'rough' but mentally sophisticated, Albanian drugs entrepreneurs are also thought to be engaged in a permanent search for autonomy. For example, after an initial phase in which drugs were purchased from Turkish intermediaries, Albanian groups are now said to access larger suppliers and producers directly. In this way, key business links with Afghanistan and other heroin-producing countries, but also with Colombian cocaine producers, were established. Large distributors residing in Italy take the consignments and feed middle-range suppliers scattered in large cities. Groups which established themselves in the Emilia Romagna region are said to be in charge of the laundering of drug proceeds by investing them in the tourist industry of Rimini and the surrounding area.

In cities such as Rome and Milan, the Albanian groups are said to have upset the old geography of criminal activity. An investigator reported that

In the largest Italian cities, Albanians have networks of rented flats. In Milan, the police found that most of the flats were rented by one person, Peschepia Ritvan. He was an Albanian politician, the son of a diplomat and member of the democratic alliance in his country, who had escaped soon after the collapse of the financial pyramids. He used his regular passport for renting the flats, and was in business with traffickers, who nicknamed him 'the falcon'.

The high degree of organization achieved by Albanian drugs entrepreneurs prompts the hypothesis that they have acquired independence from the more established Italian criminal groups. Do Albanians manage to conduct business without causing the resentment of mafia-type organizations? The evidence available on this issue is contradictory.

While traffickers from Albania have established themselves in Italy, Italian criminal groups have set up entrepreneurial outposts in Albania. Partnerships have been formed, particularly in the recruitment of irregular migrants, who constitute cheap labour for farmers and other employers in the hidden economy. Albanians, in this area, seem to have acquired the standing to negotiate with Italian mafia-type organizations on an equal footing. However, anecdotal evidence would indicate that in other areas Italian criminal entrepreneurs are unwilling to establish joint ventures with Albanians and are determined to retain their higher hierarchical position.

On the Romagna coast, two Albanians (Arben Kurani and Agim Lala) were killed on 20 May 1997. After arresting a group of suspects, detectives suggested that the two victims had tried to set up their own business in the heroin trade, and that they had consequently been punished by local members of organized crime. Albanians had to confine themselves to the importation of the substance, due to their access to producing countries and their ability to move goods and people into

Italy. They were, however, expected to refrain from wholesale and middle-range, let alone independent, distribution, the Italian groups being unprepared to share the profits of the heroin economy with the newcomers. Only at the lowest level of retailing was their presence tolerated, namely when 'running' for Italian distributors who thought it wise to keep away from the street drug scene. In this, the pattern described above appears to be confirmed.

Other episodes illustrate the problematic cohabitation of Albanian criminal groups with their Italian counterparts. The channel separating Albania from the Puglia region is not only the conduit for migrants and drugs traffickers, but also a crucial conduit for long-established cigarette smuggling controlled by Italian groups. Clashes between these groups and the new traffickers are frequent, with the former claiming that the Albanians have contributed to the militarization of the coasts, thus making the traditional business of cigarette smuggling too dangerous. In January 1999 a number of blockades were organized by Italian smugglers against migrant traffickers in Puglia. One of the leaders of this anti-Albanian protest spoke to a journalist in the following terms:

We have never seen so much control on this coast. The Albanians don't know what they are doing, they don't respect any rule, and they are in our way while we are working (Buonavoglia, 1999).

However, some local investigators believe that an agreement between Italian and Albanian groups is possible, particularly in Puglia, where cigarette smugglers are provided with radar for the interception of the customs boats patrolling the coast. If this service is rented to Albanian traffickers, it is suggested, the two parties may find it easier to cohabit.

There is only one sector in the drugs business that does not show any sign of competition between Italian and Albanian organizations. This is the marijuana sector, which traditionally has never been of interest to mafia-type groups in Italy. Marijuana, as already mentioned, is grown in Albania and sent to Italy in large quantities. In 1995 Albanian marijuana was sold for the equivalent of £700 per kilogram, while after the financial crisis its cost dropped to little more than £70 per kilogram. Very cheap and of good quality, marijuana is widely, and increasingly, available in Italian cities. Due to its low cost, marijuana is particularly attractive to small dealers, who can access the market and make a living without causing price increases which would discourage purchasers. In sum, the low market price of marijuana makes employment opportunities in its distribution very great, as the involvement of large numbers of intermediaries, each making a profit, is unlikely to produce an increase in retail prices which might keep consumers away.

The peculiarity of the marijuana market in Italy deserves further examination.

In Italy, as elsewhere, analyses of the relationship between immigration and crime offer a variety of explanatory tools ranging from 'relative deprivation' to 'stereotyping', and from 'differential law enforcement' to 'cultural difference'. Advocates of relative deprivation, for example, posit that the image of Italy in developing countries, an image associated with nice cars and elegant clothes, engenders disappointment among new settlers, who end up pursuing the official goals of consumption and success by illegal means, the legal means being unavailable to most of them (Colombo, 1998). Explanations revolving around stereotyping focus instead on the reaction of victims, who are said to be more likely to report crimes committed by immigrants than those committed by their compatriots, thus contributing to the statistical anomaly regarding the prevalence of immigrant offenders (Gatti *et al.*, 1997). In their turn, commentators resorting to explanations based on differential law enforcement pinpoint the visibility of immigrants and, consequently, the more intense police activity to which they are subjected along with the harsher responses they receive from the judiciary (Palidda, 1997; Melossi, 1998). Finally, cultural adaptation and 'ladder' hypotheses are mobilized by authors claiming that crime committed by immigrants is the result of their marginalization in the host country and that social improvement will resolve their initial cultural disorientation (Marotta, 1995).

In respect of illicit drugs, contemporary accounts in Italy echo similar accounts prevailing in other countries, whereby drugs are associated with immigrants and 'alien invasion' (Murji, 1998). Research also suggests that drug economies display a division of labour based on ethnicity so that, for example, import operations are often performed by non-Italians. As elsewhere, these poorly paid 'expendable mules' provide a service to indigenous wholesalers who are part of established distribution networks and usually are not directly involved in importation (Ruggiero, 1992*a*; 1996*a*; Ruggiero and South, 1995). On the other hand, the presence of ethnic minorities is very visible at street-level distribution, where risks of apprehension are higher and profits lower. Echoing the cases discussed above, it is frequent that immigrants are employed by indigenous distributors to deliver doses and to keep street contact with customers. In brief, in Italy too the illicit drugs economy would appear broadly to mirror the division of roles characterizing the official economy, the lower layers of both being mainly occupied by immigrants and ethnic minorities (Ruggiero, 2000).

The case of the Albanian marijuana business seems to constitute a significant anomaly *vis-à-vis* this pattern. Albanian groups are involved in the production, importation, and finally the distribution of the illicit substance (Barbagli, 1998). In an unusual role reversal, Albanian distributors sell quantities of marijuana to Italian street suppliers who are in closer contact with enclaves of users. In this sense, Albanians create job opportunities for young Italians, thus partly resolving the problem of youth unemployment in Italy. Moreover, as remarked by one of the police investigators I interviewed:

Albanian marijuana is a blessing for the Italian younger generation, as it has diverted users from crack, ecstasy, and even from heroin, whose consumption has declined.

Conclusion

The ethnic division of labour in the drugs economy across Europe entails that, in large measure, the most remunerative segments of that economy are occupied by indigenous groups and individuals. The anomaly of the marijuana market just described, with Albanian entrepreneurs offering jobs as street suppliers to young Italians, deserves a brief analysis. Marijuana is perhaps the least stigmatized of all illicit drugs in most European countries. For this reason, and therefore following an ethnic division of risks, the natives who distribute small quantities of the substance are less severely penalized than immigrants producing it and distributing it in large quantities. Again, ethnic minorities are faced with 'costs of illegal choice' which exceed those faced by indigenous populations. Moreover, an illegal economy which supplies a relatively tolerated drug should be met with appreciation for its diverting criminal activity and drug use from more damaging enterprises and more harmful substances. The costs in terms of arrests incurred by Albanian traffickers in Italy show the lack of gratitude of Italian authorities for immigrants who have caused such diversion and who act, after all, as unexpected job providers. The 'benefactors', in sum, run higher risks of prosecution than those they benefit.

Finally, there are other occupational barriers, blocking criminal careers for ethnic minorities, which precede police intervention. I am referring to the selective process whereby crimes committed by immigrants are prevented from developing into aggregate provisions of illegal services, so that they are denied the chance of assuming the stable features of illicit enterprises. Immigrants, in sum, are prevented by competing groups from setting up proper criminal economies. These competing groups are usually formed by natives and long-term residents, who report illegal activity carried out by 'foreigners' before they start displaying entrepreneurial features. In this respect, if the case study presented in the first part of this chapter shows how there can exist a drug culture virtually devoid of a drug economy, looking at crimes committed by immigrants in Europe one could suggest that we are faced with criminal activity virtually devoid of a criminal economy. The types of organized criminality accessible to immigrants in Europe are, moreover, destined to remain pariah forms of crime, due to their exclusion from the resources, the networks, the protection, encouragements, and economic dividends which only official actors are in a position to offer. Only indigenous groups have access to these 'career accelerators', and it is their simultaneous involvement in the illegal and the legal arenas which makes their criminal careers so successful.

It would be interesting to assess the degree to which criminal behaviour adopted by immigrants in Europe, which would appear to be determined by social disadvantage, is also the outcome of the amplifying role played by criminologists and their theories, particularly theories hingeing, indeed, on notions of disadvantage. I am thinking of concepts such as 'relative deprivation', according to which many immigrants, when surrounded by the wealth they are unaccustomed to, feel that they too have the right to portions of it. Hence their alleged involvement in criminal activity, the official means for achieving wealth being denied to them. It would be worth investigating whether such concepts have by now earned currency even among the police and the judiciary, who, predicting that the condition of disadvantage inevitably leads to crime, respectively arrest and convict immigrants, because sooner or later they will be forced to do so anyway.

5

From Fordist-type Criminals to Criminality 'Just-in-Time'

The formal–informal interface is usually associated with threats and opportunities. Allegedly, threats are addressed to the official economy, while opportunities are offered to individuals who are excluded from the official labour market. In this way, informal, marginal, or hidden activities come to be linked to illegal ways of obtaining income which, one could argue, make up for the loss caused to underprivileged members of society by the withering of the welfare state. Consequently, informal economies and conventional criminal activities end up almost coinciding. In effect, in many European countries the phrase 'informal economy' calls to mind conventional property crime, and is rarely associated with areas or niches which are somehow related to the official economic process. In previous chapters I have argued that conventional criminal activities intermingle with official occupations in what I have identified as the contemporary bazaar. In this chapter the importance of the informal will be examined against the background of a process that can be tentatively described as follows. The 'informal' tends to be absorbed into the 'formal', in the sense that hidden practices, parallel procedures, and forms of illicit economic conduct are increasingly required to bear fruit for the official economy. In this manner, the alleged threats posed by the informal tend therefore to be turned into opportunities for the formal. Consequently, the boundaries separating legal from illegal business practices become more blurred and beg a redefinition of classical terms such as corporate crime. This process is accompanied by changes occurring in the organization of both official productive activities and criminal activities. Examples of both types of activities will be given throughout this chapter, with the second type mainly pertaining to the illicit drugs economy.

The Hidden Economy

The study of the relationship between the formal and the informal received enormous impetus around the mid and late 1970s. This study mainly focuses on the major processes characterizing European economies which are grouped under the general definition of *industrial decentralization*. The new processes of decentralization should not be confused with previously existing forms of informal economic activity. While the previous forms took place in secondary sectors of production, mainly characterized by labour-intensive practices, the new processes I am referring to involve the core of advanced industrial production and its leading sectors.

A vast literature is available on this issue, with some authors emphasizing the aspects of *control* and some others those of *economic performance* on which the process of decentralization is said to impact. Thus, some commentators adopt a framework inspired by the hierarchical, authority-infused character of production, while others argue that the economy is driven mainly by efficiency (Putterman, 1986). The former group of commentators sees industrial decentralization as a response to labour disputes, and consequently interprets the division of large firms into smaller units as a way to dilute industrial unrest. The latter sees decentralization as an innovative process ultimately aimed at increasing profits. While drawing on both analyses, other critics argue that decentralization induces an economic 'miracle' by developing a parallel economy where statutory conditions are often ignored. Small productive units are created in which lower numbers of staff allow union rights to be suspended, with the consequence that the impact of collective bargaining is reduced. Overt illegalities are committed in many of these units with respect to working conditions: wages, security, and recruitment procedures, all precursors of what today is called flexibility.

Decentralization marks the beginning of the end of Fordism, the model of production which gave substantial incentives to the workforce in terms of salary. The Fordist model, as I have mentioned in Chapter 2, established itself within the sphere of what is termed the 'monopoly sector'. Here, relative work stability made up for the intensity of work. In the car industry of the past, for example, employees could at least temporarily avoid unemployment, as production seemed assured for ever. In the new network of ancillary production generated by decentralization, where salaries are low and job security is lacking, large firms recruit their subsidiaries, and benefit from the conditions characterizing the informal economy in which they operate. The informal economy, therefore, partially resolves problems of costs, co-ordination, and management, as segments of these are in a sense contracted out of the formal setting occupied by official business.

Adjacent to the informal economy is the criminal economy proper. Here, the drawing of a distinction may be useful. I would identify the informal economy with the production and circulation of goods whose nature is not officially defined as illegal, though their production and circulation may occur under illegal conditions. I would term the 'criminal economy' a market setting where both the goods produced (or services delivered) and the conditions in which they are produced and distributed are officially regarded as illegal. For the sake of clarity of the argument that follows, I would also like to define as the 'hidden economy' the social and productive space in which both the informal and the criminal economies operate.

Professional criminals and small non-criminal entrepreneurs are cohabitees in the hidden economy. Some of the former invest their criminal proceeds in non-criminal activities, and may periodically shift from the informal to the criminal field. Examples of these shifts are found in the literature on professional criminals who were active in the 1960s, 1970s, and in some cases throughout the 1980s. For the specific entrepreneurial character of this type of professional criminal in the UK, see Richardson (1991), Campbell (1990; 1994), and Hobbs (1995). For France, see Monzini (1999) and Greene (1982), who witnessed how the careers of robbers and smugglers evolved into those of entrepreneurs in the building industry. For a similar evolution occurring in Italy, including the development of the mafia and the camorra as enterprises, see Arlacchi (1983), Catanzaro (1988), and Ruggiero (1996a; 1996d), and the respective analyses of entrepreneurships and criminal and 'dirty' economies.

In the informal economy, as we have seen, the boundaries between legality and illegality are already blurred, a circumstance which facilitates access by entrepreneurs with all sorts of adventurous backgrounds. Decentralization, therefore, with its creation of a myriad of small factories and workshops, acts as a process for the entrepreneurial promotion of professional criminals, who finally see their dream of owning a 'proper business' come true. However, in the informal economy these criminals meet other small, 'clean' entrepreneurs, and engage in all types of joint ventures with them. In this respect, see the examples of professional criminals and 'clean' businessmen setting up joint ventures in the illicit drugs economy, in the disposal of industrial toxic waste, and, as we shall see in Chapter 7, in the trafficking in human beings and the illegal transfer of armaments.

Residues of Fordism

Paradoxically, while the growth of the informal economy signals the decline of the Fordist model of production, with parts of the work process being transferred outside the walls of major firms, it is in the criminal economy proper that Fordism seems to be revitalized. See the drug-related economic activities described in the previous chapters. The drugs economy, from the late 1970s throughout the 1980s, witnessed the participation of diverse actors with varied criminal backgrounds, who abandoned their previous activity, attracted by what promised to be a high-added-value economy. Some drug wholesalers, for example, were previously engaged in armed robberies. Presumably, they never managed to invest the proceeds of their raids in legitimate business, and their shift towards drugs was encouraged by the increasing use of firearms on the part of the police. Drugs were welcomed as a long overdue chance to put the guns away. Journalistic accounts also suggest that, after initial resistance to drug dealing, some professional criminals 'soon realised that here was a new way of making money that required no getaway car and ran less risk of informers. It had the added advantage that there was no victim running to the police' (Campbell, 1990: 5). Among this type of wholesale drug distributors, defined by Dorn and South (1990) as 'criminal diversifiers', other groups were previously active in the distribution of stolen goods.

However, as I suggested earlier, the definition 'diversifiers' also applies to 'clean' entrepreneurs inhabiting the informal economy, who came to operate in the same economic setting as their criminal counterparts. Moreover, the most striking process of diversification involved those who occupied the lower strata of the drug business. In their case, it would be more appropriate to describe this process as a 'conversion', from work or unemployment to crime. I am referring to all those drug users who had no criminal background, and whose criminal career, therefore, coincided with their drug-using career. It is my contention that these types of drug users were heavily penalized by institutional intervention, on the one hand, and by the conversion of part of the criminal (or hidden) economy into the drug economy. The internal division of labour within the latter became increasingly rigid, those who benefited from this conversion being mainly individuals who already held an entrepreneurial or managerial position in the hidden economy. In contrast, those whose role was confined to the provision of 'pure criminal labour' experienced, with the shift to drugs, an increase in their economic dependence.

The economic activities conducted by drug users and small distributors implied an immutable pattern of tasks within a virtually stagnant career. As already suggested, their frenetic activities did not translate into upward mobility: theirs was a type of motion devoid of movement. Their choices in respect of drug use and distribution produced profits which remained invisible to them; of the added value generated they enjoyed only a minimal fraction, often consisting of doses. Moreover, despite the initial enthusiasm for the new 'job' and the social scene in which it was performed, many became aware of the monotony and uniformity of the life-style embraced.

Throughout the 1980s, as I argued in Chapter 2, we are faced with a Fordist model of criminal labour, whereby the skills required to perform tasks appear to be visibly declining. Skills, in fact, are concentrated at the managerial level of the drug economy, and are ingrained in its division of labour, which is independent of those who play a part in it. In this organization, one finds an echo of Gramsci's (1951) formulation of Fordism, in the sense that criminal labour becomes increasingly abstract, as it is fragmented in a number of repetitive operations the purpose of which is lost. These unskilled criminals are young users who have not had a chance to achieve criminal apprenticeship, and whose knowledge of the economic cycle in which they are employed is reduced to the small segment they occupy. Hence their vulnerability and, like Fordist workers, their interchangeability.

It is ironic that this specific type of labour organization, which is slowly being abandoned by important sectors of the official economy, leaves residual traces in the criminal component of the hidden economy. However, it should be noted that in the hidden economy Fordist-type criminal labour finds conditions and characteristics which are the reverse of those prevailing in the official economy. In the latter, Fordism establishes itself within the monopoly sector, which serves mass consumption and responds to a relatively stable demand. Conversely, criminal economies, particularly the drugs economy, adopt a Fordist model of labour within competitive contexts, where markets are irregular and unstable, and work is often seasonal.

We shall see how changes in the relationship between the formal and the informal, on the one hand, and within the official economy, on the other, bring changes in the criminal labour market and tend to alter the specific features of its activity.

Co-opting the Informal

The relationship between the formal and the informal changed in the mid-1980s, and a process of co-optation with the former increasingly incorporating the latter started to take place. To be sure, some signs of industries incorporating the informal were already visible in the 1970s, mainly in the decentralization process started by the major car industries in Europe. These industries slowly acquired control of the small industrial units that acted as their subsidiaries. In some cases, they set up their own network of such small units which competed with their old suppliers. Such networks were established either in the same national territory as the main factory was located or in offshore territories where labour was cheaper and more disciplined. Globalization *ante litteram*? However, this expansion of the formal into the informal gained momentum in the 1980s, when most subsidiary units were financially supported by the mother industries, which also provided them with fixed capital in the form of machinery. Loyal foremen and faithful skilled workers were among those appointed as managers/directors of such subsidiary units. In these, labour was cheaper and the work legislation systematically ignored. In some European countries, due to the limited number of workers employed, the work legislation and collective contracts approved at the national level just did not apply. In other words, big industry incorporated the advantages of the informal economy within its own formal productive process.

Under such new conditions, the hidden economy as a whole became inhabited by disparate actors: small entrepreneurs formerly contractors of larger firms, new entrepreneurs promoted by large industries, and criminal entrepreneurs seeking new investment opportunities. The characteristics of the businesses conducted by such disparate actors were not easy to isolate and distinguish. In this context, the debate over what exactly constituted 'clean', 'dirty', 'legal', 'semi-legal', 'illegal', or 'mafia' entrepreneurship became particularly heated. For example, what were the characteristics distinguishing an enterprise set up through the re-investment of criminal proceedings from one set up by a major official enterprise, when both operated in the hidden sector

(Falcone, 1991; Catanzaro, 1994; Becchi and Rey, 1994; Arlacchi, 1998)?

Toyotism and Crime

The process leading to the incorporation of the informal within the formal receives unprecedented impetus with the establishment of the 'Just-in-Time' production model. Let us briefly see how.

According to what is known as the 'Toyota spirit', subsidiaries must display the same standards as the major firms they work for (Ohno, 1993). Increasingly, external independent suppliers become unable to provide what the large firms require: technology, management, flexible capitalization, versatile labour. Large firms have no choice: they are forced to set up their own suppliers and, in some industrial sectors, they virtually monopolize the informal as well as the formal. But let us briefly summarize some aspects of the 'Toyota spirit' within the post-Fordist debate which are relevant to this analysis of crime.

The new systems of production assume the fragmentation and the volatility of markets, so they abandon the central tenets of mass production. 'Lean production' is the new strategy: goods are virtually personalized on the basis of contingent demand, stocks are consequently reduced to a minimum, and production takes place 'just in time' to respond to the emerging unpredictable demand (Rainnie, 1991). Within this strategy, some authors see elements of 'vertical disintegration' emerging in industrial organization which, in their view, leave the main enterprise in control of only the final product and key technology. As non-strategic activities are presumably subcontracted, clusters of independent enterprises are said to take shape which presumably allow forms of community control over the local economies (Totterdill, 1989; Hirst, 1989). This author supports the validity of findings which run counter to post-Fordist orthodoxy. Research proves that it is optimistic to emphasize the centrality of the locality and the role of small and medium-sized firms. In fact, whilst the functions of large firms may be decentralized, with units taking on local identity, 'control still resides in the hands of a distant and global management, often overriding local concerns' (Rainnie, 1993: 53).

With deregulation, conditions in the informal economy deteriorate, while attempts are made to formalize the informal (see the case of Italy), or expand it through the refusal to establish minimum working conditions and the curtailment of union rights (see the case of the UK).

A competitive situation emerges where the distinction between the informal and the criminal, within the hidden economy, tends to become yet more blurred, with labour shifting from the former to the latter and vice versa. Deregulation, in effect, carries an ambiguous message, namely that rules and procedures are negotiable, and that the threshold separating legality and illegality is always provisional and can be moved artificially.

Similar ambiguity is found in criminal economies, particularly in the drugs economy. Drug use, for example, becomes 'chaotic', no longer implying a definitive choice, or the adoption of a specific life-style. Drugs are incorporated into a variety of life-styles: diverse substances are made available, while different markets and different consumers emerge. As with other consumables, say, clothes, food, or leisure goods, drug use diversifies on the basis of the users' income.

These developments may lead some authors to infer that an 'alarming' situation is taking shape where drug use becomes 'normalized' in the life of growing sections of the younger generations (Parker *et al.*, 1995). This interpretation seems to confirm Luhmann's (1991) provocative claim that sociologists, in order to reproduce themselves and sustain the interest of agencies funding their research, must raise moral panic. It is an interpretation which equates 'normalization' with the aggregate quantity of drugs available and the alleged total number of users, suggesting that both are increasing worryingly. Those who have challenged this suggestion have shown that available data 'do not support the contention that changes in patterns of drug use since the 1950s are indicative of major epochal change' (Shiner and Newburn, 1999: 149). It has also been noted that the main feature of current drug use is the variety of marketable substances on sale, be these licit or illicit (Power, 1998). Further, some scholars have argued that use of different types of pharmaceuticals does not necessarily lead to use of illicit drugs (French and Power, 1998), and that the aggregate health damage caused by licit and illicit drug use has not varied substantially over the last three decades (UN, 1997). The variety, rather than the number, of users is a crucial element which observers attempting to grasp tendencies should investigate. In brief, there may be more diverse customers, and these may include individuals from all age groups. However, while criminal activity is no longer a central function of drug use, drug use is becoming a function of the income available to users (Grapendaal *et al.*, 1995).

Given the diversification of drug markets and consumers, some restructuring takes place at user–dealer level, with many suppliers being 'made redundant'. Drug dealers face unemployment, unless they re-skill in supplying other legal or illegal drugs, or specialize in some other specific segment of the criminal economy. Former cannabis dealers, for example, become unemployed after the explosion of synthetic drug use, or because many groups of users start to grow their own cannabis in newly established consortia. Work in the criminal economy becomes all the more intermittent and casual, with short contracts prevailing, while flexibility, imagination, and the capacity to shift from one task to another assume a central significance in the creation of job opportunities. It is the triumph of criminality 'just-in-time', which is tailored to the changing moods of the market and volatility of consumptions.

The 'Informalization' of Responsibility

The examples provided so far pertain to conventional crime, in a way which seems to confirm the widespread view that the informal or the hidden are mainly associated with this type of criminal activity. A more detailed analysis of post-Fordism may perhaps dispel this exclusive association and allow for the inclusion of forms of corporate crime in the equation.

Post-Fordism is not only characterized by 'lean production', and associated with saturated markets, unpredictable consumers, and flexible labour. At the institutional level post-Fordism implies new procedures with respect to decision-making processes, which tend to take place in hidden settings, through obscure and distant mechanisms, and outside the traditional sites in which accountability and responsibility can respectively be assessed and imputed (Revelli, 1996). For example, let us examine the recent restructuring of the defence industry, which will be discussed in more detail in Chapter 7.

Despite the collapse of the Soviet bloc, in many European countries, particularly in the UK, there has been a virtually complete absence of conversion in the arms industry. The restructuring process taking place involves the concentration of capital, the reshuffling of sectors, and the creation of national specializations. National governments are playing a central role in privatizing formerly state-run industries and promoting a series of mega-mergers (Lovering, 1997). Governmental efforts address the promotion of arms exports, as exemplified by the British arms deals with Saudi Arabia, and later with Malaysia and Indonesia. The British arms industry now sells more abroad than to its home Ministry of Defence.

An important new feature of the emergent political economy of the defence industry is that the home state is no longer the exclusive—or even the main— political actor in the game. Defence projects are increasingly developed with a view to gaining access to future export markets, and sometimes to overseas technology. Companies are no longer agents of their home governments and armed forces, they are independent commercial actors (ibid.: 15).

While in the cold war period defence companies were typically run by managers from engineering or military backgrounds, the post-cold war industry is largely run by generic business people who are not so dif- ferent from their equivalents in any other advanced internationalized, high-tech sector. Their background is in finance, marketing, and man- agement (Hirst and Thompson, 1996). Increasingly, production arrangements are removed from the democratic process, to escape what defence companies regard as the cumbersome decision-making machinery of politicians:

Key decisions are increasingly being made within networks which have 'foot- prints' in the corridor of several Defence Ministries, several corporations, and several financial institutions. No regional, national or European institution can have a completely informed overview, or leverage, over this nexus (Lovering, 1997: 13).

In sum, greater reliance on collaborative European armaments pro- grammes implies less and less political surveillance over defence pro- duction (Hayward, 1990). The defence industry is becoming more informal and less accountable to democratic national institutions. Responsibilities regarding the amount, the characteristics, and the end user of the arms produced are becoming increasingly difficult to attribute. The development of hidden or grey arms markets and the informalization of responsibility are reflected in the growth of illicit transfers of arms and the institutional difficulties in defining such trans- fers as illegal (see Chapter 7).

The Fable of the Bees

In this chapter I have tried to describe how developments in the infor- mal economy affect both conventional criminality and corporate offending. Many of the alleged threats posed by the informal to the offi- cial economy seem to be turned into advantages for the latter, which incorporates forms prevailing in the hidden sector of productive activ- ity. We have seen how a Fordist type of labour, which is declining in the official sites of industrial production, re-emerges in the criminal economy, and how, in a sense, the new 'Toyota model' of production is mirrored by the spread of a criminality 'just-in-time'. The joint analysis of conventional crime, corporate crime, and the official economy presented above is meant to convey the necessity that any conceptualization of the informal economy should take into account the impact of such economy on a variety of actors transcending those conventionally defined as criminal. This conceptualization relates to metaphors such as that offered by Bernard Mandeville in *The Fable of the Bees* (1970 [1723]), in which street criminals are described alongside their more powerful counterparts, the offences of the former being as serious as those perpetrated by their more respected neighbours:

> These were called Knaves; but bar the name,
> The grave Industrious were the Same.
> All Trades and Places knew some Cheat,
> No Calling was without Deceit.

The second part of this book groups some essays in anti-criminology specifically dealing with a range of 'crimes of the elite'. But before that, let us enjoy an Intermezzo.

6

First Intermezzo: Drugs as a Password

There are no drugs in nature. There are natural poisons, some of which are lethal. The concepts of 'drug' and 'drug dependence' are constructed by socially institutionalized definitions. These definitions are based on culture, history, judgement, and norms grounded in an elliptic or explicit rhetoric. With this premiss, Jacques Derrida (1989) sets off on his journey through the contemporary drug phenomenon, revealing a mixture of curse and blessing, an amalgamation of destruction and *joie de vivre*. Indeed, though it is possible to identify the *nature* of a toxic substance, it must be recognized that not all toxic substances are defined as drugs. The concept of 'drug' cannot genuinely claim scientific status, as it is grounded in political and moral evaluation. In this respect, the word 'drug' conveys a notion of norm and interdiction; it alludes to something from which we intend to distance ourselves: it indicates a social separation. For this reason 'drug' is not a descriptive but an evaluative concept: it is a password automatically implying a prohibition.

The fact that in English there is also a medical use for the word 'drug' does not concern me here: first, because this double use, to my knowledge, is not found in any other European language; secondly, because I am concerned with the relationship between law as an artefact and 'drugs' as a password. In this respect, when the penal law uses this password, the social separation which the concept of drug entails is exacerbated: the impact can be tremendous. Let us bear in mind Kelsen's (1975) notion of the law as a locus which is devoid of any ontology, an artificial domain where values can never claim universal validity. In the analysis of Kelsen, law is the arena where strategies are devised with a view to impeding forms of violence from emerging. Law is therefore the place where 'claims to peace' can be asserted through injunctions which are peaceful, as law differs from violence. However, law may well resemble that which it claims to regulate, and thus become another form of violence. Girard (1980; 1987) argues that law thrives on a specific form of disregard, which is apparent in the inability of society to recognize its own violence. This self-deception manifests itself in the exclusion, separation, and social exile of some of its members: all expressions of the sacrificial practices prevailing in modern societies.

The ambivalence of law, which takes the risk of causing damage while trying to avoid or respond to the causation of damage, is associated by Resta (1992) with the ambivalence of violence itself. Violence destroys and renovates, condemns and saves, kills and cures at the same time. This combination is conveyed by the Greek term *pharmakon*, which designates a poison and an antidote at the same time, a drug which causes illness and cures simultaneously. This *pharmakon* or 'drug' allows society to look at its own violence without recognizing it as such, its ambivalence making self-deception possible. How the law lacks reflexivity is exemplified by environmental disasters: 'The society that we want to cure is the one that we are destroying; the technology that destroys is the one with which we want to revive it' (Resta, 1992: 18).

I believe that the encounter between 'drug as a password' and 'law as a drug' constitutes the drug problem as we know it today. In the following discussion of drug legalization and prohibition, the above concepts will be seen as the inescapable backdrop against which freedom of choice and the causation of harm, which form an apparent antinomy within the drug phenomenon, can be examined. This chapter will chart the key aspects of the legalization versus prohibition debate. It will then discuss the drug issue in relation to individual freedom and social harm. Finally, it will sketch a proposal of drug rehabilitation as a form of compensation to users. Let us first summarize the most relevant arguments of legalizers and prohibitionists respectively.

Legalizers

Legalizers include conservative, liberal, and radical commentators who in one way or another oppose drug-prohibition laws. While all seem to be inspired by the principle that governments should not interfere with individual choice, conservatives emphasize freedom within the market, whereas liberals and radicals focus on the sphere of personal freedom within the broader social context. In an overview provided by Nadelmann (1991), legalization strategies are located within a wide spectrum which is delimited by two extremes. At one extreme is the view that no institutional control should be imposed on the production and marketing of any drugs, and that the only prohibition should apply to the sale of drugs to children. At the other extreme are advocates of total government control of the quality and quantity of drugs produced and of agency monitoring of commercial or state-organized sale. In between lies a strategy in which 'Government makes most of the substances that are now banned legally available to competent adults, exercises strong regulatory powers over all large-scale production and sale of drugs, makes drug-treatment programmes available to all who need them, and offers honest drug-education programmes to children' (ibid.: 19).

Underpinning most legalization strategies is the belief that drug-related problems, such as acquisitive crime, violence, and to a degree 'addiction' itself, are to a large extent the result of drug prohibition rather than drug use *per se*. The availability of natural euphoriants in many Asian countries, it is stressed, never caused addiction until these countries 'learned' to use them in the way they are used in the developed countries. It is contended that legalizing drug use would not increase but reduce drug-related problems. Quality control of the type of drugs made legally available would also foil 'cutting' and dilution with dangerous additives by dealers.

Legalizing drug use is consistent with the principle that individual conduct which does not cause harm to others should not be penalized. Moreover, legalization would spare drug users the experience of prison, which in many cases accelerates drug-using careers, and provides a boost to dealing and trafficking careers (Ruggiero, 1992b). As for acquisitive crime fostered by habitual drug use, legalizers argue that, if drugs were legal, 'the price would drop dramatically, and most of those who steal and cheat in order to pay for [them] would not have to do so, and some of the worst racketeers in the world would go out of business' (Graham, 1991: 254). It is argued that this was the outcome of the repeal of the alcohol prohibition laws, an important precedent with which legalizers augment their arguments.

Several models of drug legalization have been suggested. Among these is the idea that producing countries could sell their raw materials to developed countries, with a benefit to the latter in terms of employment and profits. 'The establishment of cannabis, opium, and coca as domestic cash crops might eliminate the need for costly farm subsidies, while providing employment for farmers, unskilled labourers, pharmacists, chemists, and retailers' (Karel, 1991: 90). Nevertheless, legalizers agree that advertising of currently illegal drugs should be prohibited. In his idea of passive marketing, for example, Caballero (1989) posits that drugs should not be subject to the customary market mechanisms which impose encouragement of demand in order to produce increasing profits. A passive market implies discreet use, strict government control of production and distribution, and prohibition of advertising.

Most of the arguments used by legalizers, however, do not translate into practical proposals on how legalization could be structured and brought into effect, but are confined to the elaboration of a number of counter-arguments against prohibitionism. Among the effects of prohibition, for example, legalizers pinpoint the development of a 'barrier strategy'. This strategy imposes on users the consideration of their drug use within a dichotomy separating legal and illegal drugs. This separation renders the hierarchy of risks indistinct, and users are prevented from grasping the significance of: the diversity of substances generically labelled as drugs; the diversity of risks related to the ways they administer them; and the diversity of contexts in which they use them (Arnao, 1991). For example, when the United Nations (1987) suggested that the expression 'responsible use of drugs' be banned from the official vocabulary, the possibility for users to identify, control, and avoid the risks of abuse was implicitly denied or impeded. The barrier strategy delimiting legal and illegal drugs made all the latter equally dangerous, irrespective of quantity, quality, context, and mode of administration. One could suggest that such a strategy aims to cause damage to users, who can therefore act as living warnings to young people and novices to stay away from drugs.

Drug prohibition is also viewed as possessing a shadow agenda, in that, for example, the war on drugs gives politicians the opportunity to appear caring and protective, and to manipulate racist and xenophobic fears. Prohibition is said to mobilize activists and to trigger crusades to protect individual or group interests. For example, 'ordinary citizens who take up the drug-control banner can find meaning in political life by participating in reviving what many feel is a threatened moral consensus' (Gordon, 1994: 17). In this view, drug prohibition is a political resource or a hidden social programme which transcends the object of its apparent preoccupation. Finally, there are suggestions that the war on drugs is in reality a war declared against the ethnic minorities inhabiting the inner-city areas of Western countries, and that racial discrimination is endemic to drug prohibition. 'The fact that drug dealing in the city, unlike that in the suburbs, often goes on in public areas guarantees that law-enforcement efforts [are] directed at young black and Hispanic men' (Miller, 1996: 81).

Prohibitionists

In their case against legalization, Inciardi and McBride (1991) contest the 'enslavement theory' of addiction whereby the illegality of the drug market contributes to the increase of price, thus pushing users into committing property crimes. These authors endorse research which finds that drug use tends to intensify and perpetuate established offending behaviour, rather than initiating criminal careers: 'the evidence suggests that among the majority of street drug users who are involved in crime, their criminal careers were well established prior to the onset of either narcotics or cocaine use' (ibid.: 55). Against the argument that legalization would not cause a substantial increase in use, prohibitionists pinpoint the extraordinary power of market systems to create, expand, and maintain high levels of demand for any legitimate good.

The assumption that drug use would increase with legalization leads some prohibitionists to evaluate the potential outcomes in terms of violence if a free market of what are now illicit drugs were to be established. According to Goldstein (1985; 1986), there are three types of drug-related violence: the psycho-pharmacologic, the economically compulsive, and the systemic. The first derives from drug use itself, and is part of the effects of some specific drugs, be they legal or illegal. The second type of violence emerges when economically oriented crime committed by drug users becomes increasingly difficult because of property protection and target hardening, therefore forcing users to engage in armed robberies and muggings. The third type of violence is believed to be intrinsic in drug markets, where interactions between suppliers, between users, and between users and suppliers are said to be embedded in violent forms of regulation. Violence, in sum, is said to be a common sanction for failure to honour contracts that by definition cannot be legally enforced, and is threatened or used to deter fraud, betrayal, theft, and dishonesty (Arlacchi, 1998). Prohibitionists embrace these categories and argue that drug legalization would perhaps determine a decline in systemic violence, which is associated with the illegality of markets, but it would increase psycho-pharmacologic violence, because more people would be using psychoactive drugs. It is also argued that, unless legalization made drugs freely available to users, property crime would not decline because users would still need funds to buy doses.

While assuming that drug use is concentrated in inner-city areas, prohibitionists argue that this is hardly a reason to legalize drugs, but instead a reason to reject all legalization proposals. 'Within this context, the legalisation of drugs would be an elitist and racist policy supporting the neocolonialist views of underclass population control' (Inciardi and McBride, 1991: 65). Legalization, therefore, would be tantamount to a programme of chemical destruction of youth and minorities.

As for the aspects concerning individual freedom of choice, prohibitionists respond to legalizers by adopting the ethical framework provided by John Stuart Mill (1859) and his concepts of liberty and legitimate bases for government intervention. Ironically, these concepts, when applied in a different fashion, can also reinforce the arguments of legalizers, as we shall see later. Prohibitionists stress that government intrusion into personal choice is justifiable when such choice causes harm to others. Acquisitive crime to procure the money necessary to buy drugs is an example of such harm, while legalization would result in more harm being suffered by society in general, in terms of physiological, psychological, and private safety costs. 'Society already pays a rather high tariff as a result of the public health, safety, and violence problems associated with drug use—both legal and illicit. This would necessarily increase when levels of drug consumption increase through legalisation' (Inciardi and McBride, 1991: 69). Against the argument that alcohol and tobacco cause more deaths than heroin and cocaine, prohibitionists argue that these legal substances are so lethal exactly because they are legal, and that illegal drugs made more readily available would have the same effect.

Among prohibitionists, there are various authors who claim that coercion of users into drug treatment is likely to be more successful than voluntary treatment (Leukefeld and Tims, 1988). Some of these authors call for the criminal justice system to intervene at demand level, namely against users and street dealers. Intervention at street level by law enforcement agencies is justified by the argument that it is here that small-scale distribution and user–dealer interactions occur, and that illicit drug use spreads. Institutional response, in this perspective, is charged with the task of stopping new users from entering the market and experimenting with drugs. Moreover, low-level drug enforcement could play a major role in encouraging users to seek treat-ment. 'Stated bluntly, it is about stacking the odds through the threat of penal sanctions so that the drug user is more likely to recognise that entering some form of treatment is a rational choice: forcing people to be free, in fact' (Gilman and Pearson, 1991: 117).

As I argued earlier, the encounter between 'drugs as password' and 'law as a drug' constitutes part of the drug problem as we know it today. Inherent in this problem is a selective understanding of the con-cept of individual rights on which societies rest. It comes, therefore, as no surprise that the classics of liberal democracy and liberal law still inspire most discussions related to prohibitionism and legalization. It is exactly in these classics that the root of such selective understanding can be located.

John Stuart Mill: Whose Liberty?

'The only purpose for which power can be rightfully exercised over any member of a civilised society against his will is to prevent harm to others' (Mill, [1859] 1910: 123). In reading this passage, attention should be focused not so much on the political incorrectness of the word *his* as on the pompous adjective *civilized*. We shall return to this key word, which captures in a nutshell the self-infatuation of liberal-ism, particularly in the Anglo-Saxon world, and the longevity of which is as astonishing as it is unmerited.

The prohibitionist argument relies heavily on Mill's general princi-ple cited above. However, as I have already mentioned, this principle lends itself to a range of interpretations and also has affiliates among legalizers. Let us see why.

During the first alcohol prohibition experiment conducted in the USA in the 1850s, Mill described the prohibition law as a gross usurpa-tion of the liberty of private citizens and 'an important example of il-legitimate interference with the rightful liberty of the individual' (ibid.: 143–5). Nobody, he stressed, should be punished simply for being drunk. The desire to penalize other people's private conduct was viewed by Mill as monstrous, because such desire is prompted by pure resentment for conducts which some regard as distasteful (Zimring and Hawkins, 1992). The legalizers' endorsement of Mill's thought appears to stop here. There are in fact exceptions to Mill's principle, the first of which pertains to children and young persons. Freedom of choice, according to the father of liberal thought, is granted exclusively to human beings in the maturity of their faculties. The other exception, which is implied in the original formulation of the principle, applies to specific individuals who may infringe the wellbeing of others as a result of their conduct. The example cited by Mill concerns those whose state of inebriety triggers excitement which results in offending behaviour against others. Finally, Mill's principle is suspended in cases in which people sell themselves into slavery, a practice which should be prevented through state intervention.

It should be clear how prohibitionists find an authoritative ally in John Stuart Mill and his general principle. For example, once drug use and violence are seen as being closely associated, the intervention of the state can easily be advocated on grounds that individual choice leading to drug use has a harmful impact on others (De La Rosa *et al.*, 1990). One has to assume that violence, here, indicates physical harm against others rather than against users themselves, though prohibitionist thought on this issue is far from clear. Prohibitionists may also find support when the second exception to Mill's principle is referred to. This exception applies to persons who are regarded as incapable of free choice, and who must therefore be protected from the harmful behaviour of others whose choice affects them. In this respect, think of the way in which the lives of children bear the consequences of their parents' drug use, or of the potential effect on young persons of drug legalization. The exception pertaining to individuals selling themselves into slavery can also be mobilized by prohibitionists, particularly if drug abuse is likened to a condition of slavery (as 'addiction') against which institutional intervention is warranted (Kaplan, 1983). Moreover, the prohibitionist perspective is guided by what seems a crucial economic argument, namely that the harm caused by illicit drugs is also to be found in the health costs to which the state is subjected by users in need of care and therapy, and in the material damage caused by those who finance their drug habit through acquisitive crime. In this perspective, individual choice turns into a burden to others.

There are, finally, important implications in the recourse to Mill's analysis which may explain its appeal to prohibitionists. At the beginning of this section I highlighted the word *civilized* because it is of crucial importance for the understanding of Mill's 'map of liberty'. The author describes and delimits 'who' deserves liberty, and establishes a border between the deserving, namely the civilized, and the undeserving, that is the barbarians. *Civilization* distinguishes wealthy and populous nations from savages; it is the opposite of rudeness: 'In a narrow sense, it refers to the ontology of a place—Europe generally, and Great Britain in particular' (Passavant, 1996: 307). It also refers to specific groups and individuals, namely those who are able to engage in a dialogue and pursue 'truth' collectively. Inability to engage in dialogue entails the incapacity to exert self-control, to bend impulses to calculation: all characteristics of barbarians. 'The judge, the soldier, the surgeon, the butcher, and the executioner constitute an anomalous category to mediate between civilisation and barbarism; to protect civilisation from its own barbarity' (ibid.: 309). Hence the justification of state intervention in individual choice: despotism is a legitimate way of dealing with barbarians. Among the circumstances which warrant this legitimacy is the association of illicit drugs with violence, which deserves a brief but specific discussion.

The 'Violent' Metaphor

The cause–effect relationship between drug use and violence is extremely difficult to establish, and in many cases violent behaviour is associated less with the choice of using drugs, or with the market in which drugs are available, than with the life-style of persons prior to their involvement in the drug economy (Fagan and Chin, 1990). Research findings about the drugs–violence nexus are contrasting and inconclusive, and while in some cases they seem to prove that violent behaviour is related to a state of acute intoxication (Brody, 1990), in others it appears that the capacity to adopt violent behaviour is a prerequisite for access to drug markets (Hamid, 1990; South, 1995). Violence can also be viewed as one of the elements which are linked less to a drug-using career than to 'street lifecycles', which entail a defensive world view and a perception of society as exploitative, a place where one is either aggressor or victim (Fleisher, 1995). Violence and drugs, in this perspective, have no cause–effect correlation, but are two of the narrow options available in street lifecycles. Finally, even studies devoted to notoriously violent drug gangs seem to prove that familiarity with violence is achieved outside drug markets, and in some cases is acquired through involvement with institutional politics rather than with psychoactive substances (Gunst, 1995).

However, leaving aside contradictory research findings on this question, the very reason the drugs–violence nexus is so forcefully put forward in many quarters deserves interpretation. This nexus has gained a status of certainty in academic circles, to the point where there seems to be no need for further discussion. Christie (1996) attributes such cases of perfect consensus to the over-socialization of criminologists within their own discipline. However, looking at how the drugs–violence relationship is also predominant among the worst of media representations of drug problems, one is faced with a unique example of intellectual consensus between scholars and media representatives, who mutually reinforce their convictions. These convictions can be questioned when the relationship between drugs and firearms is examined. The existence of this relationship is widely accepted, though it is based on a sociological syllogism, in the sense that from a logical premiss an illogical generalization is drawn. A similar syllogism was prevalent in the 1960s, when drug use was associated with sex, particularly with orgiastic sex. Examples of this illogical procedure are also offered by E. Sutherland (1983), who remarked that the study of young offenders from a deprived social environment may lead to the conclusion that white-collar criminals are a figment of people's imagination, because white-collar offenders do not have a deprived background. By the same token, in studying forms of security and of property and business protection, one must reasonably conclude that workers in the world of business have more familiarity with guns than drug dealers. In fact, the possession and use of weapons are indicative of the perception of risk prevailing among different groups, rather than being suggestive of any automatic association of their business activity with them. The use of arms in drugs markets should be examined against the background of the increase in armaments available in society at large. Moreover, it should be borne in mind that the development of the drugs economy was initially hailed by armed robbers as a long-awaited occasion to do away with arms, and that, in a sense, the drug culture may be adopting a gun culture which is also developing elsewhere, at the general level. If the concerns surrounding the increasingly destructive behaviour of armed dealers are genuine, one wonders why the 'war on drugs' has not been turned into a 'war on arms'.

The analysis of violence in one specific group cannot be extrapolated from the general context in which 'violence as a resource' is distributed within a society. An assessment of the degree of visibility of the specific type of violence used by different groups, and the examination of the benefits that each group obtains from the use of its specific form of violence (Levi, 1994; Ruggiero, 1996b), would perhaps put in a different perspective the use of firearms in the drugs economy.

The *Socius* Imposed and Denied

Underlying the penalization of drugs is the tendency to impute to drug misuse all the unpleasant features of contemporary societies. We have seen the example of firearms. It should be added that penalization also entails a pre-established notion of the public–private dynamic. Users are, in a sense, accounted incapable of engaging constructively in the public sphere. We have seen how Mill regards the capacity to engage in a dialogue as one of the traits of civilized human beings. It is drug users' repetitive behaviour, one that does not lead to a dialogical search for truth, which renders them deserving of punishment. Their behaviour leads to irresponsibility and oblivion, which are the exact opposite of the qualities belonging to a disciplined self (Smart, 1984). These qualities, according to Mill, are achieved through work, particularly through the acceptance and internalization of the division of labour prevailing in manufacturing: the great school of co-operation. However, the uncooperative character of drug use is determined by the very definitions of drug and drug dependence, as we have seen. These definitions enter the private sphere of individuals because their choices are charged with a heavy social burden: users' behaviour *must* have implications for others. The variables crime, violence, and damage are the artefacts which allow official intervention to impose a *socius* on drug users. In fact, what is prohibited is a type of pleasure which is solitary and desocializing, and which therefore contaminates the *socius*. 'It is claimed that, if that pleasure were purely private, if drug users confined themselves to the use of the sacred right of property on their body and soul, then pleasure, even the most threatening, would be legitimate' (Derrida, 1989: 51). But this is denied *a priori*, because, as customers or dealers in the drug market, users are nonetheless placed in the public sphere. In fact, the public character of drug use is predominant in its forced association with crime and violence, and is implied in the very definition of 'illegal drug', which alludes to a prohibition. However, while the *socius* is imposed on users, it is at the same time denied when institutional intervention takes place. In penalizing users and dealers, one takes them away from the social arena because they are incapable of engaging in the Platonic pleasure of public dialogue, namely because they lack the *socius*.

Paternalism and Harm

According to Ferrajoli (1989, 1991), drug prohibition promotes a political use of the criminal justice system which is apparent in its propaganda symbols. These symbols are aimed at the mobilization of consensus, and are less effective in preventing harmful behaviour than in satisfying 'feelings of rejection' among sections of society. Moreover, the solemnity of the official stigma against drugs shows how the law, which implies a notion of individualism and individual responsibility, is incapable of dealing with those who bring individual choice to the extreme. Hence the imposition, as discussed above, of an artificial social dimension to unmanageable individual choices.

The prevalence of the symbolic aspect of the law in relation to illicit drugs is based on the notion of harm which, directly or otherwise, is linked to a judgement about the wrongness of drug use. It is also based on a specific hierarchy of harm implying a value judgement. Behind the condemnation of illicit drugs for the harm they cause to others lies a condemnation of drug use *per se*. The notion of harm utilized in drug prohibition, in other words, is a 'normative' one, which promotes ideals rather than protecting rights (Feinberg, 1986; 1988). This normative aspect is linked to a particularly paternalistic view of the law which can be detected in proposals for forced treatment of drug abusers.

In a definition suggested by Dworkin (1989), paternalism posits a political community in which individuals are responsible for the well-being of others. Paternalism, therefore, is not inspired by the authoritarian notion which associates law with the will of the majority, and consequently conflates 'the community' with the majority. The paternalist argument is not a winner-take-all argument, but one which appeals to the idea of the community in a more genuinely democratic sense. However, paternalism can be distinguished in two practices and philosophies. Dworkin (1989) suggests that 'volitional paternalism' views coercion as a form of help given to individuals in order for them to achieve what they already want to achieve. 'Critical paternalism' supposes instead that 'coercion can sometimes provide people with lives that are better than the lives they now think good, and coercion is therefore sometimes in their critical interests' (ibid.: 485). The intervention of the criminal justice system against drug abusers is of the second type. However, threats of punishment may corrupt rather than enhance critical judgement in users, as the metaphor of 'law as a drug', discussed above, implies. Penal threats may, in fact, persuade individuals that the life they live is better, and that the 'improvement' that such threats allegedly promise is not to be regarded as an improvement at all. It is not easy to justify making people do things against their will. In an example provided by Nagel (1987), if someone wants to pray for the salvation of someone else's soul, the beneficiary of such prayers cannot complain on the ground that he would prefer a subscription to *Playboy*. The problem arises when someone is forced to attend church and pray instead of staying at home reading *Playboy*. The author distinguishes between two kinds of disagreement: 'one whose grounds make it all right for the majority to use political power in the service of their opinion, and another whose grounds are such that it would be wrong for the majority to do so' (ibid.: 231).

Compensation as Rehabilitation

The 'disagreement' of official society with illicit drugs is expressed by its resort to the law, which, as we suggested at the beginning of this chapter, requires the use of violence in order to counter violence. This sacrificial mechanism is reproduced by popular participation in contemporary societies through the mass media. Canetti (1962) argues that sacrificial murder still involves the participation of crowds, though executions are only made public thanks to newspapers. This makes things easier. Large gatherings are no longer necessary, and crowds can now hide themselves behind the law in order to divide and arrange human beings into opposing groups. The password of 'drugs' seems to respond to such a profound need to divide and oppose. At its root lies the urge to form hostile groups and the desire ultimately to declare war against some of them.

The 'disagreement' of official society with 'illegal' drugs appears, also, to be based on a naturalistic view of humans: prohibitionists posit a pure, uncontaminated individual who achieves happiness without resorting to artificial euphoriants. However, such a naturalistic view is, in a sense, shared also by legalizers, especially those who would support a 'supermarket model' of legal drug sale whereby drugs are purchased like chocolate. These types of legalizers regard mood-altering substances as part and parcel of human needs, these substances being known, in one form or another, to all traditional societies. Surely, when the social effects of both drug misuse and drug prohibition are examined, these after all compatible views sound inappropriate.

Against this type of legalization and prohibition, I would like to propose a model of *compensation* due to users.

In most European countries, we are now faced with a situation in
which it is not so much drug use which is penalized, as drug intoxication. This is so because many users escape institutional attention and
tend to retain their drug-using habit undetected for years, some of them
for a lifetime. Users who are known to official agencies are usually
unable to manage their drug use in a safe environment, or to combine
such use with other commitments which, in a sense, would slow down
their using career. The accumulation of a number of social disadvantages leads them to intoxication, and hence to increasing involvement
in the illicit market in drugs, and inevitably to penalization. They are
apprehended, and often punished, because of the cumulative effect of
such disadvantages, because of their visibility and vulnerability. They
are punished for their state of intoxication, and for their low status in
the drugs economy, rather than for their acts.

Forms of compensation should be devised for such users, in the form
of a range of possibilities open to them. These should include resources
to establish self-managed projects aimed to redress the balance caused
by their disadvantages. Options should include: the possibility of
obtaining voluntary therapy, of independently deciding to abstain, but
also of receiving drugs on a maintenance basis. These self-managed
projects should be regarded as something which is due to vulnerable
users because of the shared societal responsibility in causing their vulnerability. Official society would otherwise be indictable for crimes of
omission, as in other cases where vulnerable individuals are denied
vital help. I am talking here of giving such users the resources to make
decisions about themselves and, as in the 'volitionist' approach
described above, giving them help to achieve that which they already
want to achieve.

This proposal is an implicit rejection of a political use of the law, and
presupposes that legislative intervention should elevate social conflicts
to the level of non-violent processes (Ricœur, 1995). Legislation should
be inspired by the notion of *capacity*, namely it should make individuals capable of acting, choosing, speaking, and taking responsibility for
their own actions. In other words, legislation should aim to provide
drug users with the capacity to recognize the effects of their actions as
their own, and thus to recognize themselves as agents. This notion of
the law excludes punishment by definition. If those involved in the drug
scene are to gain a dialogical capacity to identify the effects of their

own actions, they also 'need continuous forms of mediation in their interpersonal relationships and some forms of institutional representation which give them real power and the related rights' (ibid.: 33). Currently, punishment annuls this dialogical capacity, it constrains interpersonal relationships and eventually abolishes institutional representation, to which rights are ultimately linked. Drug abusers should be compensated for having acquired their state through the restitution of this capacity.

7

Service Providers and Criminals

The essays in anti-criminology composing the second part of this book focus on crimes committed by powerful individuals and organizations. I have already argued that the current economic situation promotes two symmetrical types of criminal activity, and that both, with the expansion of the informal, show a growing obfuscation of the boundaries between legitimate and illegitimate conduct. The movement between legitimate and illegitimate, and the consortia between actors operating in the respective arenas, shape bazaar activities which stem from constantly changing opportunities and demands. Illicit activities conducted by powerless individuals, which have provided the focus for the first part of this book, encourage and simultaneously fulfil demands for goods and services emerging in urban contexts. However, powerful individuals and organizations also possess their own bazaar, where economic initiatives are taken and constant negotiations carried out around their acceptability. In their case, as suggested in Chapter 5, legitimate and illegitimate activities intermingle thanks to the co-optation of the informal by the formal. In the following chapters, while rejecting the notion that the informal designates a vestigial mode of pursuing economic development, the notion that development itself is synonymous with harmony, progress, and legality will be contested.

Transnationality

One of the major concerns of law enforcement agencies across the world is that growing economic interdependence, while advantageous for the elites, may also bring increasing opportunities for transnational crime. On the one hand, this concern sounds like an implicit endorsement of the view that the expansion of markets is accompanied by a simultaneous expansion of crime. This view, in its turn, is an extension of analyses focusing on business as criminogenic, namely that the structure of organizations and the culture of those who operate in them create an environment in which opportunities for misconduct constantly arise (Clarke, 1990; Punch, 1996). On the other hand, this concern tends to concentrate attention on powerful criminal organizations which, it is stressed, are poised to take advantage of international deregulation. Thus, for example, the increase in goods and people crossing borders is pinpointed as the underlying condition for the growth of conventional forms of organized crime, whose 'corrosive influence on the body of Western social institutions grows exponentially' (Myers, 1996: 183).

This chapter tries a different analytical route. It considers conventional organized crime and transnational business crime within a conceptual framework formed by notions such as exchange, reciprocal entrepreneurial promotion, and mutual provision of services. These notions can be applied to cases in which the official economy benefits from goods or services provided by conventional organized crime, and vice versa. Such notions also allude to short- or long-term partnerships being established between actors inhabiting the official economy and individuals involved in criminal enterprises.

In order to pre-empt an objection which I regard as obvious or truistic, I should clarify that the following pages do not deal with 'structural crimes' inherent in the gap between price and value, or intrinsic in the economic 'lie' consisting of the extraction of surplus value and the exploitation of labour. This chapter discusses the exchanges, the partnerships, and the mutual promotion between legitimate and illegitimate actors, and the way in which the overlap between them shapes what can be termed *dirty economies* (Ruggiero, 1996a; 1996d; 1999). It discusses how the advocates of market freedom violate the very principles of 'legality and fair competition' that they officially champion and thanks to which their privileged condition is reproduced.

The trafficking in human beings and the illicit transfer of armaments will be analysed against the conceptual framework sketched above, which for the time being should only be given an ideal-typical character. As will become apparent, in the partnerships and joint ventures described below, it is increasingly difficult to establish who services whom, who learns criminal techniques from whom, and ultimately who corrupts whom. After the examination of the two cases, therefore, the ideal-typical framework of analysis will be adequately amended.

A Third-world Phenomenon?

Reports published by statutory or voluntary agencies indicate that there are today around 200 million slaves in the world. Such reports, which mainly focus on developing countries, suggest for example that between Bangladesh and Pakistan there is an intense traffic in humans who are destined to be sold. These human beings, who are often chained, are delivered to entrepreneurs who own workshops or brothels, whereas children are sent to countries in the Persian Gulf, where they are used as jockeys in camel races (Torrès, 1996; Anti-Slavery International, 1997; P. Williams, 1997; Arlacchi, 1999).

In China the process of market liberalization accelerated the traffic in women, who are sold as slave-wives to wealthy farmers in a number of small villages across the country. Adolescents and children are being sold as domestic servants in some oil-producing countries, or are bought by entrepreneurs of the rug industry operating in India, Nepal, and Morocco (Anti-Slavery International, 1978; Bouhdiba, 1982; Cross, 1991; Sattaur, 1993). Human rights organizations based in France, Germany, and the UK are trying to persuade traders to check the origin of the rugs they sell, and to adopt a mark stating that such rugs are not made by children held in slavery (Torrès, 1996).

Much of the literature available on the subject, however, seems to imply that the trade in human beings and contemporary forms of slave labour are confined to developing countries, where it is assumed that they constitute important tools for these countries to compete with their developed counterparts. Slavery, therefore, comes to be associated with primitive forms of accumulation which are likely to trigger the economic miracles observed in countries adopting an Asian model of development. Some forms of slavery do in fact seem to be compatible with this model, as they constitute an extension of the flexibility, precariousness, and over-exploitation of the workforce characterizing it. But to what extent are these forms of work relation also compatible with the economic models prevailing in developed countries? First, let us examine examples of transnational companies which displace parts of their production process abroad.

Heavens Abroad

When describing the advantages enjoyed by developed economies from the traffic in human beings, one has to consider that this type of trafficking would be redundant if Western enterprises could employ slave labour *in loco*, namely in countries where human beings can be bought and sold. However, this practice is viable only for larger enterprises which are endowed with a complex structure and a number of diversified sub-units. These enterprises, for example, might adopt different industrial practices depending on the area in which their sub-units operate. Thus, advanced marketing techniques and even forms of labour participation may be in operation at home, while labour-intensive or slave-type exploitation may be applied abroad.

Many European companies operate in South-East Asia, where they establish workshops in particularly advantageous conditions. Along with the fiscal benefits they enjoy from local governments, these companies rely on both cheap and forced labour. Examples were given by investigating judges in France who were collecting evidence for the prosecution of some entrepreneurs operating in Malaysia and Burma. These entrepreneurs had appointed intermediaries who hired labour locally in both the unregistered workshops scattered in rural areas and prison institutions.[1] Forced labour carried out in overseas penitentiaries was also exposed by German investigators, who were hampered in their attempts to bring the cases to court by the international nature of the offences they were facing. The companies they identified employed intermediaries based in Hong Kong, where they were legally registered, and from where commissions and contracts were granted to prison institutions based in the Republic of China.

As mentioned above, these practices entail a degree of diversification that only larger enterprises can afford. Moreover, they require large resources to be invested in the transportation of semi-finished and finished goods to and from developing countries. Smaller companies, which are unable to move goods internationally or to establish parts of their production where labour is either cheap or free, need labour itself to move, whether legally or otherwise. In this way, they also meet the needs of the workforce from developing countries, whose responses to the North–South divide include 'individual resistance by physical relocation':

In a world of increasing North–South polarization, with Northern demographic decline and Southern demographic expansion, how will it be politically possible to stem massive unauthorized South-to-North migration? (Wallerstein, 1995: 132).

[1] The empirical material for this part of this chapter was provided by voluntary agencies, trade unions, investigators, and lawyers.

This high demand for physical relocation is in itself a source of profits, which should be added to the profits brought by illegal immigrants to the hidden sectors of European economies.

Unregistered Work

In most European countries unregistered workshops are regularly raided and large groups of immigrants without a permit to stay or to work are arrested (Viet, 1998; Merckling, 1998; Dal Lago, 1999). Investigators across Europe distinguish between traffickers who limit themselves to the provision of smuggling services and traffickers who provide addresses of prospective employers along with smuggling services. The second type of traffickers act as intermediaries between migrants and small businesses, and can be regarded as hidden employment agents.

Examples are found in most European countries, particularly where sectors of the economy such as the textile and the building trades are largely deregulated. It should be noted that entrepreneurs, though benefiting from the labour of those who are delivered to them, are not charged for the smuggling service provided by traffickers, as it is usually those smuggled who pay. This is perhaps a unique case in which 'commodities' pay for their own circulation instead of such cost being charged to the final buyer. Refugees are also smuggled in this fashion, as is the case with individuals from Iran, Iraq, Pakistan, and Afghanistan, who often land on the island of Gotland in Sweden. They then board boats from Estonia or Latvia where traffickers act as sorting agents on behalf of entrepreneurs. The 'commodities' are then transported to Poland and Germany, where the employable and fit are selected (Silvestri, 1996). Refugees entering the UK also use illegal means of migration to flee persecution (Morrison, 1998).

Cases which came to light in Italy showed the crucial role played by trafficker-mediators. For example, in Turin an investigation started after a Chinese, who turned out to be an illegal immigrant, was found shot dead. The investigation unravelled an organization engaged in both the trafficking and employment of immigrants. These were housed under quasi-military surveillance, and worked under similar coercion in order to pay the sum due for their transportation into Europe. The murdered immigrant had failed to keep up with payments. Similar cases occurred in Milan, where a large clandestine Chinese community established itself thanks to the smuggling services provided by the group known to the Italian police as the 'Wenzhou Gang'. Dozens of immigrants are 'housed' in damp basements and cellars where they eat, sleep, and work. The handbags, belts, and clothes they manufacture under slave conditions are bought by leading companies operating in the Italian international fashion trade.

Illegal immigrants are employed in the English countryside. They pay a fee to enter the country, and are often reported by their own employers as 'illegal' when they complain about the low wage they receive. Migrants also work on British North Sea oil rigs, where they are given 'slave wages' and forced to work 28-day stretches without a break (Nelson, 1999).

Much is known about trafficking in Albanians to Italy (Mattera, 1997; Colussi, 1998; Géry, 1999; Ruggiero, 2000). Here, it is worth noting that partnerships engaged in this business include groups operating in both countries and entrepreneurs, illegal or official, who are prepared to accept the 'goods' once they reach the final destination. Albanians who wish to reside in Italy are therefore offered 'packages', which may include trafficking services together with a variety of job opportunities.

Let us now examine a specific segment of the traffic in human beings which takes place outside the illegitimate networks commonly associated with conventional organized crime. I am thinking of the myriad agencies specializing in the recruitment of men and women from developing countries who officially seek work in the developed countries. Most of them, regardless of their skills and experience, almost invariably become servants, especially women. These women are usually deceived, as they are promised the work of their choice only to find that on arrival the employer 'gives them no choice—or rather the non-choice of returning home immediately at their own expense' (B. Anderson, 1993: 24). Although legally registered, these recruitment agencies apply what amounts to a debt bondage to those seeking a job in developed countries, and threats to report their victims to the immigration authority usually succeed in keeping payments going. Many of the women fall into debt by borrowing at exorbitant interest rates to pay recruitment fees, or by taking an advance payment from the recruiter. Before they can even begin to send money to their families, which is the primary purpose of their working overseas, they have to pay their debts. In Britain, the slave condition of these domestic workers is also apparent in the ruling indicating that, on their entry into the country, the name of the employer must be stamped on their passports.

A leaflet issued by the British Home Office reads: 'The stamp placed in your passport by the Immigration Officer will record the name of your employer. You cannot work for anyone else.' In 1999 Anti-Slavery International campaigners documented more than 2,000 cases of abuse of immigrant domestic workers in Britain. Some of the immigrants, who had suffered sexual, physical, and psychological abuse, had tried to escape employers, but because their passports had been confiscated, they had been forced to live as illegal immigrants.

Similar agencies, operating in many European countries, trade in Asian women destined for marriage. An exotic wife costs between 10,000 and 15,000 German marks. Others are involved in the trafficking of sex workers, and of women who are initially unaware of the occupation for which they are destined, and upon arrival are forced into prostitution (IOM, 1996; UN, 1996; IOM, 1998; Kempadoo and Doezema, 1998; ISTAT, 1999). Some of these agencies engage in other forms of illegality when the official ways of securing entry visas for their customers are closed to them. After cases investigated in Britain, for example, a black market of visas was discovered which saw the participation of agencies based in developing countries and officials employed by the Foreign Office. Cases involving police officers in service at airports who acted as 'visa dispensers', and consulate employees devoted to the same activity, occurred in France and Italy respectively. Other agencies, though regularly registered, may find it difficult to obtain visas for their customers, and therefore resort to illegal traffickers with whom they form temporary or long-term partnerships. In many European countries such joint ventures specialize in both the procurement of work in the hidden economy and the provision of unregistered, badly paid jobs as servants.

Trafficking in servants may also involve the voluntary or inadvertent participation of foreign embassy officials in countries such as Switzerland and France. In Geneva, for example, about 34,000 individuals work in activities related to the local network of foreign embassies. Chauffeurs, personal servants, gardeners, cooks, cleaners, and so on are employed by diplomats and delegates of the UN and other international institutions. A charitable organization operating in the city, the Syndicat sans Frontières, set up by a refugee who fled Chile under Pinochet, brought to court more than fifty cases of slavery between 1997 and 1999. Some of these slaves had entered the country illegally, after payment of a fee to traffickers, and had been employed by diplomats for lower wages than those officially established. Others had become 'enslaved' after their employers had confiscated their passports or work permits. This had automatically made them illegal, and put them at the complete disposal of their owners, who could also refuse to pay them a wage.

Servants who do not bring their cases to similar organizations (because they are too scared to do so) escape from their owners and end up in the hidden economy, where the lack of a work permit or a residence permit is a guarantee of, rather than an obstacle to, employment.

Competing Agencies

It has been suggested that there are three main stages in the trade in human beings (P. Williams, 1997). There is the recruitment of illegal migrants, the shipping of them to transit points and countries of destination, and the control of immigrants once their journey has ended (Winer, 1996). Different groups can be involved in each of these stages, though not all of them are necessarily part of conventional criminal organizations. In the cases examined above all three operations were conducted by the same types of organization, namely by criminal enterprises trying to reap the profits involved in each stage of the business. However, the evidence is far from suggesting that conventional organized crime is set to monopolize all segments of the business. Agencies and organizations which are not part of conventional organized crime may become active in one or more of the stages described above. They specialize in the recruitment of men and women from developing countries seeking work in the developed countries. These agencies may limit their role to the registration of would-be migrants, with related collection of fees, and contract out the smuggling operations to organized criminal groups. The latter, under such circumstances, act as service providers by courtesy of their skills in transferring all sorts of 'goods', including humans, across borders. Under other circumstances, the opposite may be the case, with organized criminal groups recruiting, and official transportation firms being entrusted with the trafficking operations. In brief, there are opportunities for partnerships to be established between firms operating in the official arena and firms engaged in the criminal economy, thus contradicting the hypothesis that the latter tend to monopolize the entire business. On the contrary, the case presented below seems to indicate that official firms may be as keen to pursue such a monopoly as their criminal counterparts.

The case which came to public attention at Christmas 1996 offers an example of how segmented the division of labour may be, even among official firms engaged in human trafficking. The case gained media coverage only because it was unsuccessful, leading to the tragic death of almost 300 illegal migrants. The details were as follows: a group of Pakistanis were recruited in their country and transferred to Turkey, and from there to Cairo. In that city they were mixed with a larger group of Sri Lankans who had started their journey in Colombo and had been flown to Egypt. They all boarded a ship in Alexandria which sailed towards Sicily. In the Malta–Sicily channel, where the immigrants were asked to board a smaller ship, the tragedy occurred:

What is known is that the new ship was able to hold only about 100 people, but all the 300 or so tried to board it. The crew tried to force them down the ropes at gunpoint and the ship foundered (*The Observer*, 12 January 1997).

This case, if one could ignore its tragic aspects for an instant, threw light on the segmentation of the business rather than its monopolistic character. A number of operations were conducted by legally registered firms and individuals without a criminal background, let alone any direct affiliation to conventional criminal syndicates. These firms, in sum, did not employ professional criminals whose skills had developed during the course of long-term careers in illegality; they employed individuals who had refined their illegal procedures simply by operating in legitimate enterprises. The Kosovo crisis in 1999 determined yet another entrepreneurial leap among these firms, with larger transport companies gaining an edge over smaller, often amateurish, criminal groups.

Cases reported in the UK may illustrate new developments in trafficking in human beings. Such cases, again, appear to indicate that legally registered agencies, rather than conventional organized crime, may attempt to monopolize the business. Immigrants from Eastern Europe were found without a legal permit in some workshops and middle-sized factories operating in the food industry. They had arrived on a tourist visa and then overstayed. Some had been smuggled into the UK, while others had simply been driven to their destination by coach. While looking for work, they were given the addresses of employment agencies which would accommodate both the registered and the clandestine. Some migrants had been provided with these addresses before starting their journey. On arrival, they had been asked which type of work they were looking for, whether official or clandestine.[2] None of

---

[2] This case was uncovered by a journalist posing as an Eastern European migrant. The journalist taped his meeting with an employment agent, and the tape was broadcast by the ITN 'News at Ten', 23 Jan. 1997.

the individuals and agencies involved in this case had any affiliation with conventional criminal groups: they were tourist agents, employment mediators, transport entrepreneurs and employees. In brief, none of them had a criminal curriculum vitae. The functions elsewhere performed by criminal groups were taken over by legitimate business groups. It should be added that the food processed by these illegal workers was then bought by major British supermarket chains.

The examples given in the second part of this chapter pertain to the illicit trade in armaments, another sector in which, on many occasions, official entrepreneurs appear to be able to dispense with the services offered by conventional organized crime and set up their own illicit services.

Arms Traffickers: Criminals or Benefactors?

In Britain, the inquiry into the export of defence equipment to Iraq, undertaken by a commission led by Lord Scott, was unable to throw light on the normative, economic, and indeed ethical issues surrounding the manufacture and transfer of armaments.[3] When faced with objections as to the quantity and quality of the arms exported, the commission responded that both were not to be regarded as being particularly destructive. When the issue was raised that many arms transfers take place through the export of technology officially destined for civil use, the commission claimed that it is the duty of developed countries to export technology in order to help the economies of developing countries take off. Similarly, when British arms producers were accused of illegally selling their products to African countries, they retorted that, in some cases, they intended to contribute to the military and institutional stability of the importing countries, while in other cases they were keen to cause more instability with a view to establishing in those countries greater social justice.[4] In brief, we are faced with generous benefactors whose acts are hard to classify due to the uncertainty of the boundaries within which they take place.

There are some constant features in illicit arms trafficking. First, there are arms manufacturers and financial institutions supporting

[3] The 'Report of the Inquiry into the Export of Defence Equipment and Dual-use Goods to Iraq' is also known as the *Scott Report*, London, Feb. 1996.

[4] These motivations were used in relation to Nigeria and Sierra Leone respectively. In the latter case, arms producers claimed that their products were destined for the more democratic fraction of the political spectrum of the country, and that their arms would have been instrumental in overthrowing a military regime.

them. The former have permanent contact with army officials and security services, whose role includes the monitoring of the quality and quantity of arms produced. The monitoring exercise is officially aimed at ensuring that producers meet international requirements and guidelines. It must be noted that in many countries, because the arms industry is largely state-owned, managers of this industry may be former army officers. Therefore the army and the arms industry experience a permanent exchange of high-rank personnel between them. Secondly, there are mediators and wholesale traders who are closely linked to producers and also act as financial guarantors for transactions between producing and importing countries. Thirdly, there are politicians who take decisions regarding the transfer of arms abroad. They are in charge of supervising the route followed by weapons and ensure that embargoes imposed on certain countries are respected.

The arms business, therefore, may become illegal in a number of respects. The illegality may reside in the quality and quantity of arms produced, which are subject to international restrictions and regulations. Frequently, inspectors in charge of monitoring these aspects of the arms industry are members of national and international elites which are closely associated with manufacturers and may, therefore, be exposed to corruption. Moreover, in countries such as France and the UK, given the crucial importance of the respective defence industries, inspectors appear to be particularly benign towards manufacturers and exporters, who contribute substantially to the collective well-being in terms of industrial output and job provision. However, the illegality of the arms business may also reside in false claims regarding the country for which the arms themselves are destined. Finally, illegal practices may be adopted by financial institutions through which payments for illegal sales are processed. These institutions conceal the identity of purchasers along with the sums involved in the transactions.

Conventional organized crime can be a participant in the illicit arms trade when it establishes some form of partnership with one or more of the actors described: manufacturers, inspectors, importers, or financial institutions; or, perhaps tautologically, when one of its members is simultaneously one of the actors just mentioned. However, even in countries where it would not be surprising to discover that a member of an organized crime syndicate is also an arms producer, a government inspector, or the director of a financial institution, conventional criminal organizations seem to occupy the sector of the clandestine market in which light armaments and second-hand weapons are mainly traded. Under certain circumstances, conventional organized crime may limit its role to the provision of transport services to ensure that illicit consignments are safely and speedily delivered. Let us now focus on how such services offered by organized crime can become redundant.

The arming of Iraq by British producers took place through the simple artifice of claiming a false final use for the products exported. In their licence applications companies adopted terms such as 'general engineering' in order to conceal the military end-use of the products:

Although the British government had clear intelligence throughout the 1987–1990 period that the machine tools were going to make armaments, its natural inclination towards sale rather than restraint led it to maintain the fiction that, because they were destined for Iraqi plants which combined military with a modest amount of civilian production, export licences should be approved as there was no 'incontrovertible evidence' that the machines may not be put to a civilian use (Phythian, 1997a: 43).

An example of false final use is also provided by the partnership between Land Rover UK and Otokar (Turkey). The Turkish company has been producing vehicles under licence from Land Rover since 1987 (Oxfam, 1998). It is now producing the Scorpion counter-insurgency vehicle based on a Land Rover model, with which it shares around 70 per cent of its components. As these components are of a civilian nature, their export to Turkey is not covered by specific licensing requirements, though vehicles are assembled in Turkey and clearly militarized:

Vehicles on display during the 1995 IDEK Turkish arms fair had twin machine guns mounted either side of an infra-red camera system which allows groups of people to be shot in the dark, as the soldiers can take aim via an interior-mounted target system (ibid.: 18).

The other method used by British exporters consisted in sidestepping national and international regulations by concealing the end-user of the arms transferred:

The various agencies charged with responsibility for the export licensing application system continued to allow lethal and non-lethal transfers to a number of countries that were known to be diversionary routes to Iraq. These countries included, but were not limited to, Jordan, Egypt, Saudi Arabia, Portugal and Austria (ibid.: 24).

Jordan performed the function of diversionary route both during and after the Iran–Iraq conflict, when the very countries which had contributed to building up the military power of Iraq resolved to destroy it. In the port of Aqaba the warehouses containing arms destined for Iraq were obvious: 'So extensive was this trade that Iraq had a whole section of the port to itself, fenced off from the rest and known as the Iraq Ports Authority' (Phythian, 1997a: 44).

As already mentioned, similar dynamics were visible during the Iran–Iraq war, when both countries showed an insatiable need for weapons. The Bofors affair, brought to light by Swedish investigators, revealed that the major European producers of explosives had suspiciously intensified their mutual advisory activity within the professional association of which they were members. The association (EASPP, European Association for the Study of Safety Problems in the Production and Use of Propellent Powders) was established in 1975, with the manifest aim of discussing security issues related to such a delicate productive sector (Phythian, 1997b). During the Iran–Iraq war the association became the major focus for the allocation of contracts to producers, promoted the falsification of end-use and end-user certificates, and, as customary, resorted to diversionary countries to conceal the destination of arms.

Transfers of arms may also be carried out through practices which include forms of barter, offset, or cross-purchase. One such case is the Al Yamama ('Dove of Peace') contract between the British government and Saudi Arabia. In exchange for defence material and technology for its production, Saudi Arabia committed herself to the provision of 400,000 barrels of oil per day between 1986 and 1988. The proceeds of the sale of oil would then be distributed among the private and the state-owned companies participating in the deal (World Development Movement, 1995). Finally, the sale of arms may be linked to the granting of financial aid, within what could be termed coercive diplomacy. Hence the paradoxical situation whereby some countries, which on scrutiny are not among the most needy, manage to obtain finances in the form of favourable loans in exchange for their willingness to sign contracts with arms producers:

Aid is linked to commercial contracts, and in the case of 'donor' countries whose economy is strongly dependent on arms production, to military equipment contracts (World Development Movement, 1994: 13).

The development of this grey market of armaments renders obsolete openly illegal forms of arms transfer. Nor does the grey market, often deemed a necessary evil, make transactions more transparent or ethically sound. The grey market appears to have incorporated sections of the arms business traditionally occupied by conventional organized crime. However, this process does not translate into more careful evaluation of final purchasers. See the example of Nigeria, where a military coup annulled the democratic elections of 1993. The British government, as part of measures agreed by the EU, said it would withhold £65 million of civilian aid already agreed, but refused to halt the supply of tanks to the very soldiers who had staged the coup:

In the light of Britain's long and close embrace of the Nigerian military—through arms sales, military export credits and training—the move was unsurprising. Far from promoting good governments, Britain's arms sales have legitimised the Nigerian military usurping power and violating human rights. Over many years Britain's official arms sellers . . . encouraged the squandering of hundreds of millions of pounds on British arms which Nigeria could not afford—and for which the Nigerian people are still liable (World Development Movement, 1995: 75).

The sale of British armaments to Indonesia, the third highest purchasing country of UK-manufactured defence equipment after Saudi Arabia and India, presents similar characteristics. The Indonesian government, which it should be noted has been responsible for the invasion of East Timor and the elimination of more than 200,000 political opponents, purchased from British producers 'instruments for crowd control', a euphemism hiding instruments for the infliction of torture. This technology of political control, which includes electric shock batons, is also sold to Turkey. It reaches its destination as a finished product when it feeds the 'black' market, and in the form of a semi-finished product when it serves the grey market. In the latter case, consultants and instructors show *in loco* how the instruments are to be assembled and used (Amnesty International, 1997).

In the 'war markets' of transitional countries (Yugoslavia, Albania, and some countries of the ex-Soviet bloc), where international embargoes have caused the expansion of the clandestine market in arms, the services offered by organized crime are still highly valued (Ruggiero, 1996c). Being under embargo, such countries would seem unable to set up grey markets. And yet, the case of Rwanda, where Britain, France, and other European producers have sold their arms, appears to contradict this assumption. It would appear, in sum, that legitimate entrepreneurs tend to incorporate the economic procedures and sectors which are traditionally the preserve of conventional organized crime. In this respect, let us consider a final case, which again concerns transfers of arms promoted by British entrepreneurs. This case shows how the propensity of the UK to export arms illegally is not dependent on the personality of her Prime Minister, a propensity which during the Thatcher era might have been attributed to the desire to re-attach the adjective 'great' to Britain. Under Labour rule, and before the new Prime Minister started, with the Kosovo crisis, to show a belligerence similar to that of his predecessor, Colonel Tim Spicer, who had already distinguished himself in the Gulf War, became director of Sandline International Ltd., a private security firm also engaged in military consultancy services. The firm, whose operations could not be ignored by the Foreign Office and the British Embassy in Sierra Leone, sold arms and sent a mercenary army to one of the parties involved in the conflict in that country, which was under embargo:

The activities of Sandline and a UK based air company that was involved in shipping the arms to Sierra Leone, provide a good example of lax implementation of UK controls over the brokering of arms to embargoed destinations (Oxfam, 1998: 4).

In this case, however, exporters defended themselves by claiming that they were in fact benefactors: the arms and mercenaries were destined for the 'democratic' faction involved in the civil war.

Finally, attention should be given to the fact that the desire of ex-Soviet bloc countries to join NATO may foster new opportunities for arms trafficking, whether illicit or otherwise. Only countries possessing credible and reliable armaments are allowed into the alliance, a privilege which favours those who commit finances to the renewal of their military machinery. Western producers are therefore putting pressure on countries such as Poland, the Czech Republic, and Hungary to refuse Russian offers and choose their products instead. In Warsaw, Prague, and Budapest offices of representatives of French, British, and Swedish arms producers are spawning. The future will tell whether such blossoming of new market opportunities will also contribute to the development of parallel criminal opportunities.

Learning Processes

We can now return to the interpretative framework proposed at the beginning of this chapter. The evolution of transnational crime encourages, on the one hand, the participation of conventional criminal organizations, which capitalize on their expertise in transferring all commodities, be they legal or otherwise, from one country to another. Previously acquired skills in moving goods across borders put such organizations in a position to move men, women, and arms with the same effectiveness. I have suggested that final beneficiaries of the illegal transfer services offered to migrants are some sectors of the hidden economy. In these sectors, companies operate which are ultimately connected to official industries buying their products, and which indirectly benefit from the cheap labour brought in by traffickers. However, the cases examined in this chapter suggest that the analytical framework initially proposed should be revised. This framework posited an exchange of services and mutual entrepreneurial promotion between conventional organized crime and the official economy. In the light of the dirty economies analysed above this description proved somewhat rigid, and cannot be applied universally. As I have tried to demonstrate, some official industries are able to set up their own illicit services to boost their economic performance. In a sense, such industries appear to be unwilling to share the benefits of the dirty economies in which they operate with outsiders. In brief, official economies may incorporate illegitimate procedures, thus taking away from conventional criminals those business opportunities to which they perceive they are naturally entitled. In a reversible learning process, the official economy adopts illegitimate practices while illegitimate entrepreneurs strive to gain access to the official economy.

Some observers may associate the definition of dirty economy with some residual aspects of the current globalized economy, or with some secondary, unproductive, branch of the economy. According to this view, the major industries and companies operating in a global context set the moral tone for the economic initiative, leaving the dirty procedures to ancillary sectors and actors. Similarly, in widely shared analyses of political and administrative corruption, it is suggested that progress, democracy, and development are the only tools capable of defeating what, again, is deemed residual. The essays in anti-criminology which follow will try to refute the automatic association of corruption with underdevelopment, and legality with democracy.

8

Corrupt Exchange: A Victimless Crime?

The study of political corruption seems relatively unfamiliar to criminologists. This is all the more surprising as many countries offer abundant material upon which students of crime could fruitfully reflect.
Paradoxically, only some early positivist criminologists touched upon
the subject in Italy. In 1879, Pietro Ellero wrote about what he termed
'bourgeois tyranny' which causes crime and monopolizes its definition.
He named four 'passions' associated with crime, among which he
included 'criminal ambition': 'This is not a noble and dignified senti-
ment driving individuals to great achievements, nor is it akin to vanity
or pride; rather it is a vice of the soul that leads to excessive love and
appreciation of oneself and one's authority, and to yearning for yet
more authority and domination' (Ellero, 1978: 104). Seven years before
he died, in 1902, Cesare Lombroso wrote on the structural differences
between old and new crimes, and identified the new crimes as
those committed by powerful people, in some cases by politicians
(Lombroso, 1902).

With the rejection of positivism, these vague pointers to the future
study of political corruption were also discarded. On the one hand,
conservative neo-positivists were too embarrassed to take on overtly
the entire legacy of Lombroso, and in failing to do so they overlooked
some important theoretical hints. On the other, critical or new criminologists tended to ignore the phenomenon, perhaps because all 'bourgeois' states were deemed corrupt by definition.

Often the study of corruption tends to focus on precisely identifiable
individuals who play a role in a 'corrupt exchange'. The features of this
exchange are therefore examined with a view to assessing the impact
the exchange has on the specific individuals involved. In this way, political corruption frequently ends up being assimilated to a form of victimless crime, where the actors involved are equally determined to

participate in the exchange, and pursue their private, if illegal, interest. Due to the 'invisibility' of its victims, corruption has become a field of study virtually monopolized by economists, political scientists, or moral philosophers.

In this chapter I suggest that political and administrative corruption may gain criminological relevance if we shift our focus towards the study of the social damage caused by this behaviour. The impact of corrupt exchange may not be perceived when attention is centred only on the specific setting in which it takes place. In this way, corruption resembles some forms of corporate crime. In effect, the victims of both corruption and corporate crime are often unaware of their victimization, and only rarely do they engage in direct interaction with the offenders. In both instances, moreover, victims are difficult to identify because the act constituting the offence and its effect are frequently separate both temporally and spatially.

The focus on the victims of corporate and white-collar crime, and indeed on the overall social damage caused by them, has recently contributed to a substantial advancement of the study of these types of crimes (Levi, 1991; Croall, 1992). At the same time, the investigation of 'a crime problem' in legal business—its perception, visibility, and nature—has widened the field of criminological analysis. Here, I will attempt a similar route in the study of corruption, whose criminological relevance will be elicited from the examination of its costs and the tentative identification of its collective, 'invisible' victims. This chapter comprises first a section which discusses the most relevant issues arising from the international literature on political and administrative corruption. This provides the framework for the subsequent sections, in which examples of political corruption in Italy will be treated. The examples will serve as a background against which the relevant literature on the subject matter will be reviewed. It will be apparent that some of the categories suggested by this literature need to be modified when the Italian case is examined. At the same time the costs of corruption will tentatively be identified. These costs, as I will suggest, pertain mainly to the realm of human and political rights. Supplementary social costs of corruption will also be identified in the way in which this behaviour tends to be perceived—a way that, in extreme instances such as those regarding Italy, jeopardizes the possibility and the very will to tackle it.

Functional or Harmful?

A classical conceptualization of political corruption revolves around a central notion, and indeed a crucial phrase, which originally appeared in sociological theory, and was later borrowed and expanded by the sociology of deviance. I am alluding to the notion of machine politics, which was seen by Weber as indispensable in modern mass democracies. Machine politics, in his analysis, meant 'the management of politics by professionals, by the disciplined party organization and its streamlined propaganda' (Gerth and Mills, 1991: 17). Strangely, when this term was applied to the sociology of deviance, negative overtones were slowly encapsulated in it. Machine politics almost became synonymous with corruption. An explanation of this shift of meaning can perhaps be traced in the elaboration of Weber himself, when the author, in discussing the formation of bureaucracy, hypothesizes the emergence of pathologies which are likely to accompany rational efficiency. Thus, on the one hand:

Indeed, the individual cannot escape from such a mechanized organization, for routinized training puts him in his place and compels him to 'travel along'. Those who are enlisted in the ranks are forcibly integrated into the whole (ibid.: 255).

But on the other hand, mechanized organizations may lead to a situation where 'the ruling and bureaucratically articulated group may occupy a quite autocratic position, both in fact and in form' (ibid.: 226). It is on this aspect that sociologists of deviance focused their analysis. Bureaucracy, which ideally permits regularity of the execution of authority, may become independent of its original function. It may end up reproducing itself, its own mechanical interests, and consequently the interests of some individuals who occupy a leading position in it.

Merton (1968: 125) introduced his analysis of 'political machines' with a distinction between the manifest consequences of a practice or code and their latent functions. The analysis of these functions, he argued, 'at times runs counter to prevailing moral evaluations'. Given that attention is focused on manifest consequences, he argued, the political machine or the 'political racket' is judged unequivocally bad and undesirable. The grounds for such judgement, he noted, consist substantially in pointing out that political machines violate moral codes. For example: political patronage violates the code of selecting personnel on the basis of impersonal qualifications rather than on grounds of party loyalty; bossism violates the convention that votes should be based on individual appraisal of the qualifications of candidates, and not on abiding loyalty to a feudal leader; and so on. It is known how Merton attributed to the political machine the role of satisfying basic latent functions. In his view, the

structural function of the Boss is to organize, centralize and maintain in good working conditions 'the scattered fragments of power' which are at present dispersed through our political organization. By this centralized organization of political power, the boss and his apparatus can satisfy the needs of diverse subgroups in the larger community which are not adequately satisfied by legally devised and culturally approved social structures (ibid.: 126).

It is interesting to note that among the sub-groups identified by Merton as those benefiting from the political machine are not only the deprived classes, but also business groups for which 'the political boss serves the function of providing those political privileges which entail economic gains' (ibid.: 129). In other words, the political machine provides alternative channels of social mobility for those excluded from more conventional social advancement, and at the same time it rationalizes the relations between public and private business. In brief, even corrupt political machines and rackets represent the triumph of amoral intelligence over morally prescribed failure.

Merton's functionalism inspired several authors according to whom corruption is mainly found in transitional societies, where it contributes to the humanization and personalization of the new social relationships (Bailey, 1966). From this perspective, political machines are said to flourish during periods of rapid growth, when the sense of community is weakened and fragmentation makes particularistic ties virtually the only feasible means of co-operation (Scott, 1969). It is worth noting that, while in Merton diverse social sub-groups are the clientele of political machines, in later functionalist analysis the stress is mainly laid upon the underprivileged. Thus:

Perhaps the most fundamental quality shared by the mass clientele of machines is poverty. Machines characteristically rely on the suffrage of the poor and, naturally, prosper best when the poor are many and the middle-class few (ibid.: 1157).

While retaining the focus on poverty, more recent analysis moved a logical step forward by arguing that a tolerant attitude towards corruption is the only way in which institutions geared towards economic

and social progress can be established. These institutions provide conduits of integration for individuals who would otherwise systematically resort to violence in order to express their political and social
demands (Huntington, 1968). 'He who corrupts a system's police officer is more likely to identify with the system than he who storms the
system's police station' (ibid.: 65). Corruption may therefore be functional to the maintenance of a political system in the same way as
reform is.

James Q. Wilson (1990) maintains that corruption is part of a vestigial survival of the past, and is destined to be swept away by progress
and development. He argues that there is a reduction in the demand for
and tolerance of corruption

owing to the massive entry of voters into the middle class; the nationalization
and bureaucratization of welfare programs that once were the province of the
political machine; and the greater scrutiny of local affairs by the press and civic
associations (ibid.: 593–4).

It is by courtesy of a series of economic studies that poverty was temporarily withdrawn from the limelight. These studies drew attention to
'choice', whereby individual acts are explained in relation to the objective of maximizing one's well-being within an environment characterized by scarcity. Poverty, and indeed morality, do not play a significant
role in these choices, the only restraint being identified in the potential
cost for the agents of corruption in terms of prosecution. In this perspective, corruption is to be tolerated if its financial cost does not
exceed the cost of law enforcement addressed to its control (Becker,
1968; Stigler, 1970). Corruption is deemed too important a phenomenon to be left to moralists: its cost, especially in less developed countries, does not exceed its benefits when it 'provides the only solution to
an important obstacle to development' (Nye, 1967: 425).

Orthodox cost-benefit analysis is criticized by other authors, who
claim that the economics of corruption are underpinned by systems for
the allocation of resources which determine the prices of goods in a
different way from the systems operating in the official market
(Rose-Ackerman, 1978). There are specific 'corrupt incentives' which
can only be highlighted if the type of bureaucracy or organization in
which they germinate is thoroughly investigated. Public, private, and
illegal settings differ in terms of opportunities for and the impact of
corrupt exchange. So do bureaucracies, which present their members

with diverse 'incentives' according to their specific structure: fragmented, sequential, hierarchical, or disorganized (Rose-Ackerman, 1978).

Undoubtedly, Rose-Ackerman's analysis represents a notable theoretical advance in the face of early economic studies of corruption. These seemed to rely too heavily on individual, almost universal, motivations supposedly leading people to an instinctive maximization of their material possessions. However, the shift from individual motivations to organizational opportunities leaves one aspect of corruption uncovered—namely the nature and the dimension, if any, of the damage it causes. Surely, as Johnston (1986) argued, it makes little sense to ask whether corruption is inherently good or bad. For some, the fact that it is a departure from established rules is sufficient to make it harmful by definition. A normative approach to corruption requires a presupposed standard of 'goodness', and a universal behavioural model: 'One does not condemn a Jew for bribing his way out of a concentration camp' (Rose-Ackerman, 1978: 9). But the refusal of a normative, universal approach does not justify the striking absence of any aspect of victimization in many economic studies of corrupt exchange. Nor can the victims of corruption be solely identified, as some authors suggest, with abstract entities such as development, fair competition, productive investment.

I will discuss aspects of victimization after describing ten cases chosen at random from the abundant chronicle of corrupt exchange in Italy.

Phenomenology of Corruption in Italy

In presenting the limited sample of corrupt exchange which follows, I will proceed from top to bottom, that is to say I will consider cases where actors holding decreasing social power are involved.

Case 1: A government member was arrested for soliciting payments from American aircraft manufacturers in order to guarantee the purchase of their goods by the Italian government. The involvement of mediators, both on the part of the American company and on the part of the cabinet member, namely the Minister of Defence, was in this case crucial. Among these mediators were American sales promoters on the one hand, and army generals, personal secretaries, and cabinet consultants recommending the importance of the purchase on the other (G. Green, 1990; Caferra, 1992).

Case 2: A group of MPs was brought to court, after the suspension of their parliamentary immunity, in what became known as 'oil scandal No. 1'. The owners of oil companies made payments to all government parties in exchange for a number of legislative measures which favoured them. These included compensation for the effects of the petrol crisis during the Arab–Israeli conflict, a discount and extension of the deadline for the payment of taxes, and the increase in the price of oil purchased by state-owned power companies. 'Oil scandal No. 2' involved the Customs authorities and a number of Inland Revenue officials: the former turned a blind eye to counterfeit invoices claiming oil exports in order to gain state subsidies, whereas the latter accepted forged receipts for tax payment (Turone, 1984).

Case 3: A number of major state-owned companies were found guilty of running two sets of accounts, one for official monitoring, another for their own internal records. Among these companies was a state energy conglomerate managed by officials directly appointed by political parties. All government parties were represented on the executive board in proportion to their respective electorates. Funds were regularly channelled to government parties, again with proportional criteria, via secret Swiss accounts (Pansa, 1987, 1989).

Case 4: A major building business contracted for the construction of four model prisons. This case became known as the 'golden prisons scandal'. Forged invoices claimed three times the real costs incurred. Charges mushroomed while work was in progress, as new features were added to the original plan. These were not only accepted but in some cases solicited by the politicians who granted the contract. The building firm kept on computer disk details of kickbacks given to party representatives, mediators, and government officials. In his colourful comment on the case, a judge remarked: 'There are kickbacks for all tastes, to be paid in percentage or pre-arranged lots, cash or instalments, indexed to the dollar or the mark' (Caferra, 1992: 56).

Case 5: Here I will group a cluster of episodes belonging to the same type. These came to worldwide public attention between 1992 and 1993. Almost 2,500 politicians, businessmen, and civil servants were served with warrants informing them that they were under investigation for taking bribes. The whistle was blown by a small businessman operating in Milan who contracted to supply cleaning services in a home for the elderly. He reported to the police the incessant requests by top administrators of the home for a percentage of his profits. Previous contractors had all accepted the deal, their payments being channelled to the political party of which the administrators were members. Thousands of similar cases, of equal or greater gravity, were denounced afterwards in all Italian regions.

Case 6: Five police officers were arrested for asking for money in exchange for work permits issued to Arab immigrants. Four *carabinieri* were arrested for forcing owners of electrical goods shops to grant payments and 'gifts' in exchange for ignoring licensing irregularities. A *carabinieri* officer was brought to court for leaking information regarding judicial investigation to members of organized crime syndicates. In exchange he had required a sum of money and a Fiat Regata. Three traffic police officers were reported by lorry drivers for asking for money in exchange for turning a blind eye to alleged road traffic offences.

Case 7: The local administration of a ski resort in the Apennines financed the construction of a number of council houses and flats which were allegedly meant for the local homeless. In fact, the resort did not have homeless people. The houses and flats were sold as second homes to non-residents living in neighbouring towns or to tourists. This gigantic fraud involved urban planners, local administrators, and potential purchasers (Cazzola, 1992).

Case 8: Another cluster of episodes concerns bribes paid to employees and low-grade administrators. In these cases, the payment of bribes allows for formal procedures and official rules to be sidestepped or suspended. Payments are required for: exemption from military service, permits to drive in pedestrian areas, the suspension of driving bans, disabled certificates for healthy people, a false report on the hygiene standards of a food retailer, a school certificate for an undeserving student, and so on (Cazzola, 1992).

Case 9: Here, cases in which procedures and rules are activated can be grouped. In these cases, bribes are paid for rights to be recognized and services provided. Rights and services sanctioned by law would not be recognized or delivered without the payment of incentives to those who are in the position to do so. Therefore bribes may be paid in exchange for speeding up the granting of a building permit, a driving licence, a birth certificate, a telephone line connection, a pension, a job, a place in the municipal cemetery, and so on (Signorelli, 1990). Employees who indulge in these practices feel entitled to extra payment for speeding up their pace of work in a sluggish bureaucracy. An example illustrates how bribes, in this context, tend to be perceived as a right by those who receive them. In a northern Italian city, the manager of a municipal bureaucracy issued a notice addressed to the public. Ostentatiously displayed at the entrance to the office, this stated that no payments were due for services provided there. The protest by the personnel was immediate. They started working to rule, and by applying procedures *ad litteram* they brought service to a halt.

Case 10: This episode epitomizes the lowest level of corrupt exchange, and is based on personal communication. A gentleman employed by the municipal department of education of his town applies for early retirement. He knows that at least a year can elapse between the time of application and the granting of his pension. It is the duty of his colleague, an accountant who works on the desk next to him, to prepare the papers and work out the amount due. This colleague postpones the operation for months. Fellow employees get the message: they collect money among themselves (the equivalent of £50 each) and give the sum to the accountant. The task is finally performed. I deliberately omit an important detail of this case, which I will reveal later when a crucial aspect of corruption in Italy will be discussed.

Corruption and Development

The dynamics identified in the first part of this chapter do not seem to apply to the above, non-exhaustive, description of corrupt exchange in Italy. Poverty and lack of development, for example, certainly do not describe Italian economic history of the last fifty years. Estimates of the annual rate of income increase per person between 1950 and 1973 see Italy as second only to Japan. For the period from 1973 to 1988 Italy and Japan show an identical rate of increase (2.8 per cent), well ahead of the USA (1.4 per cent), Britain (1.7 per cent), France (1.8 per cent), and Germany (1.9 per cent) (Zamagni, 1990). Similarly, the expansion of the middle classes and the nationalization and bureaucratization of welfare programmes did not cause a reduction in the demand for and tolerance of corruption (Wilson, 1990). The reverse seems to be the case. The demand for corruption increased along with the reduction of the industrial working class on the one hand, and the expansion of state intervention on the other (Paci, 1992). As regards the latter aspect, the Italian state performed as a crucial economic actor throughout the last half century. Its role was not and is not confined to the ownership of important industrial conglomerates, but includes the direct provision of income in the form of jobs, aid to needy areas, and a wide range of benefits. During the early 1990s the state contributed to the production of income in the region of an average of 40 per cent per person. In the south of the country more than half the income of each person came from public finance (Trigilia, 1992).

The list of examples provided above aims to emphasize how development in Italy fostered a 'learning process' whereby corrupt exchange moved from the apex to the bottom of society. Contrary to E. Sutherland's (1949) theorization, deviant techniques and behaviours were not only 'learned' by members of specific and homogeneous enclaves or professional groups, they were also translated into tools adaptable to a variety of social groups. Against the background of tumultuous economic development, corrupt exchange crossed the boundaries of occupational groups and subcultures.

As stressed above, economic studies of corruption often fail to identify the nature of the social damage caused by it, especially when abstract economic variables (that is, harmonious development, fair competition, and so on) are given the status of victims. It is to a tentative description of this damage that the following pages are devoted.

The Commodification of Rights

In Italy, the development of public intervention led to the parallel development of private entrepreneurship and market forces. It also fostered the growth of what could be defined as interstitial market forces. The increased presence of public resources, in sum, spawned opportunities for market forces to integrate, or even replace, the public system itself. This process, perhaps, bears a vague resemblance to that of deregulation occurring in other countries. Italy, where deregulation in a strict sense is only just starting, experienced the extension of a private market culture into the domain which supposedly belongs to the public authority. Cazzola (1988, 1992) described this process in the following terms. There are a multiplicity of rights/duties which pertain to the sphere of citizenship and the law: the right/duty to work, education, housing, health care, free expression, etc. Many of these rights/duties (or goods) are by now guaranteed, in the sense that, being outside the market, they are not negotiable. This makes our relationship with them relatively predictable, in that a custom is in place which governs their allocation and guarantees their enjoyment. These rights/duties can also be defined as value goods, as opposed to commodity goods, which are instead negotiable within the market. In Italy, the expansion of value goods was accompanied by their relentless transformation into commodities. Goods which should be exempt from market dynamics indeed became marketable. Corruption was both a consequence and a feature which accelerated this process. On the other hand, as corrupt exchange moved downwards in the social echelon, all rights (value goods) therefore became negotiable, discretional, uncertain, sometimes invisible.

An important aspect of victimization can be identified here. The transformation of value goods into commodity goods—in brief the commodification of rights—distorts social justice, the characteristics of which are ideally rational calculability and predictability. The administration of social justice becomes riddled with arbitrariness, lordly grace, oracular authority—all traits which Weber attributed to pre-modern justice systems and to which he gave a concise definition: 'Kadi-justice'.

The Tyranny of Stagnant Procedure

In Italy, corruption as a method of conducting business and managing public interest resulted in widespread mistrust of the economy and politics. However, it did not lead to the delegitimization of the entire political and economic system in the eyes of all social groups. Corruption in a sense also mobilized numerous people into political activity and into economic venture. Italy still holds the European record for electoral turnout, which can evidence the desire to change but also its opposite. Despite generalized awareness of political corruption, the same political parties have won the favour of the electorate for almost half a century. Furthermore, the expansion of self-employment and small businesses in the country attests to the trust enjoyed by the economic system. In a panorama of widespread corruption and total awareness of it, what is striking therefore is the degree of participation in—rather than alienation from—economic and political activity. However, the nature of this participation deserves brief discussion.

The procedure and rules governing corrupt exchange, as revealed by judicial investigation, were devised at the elite level first, and were afterwards imposed on the majority of interactions taking place between private and private, private and public, public and public actors. To participate required the adoption of precisely that procedure and those rules. The rigidity of these rules denied one elementary right to the more vulnerable actors: that of negotiating, and sometimes even changing them. Habermas (1988, 1992) sees in the constant possibility of altering the procedure whereby resources are allocated a crucial characteristic of democracy. With the decline of agreement on universal values, and the disappearance of the ethical state acting as the repository of the general will, the only source of legitimation and consent, he argues, is to be found in the procedure whereby power is exercised. This must be flexible, negotiable, diversifiable. Corruption in Italy affected these attributes, as it made procedure and rules sclerotic and impervious to innovation.

I believe that this lack of innovation and the rigidity of the procedure whereby resources are allocated constitute an important aspect of victimization. However, whether these, and indeed corruption, are part and parcel of the evolution of democracy or pathological traits of it is a matter for discussion. In order to clarify the relationship between corruption, victimization, and democracy itself, the notion of citizens' participation and that of elite need to be revisited. In this respect, Vilfredo Pareto's (1966) 'pessimistic' analysis seems as apt to describe the political apparatus of the country in the early decades of this century as it is fit to describe it now. Pareto saw all societies, irrespective of the regime, governed by a minority elite. The governing class, he argued, is not a tight, well-knit, and clearly circumscribed organization. It is a very unsystematic system—much like the feudal system. 'The essence of democracies is the patron–client relationship, a relationship based for the most part (and increasingly) upon economic interests' (ibid.: 67). In such systems, democratic participation is achieved by courtesy of 'a vast number of mutually dependent hubs of influence and patronage, which keeps together by the fact that each hub is dependent to some extent on the good graces of another such hub'. Corruption is therefore the permanent and central feature of all representative systems. The task of these systems, in order to maintain their stability, is to aggregate the various centres of patronage, the various clienteles, in such a way that they are all satisfied. This requires rigid rules within a flexible setting where alliances may constantly change. The governing class is not a concrete unity, a person. It does not possess a 'single will'. Unity and singularity are instead to be found in the procedures which allow its reproduction.

It has to be noted that what Pareto saw as the attributes of all democracies, contemporary theorists such as Habermas see as salient features of declining democracies only. Which leads us to examine other theoretical contributions on the relationship between democracy and corruption.

Democracy and Despotism

Corruption is said to affect the conditions in which political activity is conducted. These conditions, which are deemed inherent in any democracy, include transparency, visibility, equality of political rights, equality in gaining access to the benefits produced by the activity of the state (Pizzorno, 1992). Corruption is by definition the denial of transparency in that, supposedly, it takes place in conditions of secrecy. As I have tried to argue, this is not necessarily so, the visibility and widespread awareness of corrupt exchange in Italy being a case in point. However, in Pizzorno's analysis, transparency and secrecy are instrumental in tracing some important aspects of representative democracy and its relationship with corruption. Let us follow his argument.

Democracy is characterized by the presence of political mediators between citizens, their needs and interest, and governments. Frequently, this type of political mediation is not separate from the activities aimed at gathering resources for mediation itself to be carried out. This is so because mediators are private individuals who invest their own resources in the achievement of a political career. Even when established, Pizzorno argues, mediators continue to play their role at their own costs. When some representatives of the Italian Socialist Party were prosecuted, they claimed that the amount of money they needed to 'work' as party representatives was three times larger than the sum granted by the state-funded system. The remaining part of the money, they lamented, had to be collected privately. Corruption, therefore, seems to amount to no more than unofficial fund-raising for political activity to take place. Cases where unofficial fund-raising does not benefit a political party, but the private sphere of individual mediators, are interpreted by Pizzorno as the outcome of the immorality of the emerging political class. This new rampant class, unlike its predecessor, finds the moral costs of corruption very low due to the low status of and the relative lack of disapproval within its group of origin. 'It costs the newcomers less to be corrupt than it does those who already hold a recognized status' (Pizzorno, 1992: 44).

At first sight, in this analysis, the cause of corruption appears to be twofold. On the one hand, it appears to be inherent in representative democracy, with the development of political mediation being part of its natural evolution. On the other hand, it appears to be the outcome of new classes gaining access to political power, namely classes which have no status and reputation to safeguard. However, one could conclude that these two causes in fact amount to one. The process whereby new classes which have no previous status gain access to political power may in fact also be regarded as inherent in representative democracy. Thus corruption and democracy end up by coinciding. Classical thinkers hold a different view on this point. For example, Alexis de Tocqueville (1956) linked corruption with the prevalence in a system of what he defined as office-hunters. These, he argued, strive to gain privileged positions in places where public resources are collected and distributed. Office-hunters have a realistic chance of succeeding when their background offers financial and cultural means of doing so. De Tocqueville's argument is the reverse of that sketched above: it is the accumulation of power among those who already hold a degree of it which may constitute a danger for democracy. It is centralization which poses a threat to governments, not its opposite:

> Thus, when public appointments afford the only outlet for ambition, the government necessarily meets with a permanent opposition at last; for it is tasked to satisfy with limited means unlimited desires (ibid.: 262).

As we have seen, the state acts as one of the most important economic forces in Italy, both at the national and at the local level. The degree to which its economic power is centralized makes the Italian state fit the description of de Tocqueville, who warns that a consequence of excessive centralization may be the destructive greed of office-hunters:

> Whatever endeavours are made by rulers, such a people can never be contented; and it is always to be apprehended that they will ultimately overturn the constitution of the country, and change the aspect of the state, for the sole purpose of making a clearance of places (ibid.: 262).

It is worth noting that these characteristics were regarded by de Tocqueville as 'novel features under which despotism may appear in the world' (ibid.: 303). Despotism, with a virtual monopolization of offices, presents itself as an immense tutelary power. Despotism is absolute, minute, regular, provident, and mild. It degrades people without tormenting them. This power could be compared to the authority of a parent if, like that authority, its object were to prepare children for adulthood; but this power seeks, on the contrary, to keep them in perpetual childhood. In this analysis, corruption is the outcome of despotism, and it victimizes citizens by infantilizing them:

> It is in vain to summon a people, who have been rendered so dependent on the central power, to choose from time to time the representatives of that power;

this rare and brief exercise of their free choice will not prevent them from grad-
ually losing the faculties of thinking, and acting for themselves (ibid.: 306).

Moral and Political De-skilling

It is not easy to say a final word on the relationship between democracy, despotism, and corruption. Reading the work of contemporary
critics of representative democracies, one finds only hints which need
thorough elaboration. However, some of these hints may help identify
yet another aspect of victimization caused by corrupt exchange.

Offe and Preuss (1991) suggest that in liberal democracies a mechanism is at work whereby there is always a difference between the formal
purpose of the decision-making process and the outcomes of the decisions themselves. This, which the authors identify as the source of
political alienation, is said to be a characteristic of all democracies, and
to cause the depletion of the moral resources of citizens. Their mandate, it is argued, is valueless because decisions on issues will be made,
the nature of which is entirely unknown at the moment of voting, and
in which voters can play no role (Offe and Preuss, 1991). Policy-
makers and administrators, who make choices and control decision
outcomes, acquire skills which increasingly separate them from ordinary citizens. In my view corruption accelerates this tendency and
sharpens its features. The mandate of citizens, in a corrupt political
system, faces a situation where not only is the outcome of decisions
uncertain, but the real power of those making decisions is unknown.
Decisions, their effect, and even the possibility of their being made
depend on the resources that political parties accumulate outside the
formal and legal sphere. Voters will therefore ignore the amount of
power held by parties and their very capacity to make decisions, let
alone the outcome of those decisions. Corruption exacerbates the
moral and political de-skilling of the electorate.

In the Italian context, as I have already argued, corruption is characterized by a multiplying effect which is felt in all positions of the social
hierarchy. It is interesting to investigate how corrupt exchange involving the elites and that involving ordinary citizens feed upon each other.

The Acceptance of Higher Immorality

In Italy, as corruption spread from the elite downwards to other social
groups, impunity seemed to increase its multiplying effect. One could

apply to this the explanatory metaphor of the 'broken window'. As Wilson and Kelling (1982: 33) argued:

Window-breaking does not necessarily occur on a large scale because some areas are inhabited by determined windowbreakers whereas others are populated by window-lovers; rather, one unrepaired broken window is a signal that no one cares, and so breaking more windows costs nothing.

In witnessing a variety of corrupt exchanges, social groups and individuals, whether taking part in corruption or not, may have become unaccustomed to public welfare. Arguably, this process was favoured by the limited benefit that even people not belonging to the elite might enjoy from corrupt exchange. Mills (1956) observed a similar pattern in North American society of the 1950s, when he remarked that the amoral tone of that society also involved the lack of public sensibility when confronted with corruption. 'Effective moral indignation is not evoked by the corrupt public life of our time; the old middle-class moralities have been replaced by the higher immorality' (ibid.: 341). Similarly, in contemporary Italian society, it seems that the opportunities granted to ordinary citizens to benefit from minor episodes of corruption led to the partial condoning of large-scale corruption. The tolerance of petty immorality on the part of the elite, to use Mills's expression, paved the way for the acceptance of their own higher immorality by the non-elite. In fact, the elite encompassed in their tolerance not only petty corrupt exchange, but also petty illegal activities. In places such as Naples, Rome, and others, for decades the authorities turned a blind eye to small commercial illegalities, unlicensed retailing, even contraband. This permissiveness in the face of small-scale criminal activity was perhaps due to its being vaguely regarded as a substitute for the ineffective welfare state. A healthy person granted a pension for disabled people did not epitomize, as Merton would have it, the 'trained incapacity' of public employees, but their flexibility.

This mutual acceptance between different social groups affected the perception of corrupt exchange as a whole. Corruption lost an agreed yardstick whereby its impact could be measured. The involvement in it of non-elite groups contributed to this process, which resulted in overlooking the quality and quantity of social damage caused by different episodes. As Paci (1992) remarked, if a person pays a £10 bribe to obtain a birth certificate quickly, he or she will probably condone the behaviour of the entrepreneurs who pay millions in exchange for a contract. In this sense, the following metaphor seems to apply: 'Social opposites meet in the smoke filled room of the successful politician' (Merton, 1968: 135). But it is indeed in that room that the victims of corruption miraculously disappear, while the degree of harm respectively caused, which is incommensurable, becomes symbolically equal. In the perceived equality of incomparable entities, another aspect of victimization of the more vulnerable can be detected. This relates in a curious way to the well-known techniques of neutralization suggested by Sykes and Matza (1957). Among the 'excuses' by which the norms are temporarily neutralized, and therefore corrupt exchange easily takes place, is somehow the reverse of the 'condemnation of the condemners': it is the condoning of the condoners.

The Prince Restored

Mills's (1956: 355) emphasis on the participation of the 'men in the mass' in shaping the social perception of corrupt exchange should be borne in mind. The author argues that the absence of any firm moral order of belief makes ordinary citizens all the more amenable to manipulation by 'the world of the celebrities':

In due course, such 'turnover' of appeals and codes and values as they are subjected to leads them to distrust and cynicism, to a sort of Machiavellianism-for-the-little-man.

I suggest that the version of Machiavellianism which is adopted by ordinary citizens in the face of corruption is more extreme, as it goes beyond cynicism and alienation from the political arena. It is an unwitting espousal of the more pessimistic, and indeed the core, aspect of Machiavelli's analysis, namely the assumption that corruption is the main characteristic of those who are governed rather than those who govern. Corruption is part of the natural inclination of the masses, and it is against this inclination that the virtues of the Prince are required to intervene. In sum, citizens involved in corrupt exchange end up perceiving themselves as the real cause of corruption, thus legitimizing all solutions adopted by the Prince. As no opposition to him is legitimate, he can therefore resort to any means in order to make the cohabitation of his unruly subjects possible.

I can now return to Case 10 of the examples of corrupt exchange in Italy. The employee who applied for a pension was not surprised by the corrupt behaviour of his colleague who, in exchange for performing what was part of his job and at the same time part of his colleague's rights, expected the payment of a bribe. The would-be pensioner was in fact applying for early retirement as a disabled person, which he was not.

9

Corruption as Resentment

This chapter examines episodes of political and administrative corruption which occurred in France in the 1980s and the 1990s.[1] In discussing the French case corruption will be defined as occurring when one or more actors involved in, or witnessing, corrupt exchange have reasons for resentment and therefore permit corruption to come to light. The adoption of this framework of analysis constitutes an implicit refutation of views which associate corruption with variables such as economic underdevelopment and social backwardness. The choice of the formula 'corruption as resentment', in other words, permits the exploration of how corrupt exchange also takes place in highly developed and advanced social contexts.

In the previous chapter corruption was analysed with a view to uncovering some aspects of victimization caused by it. It was argued that a number of actors, endowed with varying degrees of resources and power, participate in corrupt exchange, and that only a deeply rooted optical illusion enables us to see these exchanges as victimless. In that chapter, without analysing why corruption occurs, an attempt was made to show why, when, and for whom it is harmful. In what follows, similarly, I do not propose an aetiological view: the existence of corruption is treated as a given, while questions are posed regarding how it is perceived. In brief, an explanation is attempted of its public manifestation, rather than of its 'true' prevalence, of its very definition as corruption, rather than of its causes.

This avenue has also been taken by other authors, who have argued that scandal, like treason, exists only when something goes wrong (Frears, 1988). This is to say that abuse of power, governmental malpractice, and incompetence emerge only when they are exposed. However, when this avenue has been explored, the emergence of corruption

[1] I would like to thank Laurent Joffrin, editor of Le Nouvel Observateur and now of Libération, together with a group of lawyers of the Syndicat de la Magistrature, for their suggestions and observations.

and its concealment have mainly been associated with, respectively, the efficacy or lack of scrutiny of political and economic power. This perspective appears to entail that there would be less corruption if some actors—usually the judiciary, the media, and the public—exerted stricter control over others—usually politicians and entrepreneurs. In the following pages, emphasis will be placed on interactions between these actors and, crucially, on the resentment that corrupt behaviour produces in some of them, a resentment which translates into the exposure of that behaviour and its definition as corrupt.

A related assumption to this approach is that corrupt activities, albeit unorthodox or even illegal, may be tolerated when they appear to generate benefits for all those participating in or witnessing them. Resentment and, therefore, corruption emerge when these activities are no longer perceived as generating acceptable benefits for everyone; or when the previous role division and related expectations are no longer accepted. In some cases, which will be mentioned later, some of the actors involved may find the 'diseconomies' of corrupt exchange too costly to endure, and begin to perceive that exchange as tantamount to extortion. In the present chapter politicians, entrepreneurs, judges, and the media are identified as the main actors contributing to the definition of certain behaviour as corrupt. It is in the light of the interactions taking place between these actors, which periodically oscillate between mutual acceptance and competition, that corrupt exchange in France is examined. In a brief conclusion, the reasons for the exclusion of 'public opinion' from the dynamics described are clarified.

Politicians and Entrepreneurs

The predominance of the executive power is among the legacies characterizing contemporary France, a legacy which Michelet (1981) traces back to the republican Constitution of 1793. However, the recent history of the country reveals a pendulum-like movement between concentration of power and its distribution. According to Mény (1995: 23):

Since the Revolution, all authoritarian regimes have tried to put power in the hands of one person: the dictator, the emperor, the head of state at central level, the prefect and the mayors at the local level. Conversely, democratic regimes have tried, sometimes going too far, to fragment power.

During the Third and Fourth Republics, for instance, the central power of the executive was weakened, while the power of local administrators was strengthened. Opportunities for corrupt exchange were therefore mainly located within the domain of the legislative power, where economic decisions were made. Lobbying Members of Parliament was among the activities of powerful entrepreneurs, who were deemed the victims of the corrupting influence of Paris. The Panama scandal exemplifies this type of corrupt exchange. It began with a project to build a channel through the isthmus of Central America in order to join the Atlantic and Pacific oceans. Difficulties and incompetence repeatedly interrupted the work, while the budget grew disproportionately higher than the costs initially envisaged. The company needed constant refinancing, until a final parliamentary vote was required to authorize a large loan. More than 100 deputies were accused of having taken bribes in exchange for a 'yes' vote for an undertaking which they knew was bound to fail (Cornick, 1993).

During the Fourth Republic, however, the involvement of politicians in corrupt exchange was also traced in local clientelism. Politicians owed their presence in Parliament to the financial support of local notables, with whom they had ties of mutual interests: once elected, they would exchange the support received for favouritism in the concession of local contracts (Jenkins and Morris, 1993). The Fifth Republic inherited the strong executive advocated by Montesquieu and Robespierre, with power being concentrated in the presidency. However, along with the national, regional and city authorities also took on unprecedented decision-making powers. This 'monarchic model', with the executive power being strong both at the centre and at the periphery, resulted in the multiplication of corrupt opportunities (Gaetner, 1992).

Opportunities for corrupt exchange to take place at the local level increased with the legislation passed in 1982 which accorded relative autonomy status to regional executives and mayors. From 1982, the decentralization process endowed local authorities with such crucial prerogatives that local politicians soon resembled 'feudal seigneurs'. The power of mayors, for example, included full responsibility with regard to all aspects of urban development, town planning, property and planning permission, health (with mayors sitting on executive boards of public hospitals), social welfare, education, and environment. Decisions taken in these fields were not subject to *a priori* scrutiny by national bodies, but only to *a posteriori* control on the part of regional authorities. These would forward the relevant information to the prefects, the representatives of government at local level, only after contracts with local businesses had been signed (Etchegoyen, 1995). It should be added that most members of the French Parliament held, and to a degree still hold, local office in their constituencies, and that about three-quarters of them are mayors:

> To combine the role of *député* and mayor gives much greater control over the local political sub-system, gives one more influence when it comes to obtaining grants or subsidies from central government, gives one, as a notable, a better chance of being elected (Frears, 1988: 308).

French Members of Parliament, therefore, may devote more time to their local concerns than to their parliamentary responsibilities as controllers of the executive. On the other hand, they may be part of the executive itself, albeit at the local level, thus acting as both controllers and controlled.

Under the influence of Gaston Defferre, both mayor of Marseille and Minister of the Interior, the socialist government played a central role in devising the 1982 legislation on decentralization. Inspired by the apparent desire to realize forms of local democracy, and to bring citizens closer to decision-making bodies, this legislation in fact favoured the large entrepreneurial groups which surrounded and supported local politicians. Virtual monopolies were established, with some loyal entrepreneurs attracting the most lucrative contracts from local authorities. It should be added that in France, over the last fifteen years, the majority of public contracts, consisting of major urban works, were issued by local authorities, with funds being released by mayors (Mény, 1992). This fact led entrepreneurs to focus their activity on municipalities and regions, where funds were more easily available. The 'local choice' was also prompted by the rule whereby those winning contracts were required to pre-finance the works or services undertaken and accept delayed reimbursement. This considerably reduced the number of firms which were in a position to bid, and only groups already strong nationally, namely those endowed with national credentials and collateral, had a realistic prospect of winning contracts. In their case, credibility at the national level turned into opportunities at the local one.

In this respect it may be of interest to draw a comparison with the Italian situation. By contrast with the Italian context, corruption in France does not necessarily rely on mediators who act as informal contacts for politicians and entrepreneurs. In Italy, these mediators are unelected figures who are active in both the public and private spheres, moving as they do between the two. In France, instead, relationships between the political and entrepreneurial worlds seem to be more direct, with mayors, deputies, and ministers in a position to relate to entrepreneurs in a more independent fashion. This suggests that corrupt exchange in France is less dispersed, and that corrupt income is concentrated among limited elites. As its proceeds are less 'socialized', corruption in France appears to entail lower costs.

The dynamics described so far may lead one to over-emphasize the role of local authorities in the building of a corrupt system and, more specifically, the role of the political Right, which controls the majority of local administrations. Did the Right take advantage of a piece of legislation, namely a well-intentioned decentralization of power, designed by the Left? This assumption is challenged by facts. The Pechiney–Triangle affair shows how corruption in ministerial circles can proceed simultaneously with locally based corruption. The state-owned Pechiney group acquired the US company Triangle in 1988, with the encouragement of Ministry of Finance officials. Immediately after the government had secured the go-ahead for the takeover, a businessman closely linked with the Socialist Party bought 32,000 Triangle shares, while a close friend of the President purchased a further 20,000. The profits were laundered through businesses set up in Panama and returned to France, allegedly to the Socialist Party (Maclean, 1993; *Le Nouvel Observateur*, 6–12 October 1994). The Urba affair, which will be discussed below, is another notorious example of socialist involvement in corrupt practices, and, most importantly, of local–national co-ordination of corrupt exchange.

It has been suggested that corruption in France is to be analysed against a crucial characteristic of the political apparatus. This is that political parties are financially and socially weak. Numerous and undisciplined (with the notable exception of the Communist Party), they have never achieved the features of hierarchically structured machines set in motion by the efforts of branches, representatives, and members. Lacking in human and financial resources, parties traditionally resort to informal donations and opaque contributions given in exchange for 'influence'. The example of Urba is illuminating. In President Mitterrand's ambition, the Socialist Party was to evolve into a modern party of the Left, though it was unable to gain the support of active members and generous entrepreneurs. The establishment of a network of *sociétés d'études*, which would attract funds officially earmarked for research and cultural development, was thought to serve the purpose. These *sociétés d'études* had to ensure an intermediary function between those who controlled the resources (the firms) and their beneficiary (the Socialist Party), thus making obligatory a movement of funds which had never been spontaneous (Della Porta and Mény, 1995). Not completely new, this system reached organizational perfection with the socialist government, with percentages on the contracts granted being paid to commissioning politicians and their parties.

However, the weakness of political parties may explain only the causes of specific episodes in the French context, and should not be regarded as a universal causation of corrupt activities. For example, in the face of the Italian case, one might endorse a completely opposite aetiology, the country being characterized by extremely powerful political parties. In this respect, the 'Republic of Parties' is a shared definition, one which retains derogatory as well as aetiological significance when applied to Italy. But to attribute to the weakness or to the power of political parties the causes of corruption is to overlook the interactions of political parties themselves with other actors who contribute to the definition of some activities as corrupt.

The next section is devoted to such actors, in particular to the judiciary and the media, and to the way in which they have long been unable to perceive corrupt activities as being corrupt, or have been prevented from expressing their resentment over them.

Privilege of Jurisdiction

A number of articles included in the code of penal procedure allow the executive to deprive judges who conduct delicate investigations of their investigative power. For example, legislation passed in 1974, and in place until 1993, established that public prosecutors could not investigate offences committed by mayors within the sphere of their public mandate, but had to hand such cases to the Cour de Cassation, where an appropriate investigative judge would be designated. The designated investigator had to be one of the high judges sitting in the Supreme Court. This prerogative is inscribed in the procedural code, according to which the Cour de Cassation can suspend the validity of decisions taken by lower courts and tribunals, and is required to ensure that legal proceedings adhere to the existing legislation. The 1974 legislation also implied that whenever in investigative documents the names of public administrators were mentioned, examining judges were required to hand the investigation over to the higher ranks of the judicial hierarchy. If they failed to do so, the Cour de Cassation, after taking charge of the investigation, could annul all the previous procedural acts and findings, before transferring the proceedings to the Supreme Court. However, only cases not dismissed by the former court would be handed to the latter.

The immunity enjoyed by cabinet ministers dates back to 1958, when the Supreme Court was established. This court, elected anew by each newly formed parliament, dealt with crimes committed by government members in relation to the exercise of their functions. But before legal proceeding could be initiated, permission had to be granted by Parliament through a formal resolution of *mise en accusation*. During the thirty-five years of its existence, the Supreme Court, this 'archaic institution formed of 12 senators and 12 deputies' (Maclean, 1993), heard only two cases from those selected by the Cour de Cassation and approved for examination by Parliament (Vogelweith and Vaudano, 1995). This *procédure du privilège* came to an end not least because of its indirect, catastrophic judicial effect. The privilege of jurisdiction also applied to police officers and detectives. In a number of investigations of drug-trafficking offences, some officers were charged with malpractice or even complicity with offenders. The transfer of the investigation to a higher judge meant a delay which resulted in alleged drug traffickers being granted conditional bail.

'Little' and 'Big' Judges

According to critical commentators, those occupying the high ranks of the judiciary 'have never changed': they were there before, during, and after Vichy, and allegedly they all have very correct Republican views. Vogelweith and Vaudano (1995) term the culture characterizing senior judges a 'subservient one', and see the intermediary and low ranks of the judiciary as more susceptible to change and more independent.

The lowest positions in the judiciary are occupied by the *juges d'instruction*, examining judges who are charged with the gathering of information and evidence relating to criminal offences. Above them are the judges of the public prosecution service (also termed the *parquet*), who are required to supervise the legality of the examining procedure. The presidents of the *parquets*, or public prosecutors, have the prerogative to designate which examining judge (*petit juge*) will be entrusted with the investigation of which case. They also have the power to appoint one or more examining judges under their supervision as experts in financial and administrative crime. Data produced in 1994 indicate that an elite of eleven investigative judges was dealing with about 7,000 cases each year.

Although their action is dependent on decisions taken by their public prosecutors, it is common for examining judges to be accused of wielding too much power. In effect, once they obtain permission to proceed, they become responsible for both the investigation and the treatment of those investigated. For example, they can remand suspects in custody until they believe all evidence has been examined. This, however, does not apply to proceedings in which public political figures are involved, as these cases are dealt with according to the procedure described above.

The career of an examining judge offers limited promotion opportunities, especially when his or her activity generates embarrassment and is regarded as inimical. This organizational set-up lends itself to potential abuse, as examining judges who intend to advance in their career are required to be obsequious towards public prosecutors in order eventually to join the *parquet*. There is also scope for 'punitive' promotions, whereby 'stubborn' individuals are removed from their investigative role and assigned a higher rank in a less problematic region of the country. Finally, some judges may 'choose' to abandon their career altogether when the feeling that their hands are tied becomes too unpleasant to bear. The following is one such case.

Jean-Pierre Thierry was handling the Urba affair in the capacity of *juge d'instruction*. He was gathering evidence concerning the illegal funding of political parties. In particular, his investigation began to suggest that a part of the funds used to finance the 1988 election campaign of the Socialist Party had been illegally obtained. The funds had been diverted from a construction company, and via the intermediary Urba network of *sociétés d'études* forwarded to the Socialist Party, which was in government at the time of the investigation (Trouille, 1994). Thierry was accused of having taken the law into his own hands because he had failed to report back to the public prosecutors about his investigation, and had not received the necessary permission to continue his investigation of the case. Thierry was immediately removed from the case by the *procureur général* (the head of the public prosecution service). He decided to abandon his career as a judge and became involved in politics.

At the two extremes, the investigating judges and the heads of the prosecution service occupy the most controversial positions. The former are deemed too young and inexperienced to hold a position which entails too much power. However, we have seen how this power can be curtailed and bridled. The latter, who are directly appointed (and disciplined or fired) by the Ministry of Justice, may be under attack for their close relationship with the executive, as their very career depends on the will of government. This is exemplified by the fact that all criminal proceedings initiated by prosecutors must receive official approval from the Minister. Theoretically, prosecutors can inform the Minister that proceedings are being undertaken rather than that they have intention of undertaking them. However, in practice, before sensitive proceedings are started, consultation with the Ministry is essential, in particular when cases are investigated which could cause distress for government and affect public opinion. When prosecutors are instructed by the Minister in relation to sensitive affairs the problem is not whether or not to pursue a case (*vis-à-vis* the law), but whether or not to obey (*vis-à-vis* the instructions received) (Lorenzi, 1995).

The only avenue available to public prosecutors, and for that matter to *petits juges*, to pursue a case entails the media enlarging upon the case being investigated. Once the media divulge information relating to an affair, it is more difficult for the Ministry to deny permission to proceed. But with this we are entering the role of the fourth actor involved in the definition of certain activities as corrupt.

The Media

The French media have never been regarded as particularly effective in their watchdog role. This applies in particular to television, whose coverage of news was under direct government control during the de Gaulle and Pompidou presidencies. With Giscard d'Estaing, 'direct control was replaced by patronage: associates of the President were put in charge of television and radio organisations' (Frears, 1988: 323).

Before the scandals of the last decade were unearthed, the press was also noticeable for its investigative inefficiency in exposing abuses of power. The vigilance of newspapers such as *Le Canard Enchaîné*, along with the work of a few independent journalists, was sufficient to bring abuses to light, but was incapable of following up enquiries or forcing the judiciary to act, let alone to sustain generalized public interest. In its turn, television, too timid to deal with the malpractice and offences of the elites, applied self-censorship as its rule. In choosing the items for evening news, for example, 'delicate' affairs and their critical discussion were relegated to the midnight programme, while pre-arranged interviews with politicians involved in those affairs were given prominence in the six-o'clock programmes.

There is a media network of trusted journalists who are omnipresent, on television and in the press. According to Halimi (1995), they amount to no more than a dozen, and their presence and opinion can never be done without. Connivance and uniformity of views are the consequence: they meet, exchange information, support each other, and end up agreeing on everything. They write a leader in a weekly, give an interview to a monthly, talk on the radio and appear on television, and publish the inevitable book every year. Funded, as elsewhere, by financial groups and sustained by their advertisement money, newspapers and 'independent' television stations were, and to a degree still are, under strict control. Financial groups do not hide their political sympathies, nor do they conceal which newspaper they find most congenial, and therefore worthy of support. Newspapers sell advertising space to political parties and also to individual politicians engaged in their electoral campaigns. Moreover, political parties themselves own papers and magazines, and sometimes set up their own radio stations. See the example of Radio Nostalgie, the programmes of which contained only indirect political propaganda for the Socialist Party, but which was proved to act as a conduit for channelling illegal funds to the party (Gaetner, 1992). Ironically, the companies which were eventually to be exposed for their role in illegal party funding were the same as those which sustained newspapers such as *Le Monde*, *L'Express*, *Le Point*, and *L'Expansion*.

Resentment

The exposure of political scandals and corruption was the result of the resentment of one or more of the actors described so far. Before briefly sketching the institutional reaction to the onslaught of accusations, let us see how this resentment found its expression.

The exchange of public contracts for bribes (whether for personal gain or illegal party funding) may not be a widely accepted practice among enterprises. This implies that only 'trustworthy' companies can be expected to participate in the exchange. For this reason politicians' choice of the type of service or work to contract out may not depend on the actual need for that service or work, but on the offer of money made by entrepreneurs. Resentment may therefore be expressed by firms offering services which, though needed, are nevertheless never asked for. The example of service privatization offers an illuminating extension of this. Here it is not only the nature of the service privatized, but also the costs incurred by private providers, which may cause resentment. Private firms contracted may apply higher costs than their competitors, because they are, in a sense, assisted enterprises (Barca and Trento, 1994). The resentment of competing firms arises, therefore, from the diseconomy caused by both the type of service contracted out and its cost. The former is in fact determined by the loyalty manifested by firms to politicians, the latter by the cost of this loyalty.

Other sources of resentment may come to light when the relationships between small and large firms are analysed. The system of illegal party funding created a *de facto* corrupt monopoly which in the main benefited the large groups more closely associated with the executive, be this locally or nationally based. The organizational structure of these groups was decentralized enough for them to obtain contracts in different business arenas and geographical contexts. For example, a large firm could offer building work to one local authority and furnish hospital equipment to another. This flexibility was promoted, among other things, by the wide range of public contracts granted in France to private companies, and received a boost from the related process of decentralization described above. Moreover, French firms seem to have stretched the concept of flexibility to embrace the political arena, with work and services being offered to local authorities controlled by both the Right and the Left. Finally, flexibility also informed the ethical sphere, in the sense that rules and procedures would be stretched to tally with those adopted by those granting contracts. This diversification allowed large firms to be competitive in both national and local markets. In the latter markets they encountered the resentment of smaller firms which were unable to achieve similar organizational complexity.

One of the first large scandals uncovered in the 1980s involved one such small enterprise. The scandal came to light by pure 'judicial accident', during the course of investigation into the death of two workers on a building site. Following pressure from the union, examining judges found that working conditions in the company involved were poor and safety regulations ignored. The market for public contracts in the region where the accident took place was characterized by a situation of oligopoly shared by large firms connected with local politicians.

Smaller firms could obtain contracts only by applying significantly lower costs, thus cutting safety expenses. The resentment of the firm under investigation was expressed through the claim that it had incurred high costs for the 'privilege' of winning the contract:

> The accident in the workplace had occurred because the firm had had to pay a backhander to politicians in order to win the tender, a circumstance which had deprived the firm of the financial means necessary for the respect of safety regulations (Vogelweith and Vaudano, 1995: 22).

The investigation, eventually, uncovered a wide network of enterprises adopting the same procedure: the Urba affair was born.

It is worth noting that the Italian 'clean hand' operation started on a similar note. The whistle was blown by a small entrepreneur operating in Milan who had a contract for the supply of cleaning services in a home for the elderly (see Chapter 8). He reported to the police the incessant requests by top administrators of the home for a percentage of his profits. Because this percentage was increasing, the entrepreneur could no longer guarantee the quality of the service he was providing.

Resentment against companies engaged in corrupt practices may also be expressed by shareholders. Again, this may result from 'accidents' such as unexpectedly poor financial returns to shareholders or even the sudden bankruptcy of a company. In France, this was the case with a number of allegedly stable companies suddenly going into receivership. Pressure by shareholders led examining judges to uncover illegal transfers of finances, displacement of funds, false invoices, and so-called 'taxi companies', whose role consisted solely of delivering money to political parties.

It remains to be seen whether, in the near future, the internationalization of markets will lead to new forms of resentment. This might be expressed by non-French companies attempting to operate in France, where they will be likely to find unfair competition from 'protected' firms which enjoy the support of the domestic political class.

The Judiciary–Media Alliance

The resentment of the judiciary went hand in hand with that of the media. The bargaining power of judges mainly stems from their ability to make investigation findings public. In this they may also be helped by the defence lawyers of those under investigation, as is the case with politicians and their counsel calling press conferences to reveal the 'absurd charges' brought by judges. For example, when the first large financial scandals of the 1980s exploded, the TF1 channel launched a serial programme against the 'witch hunt' mounted by the judiciary. One of these scandals involved the Alcatel group which, under investigation on corruption charges, pre-empted the judiciary in making the content of the accusations public, presumably in an attempt to keep control of the information revealed. This move proved beneficial to the examining judge, who could rely on the support of the media and obtain permission to carry on with the investigation from the *procureur général*.

In other cases publicity was sought by investigative judges themselves, but in doing so they could be accused of non-compliance with the secrecy principle governing the investigation process. This happened in relation to the Henri Emmanuelli case, when the media revealed corruption charges brought against this Socialist Party politician before he had received any official notification from the examining judge.

This judiciary–media alliance triggered the reaction of politicians and entrepreneurs, who felt they were being treated as guilty before their guilt had been proven. Judges were likened to contemporary Saint-Justs, and convictions were said to emanate from the press. Obscure investigators and journalists were accused of pursuing fame, of acting as stars, in a spectacle which some commentators equated with a 'judiciary–media circus' (Lorenzi, 1995).

Institutional Responses

According to the influential writer Alain Minc (1995), France is experiencing a misguided 'democratic inebriation' which will lead to a new public individual: one who is obsessed by external observers and is therefore bound to lose reflexivity and tolerance. The new public individuals, namely the politicians, will be required constantly to fight those who accuse them: a Holy Trinity formed by judges, public opinion, and the media. France has become a 'government of judges', the damning phrase with which the accused mount their counter-attack against investigators.

In July 1988, in the wake of the presidential election, along with a new piece of legislation establishing the funding of parties by the state, an amnesty was given to all politicians charged with malpractice and corruption. The amnesty covered all offences committed in relation to electoral campaigning and political party funding. In that year big cases such as the Urba affair had not yet come to light. After they had, a second amnesty was granted in 1990 for all those who had not benefited from the previous one, but corrupt politicians who had pursued personal gain, rather than party funds, were excluded. This second amnesty was presented as an inevitable measure, when legislation regulating political party funding was non-existent or vague. Therefore, new legislation regulating the financial aspects of political activity was introduced with the amnesty. This reduced the amount of funds each campaigning candidate was allowed to spend, and decreed that private donations to parties be given a pre-established ceiling, be precisely recorded, and be made public. This piece of legislation was regarded by critics as a *de facto* decriminalization of formerly illegal practices. Currently, it is argued, if politicians still intend to pursue their personal gain, they may well continue in this practice by resorting to falsification and forgery, as they did before. If funds exceeding the legally set ceiling can still be channelled to parties by means of forged invoices, individual politicians may well 'forge the forged invoices' to pocket money destined for their party. On the other hand, with the state-funding system, improbable political parties and even 'unipersonal parties' are said to crop up with the sole purpose of attracting state funds (Imerglik, 1994).

The 1990 legislation marked a shift in the legal perception of corruption. Amnesties granted in 1947 and 1953, for example, were not intended for politicians, who were deemed passive parties in corrupt exchange. Their behaviour was only regarded as complicity with corrupt individuals. Moreover, politicians using mediators in their corrupt practices could escape prosecution because they would be defined as 'accomplices of accomplices', a byzantine category devoid of juridical significance. Finally, 'attempts to corrupt' could not be prosecuted because 'attempting to become an accomplice in crime' was an even more byzantine juridical category. Changes introduced by the 1990 amnesty abolished these privileges.

In 1993 the Bouchery report was published, which addressed three of what were believed to be the deep-seated problems of France: unemployment, street crime, and corruption. The report described corruption as a gangrene devouring society, but failed to identify new rules for its prevention. Too many rules regulating the relationships between politicians and enterprises, it was argued, would hamper competition and benefit companies from other European countries, unless all countries of the Union agreed to introduce similar rules.

Organizational reform of the judiciary was one of the responses to assuage resentment. In 1993, a number of amendments to the code of procedure were passed. The *privilège de juridiction* was abolished, although Members of Parliament took a precaution: the *procureur général* maintained the power to remove a judge from a case when this was in the best interest of the administration of justice. In 1992 a new piece of legislation made concessions on two important issues. First, it made the procedure related to the career of judges more transparent, with new powers being given to their national professional body. This body, elected by judges themselves, was made responsible for transferrals and promotions. Secondly, it issued a series of statutory guarantees aimed at reducing the influence of the executive on the judiciary.

Concessions were also made to journalists. Their resentment had induced Mitterrand to create the 'High Authority for Audio-Visual Communications', allegedly independent of government, to supervise radio and television programmes and make appointments to top jobs. Abolished by Chirac in 1986, and replaced by his CNCL (National Commission for Communications and Liberties), the 'High Authority' did not 'free' the press: when *Le Monde* started covering the Alcatel affair, the newspaper's advertisement contract with that company was suspended.

Finally, responses to the resentment expressed by small firms, which remain excluded from large public contracts, took the form of governmental tolerance towards their illegalities, namely their employment of unregistered workers and violations of trade union rights. This tolerance may soon translate into the abolition of minimum statutory wage levels, and related forms of deregulation, therefore into the virtual decriminalization of all their practices.

Conclusion

It is difficult to assess the extent to which the institutional responses sketched above will reduce resentment and thus exposition of corrupt activities, let alone reduce corruption itself. The actors involved in identifying what constitutes corruption may temporarily be satisfied by the concessions obtained, but may soon discover new reasons for being dissatisfied.

It should be noted that resentment alone does not explain the success of those exposing cases of corruption; resentment is merely the motivation for exposure. The multiplication of cases of corruption revealed over recent years, and the success of the media and the judiciary, are perhaps due to the fact that all political parties were accused, sooner or later. This may have reduced the embarrassment of individual parties, and consequently tempered their willingness and capacity to halt the anti-corruption onslaught. It is worth remembering that the Right came to power thanks, among other things, to its exposure of corrupt episodes in which the Socialist Party had been involved. When the Right itself was charged with corrupt practices, it could not replicate the responses given by its socialist counterparts. For example, it could not claim that there was a political conspiracy against it, nor that judges and journalists had hidden agendas, because these were the same agencies that had indicted their predecessors. In a sense, the alternation between political parties created a climate in which it became easier to expose corruption. Similarly, after the initial reprisals by firms against the press in the form of curtailment of advertisement contracts, things returned to normal because too many firms came under investigation. Soon the issue became how to impose limitations on the press when individuals not found guilty of an offence were mentioned.

This chapter does not include public opinion among the actors involved in corrupt exchange and its exposure. It is time to explain why. It is a characteristic of representative democracies to create an increasing distance between electoral decisions and policy decisions. Elected politicians are the recipients of power conferred on them by citizens. As with banking institutions, once they have received this 'deposit' of power, politicians can invest it in enterprises which are out of the control of depositors. Increasingly, decisions affecting all are made in places and times known only to a few. It is the awareness of this distance between the 'public' and its political representatives which makes the role of the former in exposing corruption a secondary one. This distance is perceived as the cause of corruption, or is even itself deemed corruption. To use Geertz's (1988: 18) metaphor: as in the past crowns and coronations, now limousines and conferences 'mark the centre as centre and give what goes on there its aura of being not merely important but in some odd fashion connected with the way the world is built'. Paradoxically, this distance does not shelter politicians from 'public' scrutiny, because the behaviour of politicians will be assumed to be corrupt even when it is not. The slogan 'tout est pourri' was not coined to describe the scandals of the 1980s and 1990s, but dates back centuries. But this slogan, applied to all regimes and governments, makes it impossible to establish the limit within which corruption is acceptable and beyond which it must be exposed. For example, in opinion polls conducted in France, respondents were asked to choose whether they would rather be governed by corrupt but effective politicians or by honest and ineffective ones (Etchegoyen, 1995). As politicians are not expected to have both attributes, the belief that it is impossible to get rid of the former led the 'public' to opt at least for the latter.

The analytical route chosen in this chapter has permitted us to sidestep the obstacle represented by public opinion, among which the relationship between politics and corruption is undeserving of analysis, being somewhat axiomatic.

However, as we shall see, this obstacle will return, thus invalidating the analysis conducted here. In the chapter that follows, public opinion, in the form of common feeling and sense of the state, will claim back a crucial role.

10

Crime as Sense of the State

In Italy, as I have suggested, the spread of corrupt exchange was accompanied, first of all, by the slow disappearance of the victim. The participation of diverse actors and groups in some form of corrupt practice encouraged a collective denial of the existence of the victim and the adoption by many of the characteristics, and the self-perception, of offenders. Notwithstanding the extraordinary differences between the gains of the various actors involved, these became comparable and, miraculously, their respective corrupt profits commensurable. This equitable partition of guilt, in its turn, allowed everyone to attribute the criminal label to someone else, usually in a higher position in the social hierarchy. In this case, which is perhaps unique, one is forced to conclude that the disappearance of the victim ultimately led to the simultaneous disappearance of the offender.

In France, where the cases of corrupt exchange appear to involve the participation of a more limited number of actors and groups, one could lament that corruption is not an offence open to all, that it is not an equal-opportunity criminal behaviour. Resulting from negotiation and agreement among groups endowed with resources to invest and valorize, corruption is a tool which strengthens their position in the market, making them more competitive. When the distribution of corrupt proceeds is perceived as unfair, that is to say when participants develop reasons for mutual resentment, episodes of corrupt exchange come to light, in the form of reporting or self-reporting. Among those who report episodes of corruption are often individuals and groups who, implicitly, seem to claim wider access to illegality, the opportunities for which they regard as being unjustly distributed.

In both cases examined, mainstream analysis posits the existence of a background situation in which politics is deteriorating, as it is no longer capable of utilizing human resources and mobilizing hope. In this respect, the practices of contemporary socialist parties in Europe are deemed exemplary. These political parties, which are judged unable to attract activists, members, or even donors who believe in the 'cause', are forced to find the finances for their reproduction elsewhere. As for corrupt entrepreneurs, it is commonly suggested that their conduct damages the market or, in some cases, victimizes the state and contributes to lowering the moral tone of a country. In the last analysis, political and administrative corruption, along with the range of collusive opportunities offered to entrepreneurs, become associated with 'lack of solidarity' or 'want of a sense of the collectivity'. In extreme cases, such as the Italian case, commentators are inclined to relate corruption to the lack of a 'sense of the state', a legacy, it is assumed, of a hasty, recent, artificially imposed national unification.

In this chapter, I will try to analyse corruption in England moving from exactly opposite premises. Can a deeply rooted sense of the state, and a sense of one's nationality which oscillates between complacency and glorification, hide the existence of corruption, deform its features, render it unrecognizable as such, and at times even encourage it?[1]

Brief Phenomenology

In a sort of league table of shame, elaborated by Transparency International, the UK occupies an intermediate position, slightly above countries such as Chile and the USA. This organization, which publishes an annual corruption perception index, and which was founded in Berlin in 1993, puts Italy on the lowest rung among Western countries, giving her a degree of shame higher than that of Nigeria, Russia, and Colombia (McCormack, 1996; Leiken, 1997). Italian observers, and for that matter Italians in general, feel that their political and business elite genuinely deserve such a position. Let us try to unravel some of the elements which underlie the position occupied by the UK.

For some decades, during the successive Thatcher, Major, and finally Blair governments, for technical—which as we shall see are also social—reasons, transactions between entrepreneurs and politicians have enjoyed particular protection and secrecy. The British state has fed the productivity of the major industries through an incessant demand for goods and services. Among the main beneficiaries were, and to a degree still are, companies which guarantee relative stability in the workforce, a fact which renders the alliance between politics and

[1] I would like to thank John Mason and Francis Mulhern of Middlesex University for discussing with me the content of this chapter and for some important bibliographical suggestions.

business somewhat 'noble'. With the manifest purpose of averting tensions in the labour market, this alliance looks leniently at irregularities committed abroad, provided business initiatives accompanying such irregularities translate into wealth for the country as a whole. In the past, the prevailing condition was one characterized by what I would term a *customer monocracy*: a specific market situation in which there was only one purchaser and in which the monopoly belonged to those who bought rather than those who sold. This is the case with the armaments industry (extensively examined in Chapter 7), whose main customer has for years been the Ministry of Defence, and also with the powerful pharmaceutical industry, linked to the National Health Service and its political representatives in Parliament.

This mingling of the public and the private spheres, sometimes felt to be ineluctable, is part of the connatural features of the English elites, which are bred, nurtured, and 'manufactured' within networks of affiliation inaccessible to most. In such networks, corrupt exchange may not be perceived as such because it takes place in 'invisible' locations which are as distant from civil society as the elites promoting it. The elites, in turn, even when engaged in corrupt practices, may well feel that rule-bending is a venial fault when weighed against their important mission, namely the reproduction of roles and hierarchies which, for centuries, guaranteed international power, domestic stability, and a good dose of widespread admiration which was given the name of 'Anglophilia'.

Invisibility for centuries characterized the financial world. The City could be described as a gentleman's club, relying on self-regulation performed within a network of families, friends, and business contacts. Penalization of unacceptable business practices was reduced to 'moral suasion, raised eyebrows, the stern rebuff over drinks' (Stanley, 1996: 81). A distinctive class as well as a distinctive cultural enclave, the City was the site of interlocked powerful groups including industry, the state, and the Church. The development of global financial markets may have changed this in part, making provincialism a hindrance to business. Foreign investors cannot easily adapt to a system requiring 'a stock of socially accepted competencies all the way from a family name through ownership of "appropriate" goods to formal educational qualifications' (ibid.). However, despite changes triggered by business internationalization, the invisibility of the financial world persists as business practices are still monitored through quasi-legal regulations which do not include precise definitions of fraud and business crime. 'In the absence of a general definition there is scope for liberal interpretation of what will and what will not constitute fraudulent behaviour' (ibid.: 96).

A contemporary example of the secrecy in which the elites operate is provided by financial agencies located in the Channel Islands. Here, the confidentiality of records, the low costs of operations, and the general absence of regulations allow for both money laundering and tax evasion to go virtually undetected (I. Taylor, 1992). The role of financial experts, lawyers, and accountants in this activity was denounced by the Association for Accountancy and Business Affairs, which suggested that these professionals create and manipulate complex transactions, making it difficult to identify the origins and trace the ultimate destination of illicit funds. Moreover, 'when acting as auditors, the accountants are also incapable or reluctant to report such activity' (Mitchell et. al., 1998: 3). Due to the customary reliance on self-regulation, it is expected that these professionals help in the fight against money laundering, and that they investigate their own involvement in such illicit activity. In the Channel Islands there are an estimated 100,000 offshore companies, and authorities and bank directors refuse to breach confidentiality over their customers when required by foreign investigators and governments. Changes in the legislation allow for the criminalization of bankers and professionals who fail to report suspicious customers and transactions, but such changes are aimed specifically at illicit drug entrepreneurs and organized transnational criminals. The legislation, in other words, is focused on conventional criminals, and is the result of a general reluctance to tackle corporate and white-collar offences. Hence the exclusive identification of 'dirty money' with 'drugs money':

At stake is partly the concern that they might come under pressure to stop laundering each other's tax evasion money—an argument that can be discussed publicly in international meetings, under the 'well-established' international principle that countries are not obliged to enforce each other's tax laws—and partly . . . the fear by local elites that their own income from corruption might be exposed and that white-collar crimes will be incorporated (Levi, 1997: 3).

Money laundering is not the exclusive domain of offshore financial centres:

Even in the major international financial centres, such as London, companies can be formed with minimum issued share capital of just £1 and used for legitimate and illegitimate purposes. The ownership of these companies can remain secret with professional nominees and agents providing respectable fronts. Some of these companies never undertake any trading and have little direct contact with the public. Instead, they can easily be used to launder the proceeds of drug-trafficking, robberies, smuggling, terrorism, tax evasion, bootlegging, art theft, vehicle theft, fraud and other anti-social activities (Mitchell *et. al.*, 1998: 6).

While in the past the business–politics interface was legitimized by its alleged capacity to provide job opportunities and augment national wealth, in more recent times it revealed less noble motives. The incessant need for finances for the political machine became apparent and, at the same time, the use of such a machine as a tool of sheer internal competition within the political and the business arenas emerged. Let us consider, for example, the case of Al Fayed, the owner of the Harrods store, and his liaison with Members of Parliament. Al Fayed, who intended to undermine one of his business rivals, managed to obtain the asking of a parliamentary question which had the ultimate effect of penalizing that rival, forcing him out of business. The parliamentary question was literally bought, as the owner of Harrods 'donated' a large sum of money to the Conservative Party.

When we observe the funding of political parties in the UK labelling theories appear to receive sensational confirmation: crimes are those acts which institutional intervention defines as such. One of Cesare Beccaria's enlightened mottoes, in turn, seems to be validated yet again: *nullo crime sine lege*. It is true that, in the history of the country, there have been attempts to regulate the income and expenses of political parties. A piece of legislation introduced in 1883, for example, established the maximum sum to be spent in electoral campaigns in every constituency. It has been suggested that this legislation was inspired by the desire of the Crown to save money, as political activity received funds, though indirectly, from the royal family itself (Doig, 1995).

In the last update of the indexes, in 1994, the sum of £5,000 was laid down as the maximum amount of funds to be invested by individual candidates in their political propaganda. Such regulation, which is extremely hard to enforce, leads to the predictable practice of double accounting, a practice brought to perfection by Italian, French, and Spanish political parties. In a typical episode, when a popular newspaper publicly supported one of the main parties at the national election, it is easy to figure out the type of financial transaction occurring between that newspaper and that party.

Another means of obtaining hidden funding for political parties revolves around the extravagant distribution of honours and distinctions, which are awarded by political parties in exchange for financial

support. Although traditionally it is a prerogative of the Crown to dispense decorations and honours, since last century this prerogative has
been informally shared by the Prime Minister, who designates the individuals who deserve medals, titles, and finally a place in the House of
Lords. A study conducted during the Thatcher era (1979–90) found
that eighty-five of the 174 entrepreneurs who had been given knight-
hoods or peerages were connected to private companies which had
donated a total of £13.6 million to the Conservatives. Funds were
entrusted to intermediary agencies which then transferred periodical
instalments to the party or individual politicians. In this respect, one
could suggest that the preference of businessmen for the Conservative
Party is not only due to the certainty that the party will implement policies and economic measures favourable to them, but also to a form of
frivolity underlying their pursuit of a 'title', which of course, sooner or
later, is also destined to 'pay' in economic terms. The Conservative
Party, while being (presumably) ideologically closer to entrepreneurs,
is also more successful in its lobbying of the Crown when honours are
conferred.

A piece of legislation introduced in 1925, which aimed at curbing the
scandalous practices of Prime Minister Lloyd George in relation to the
sale of honours, abolished the 'vile list of tariffs' which established
the price of titles such as baron, knight, and lord. However, with the
introduction of the new legislation, the criteria for the granting of titles
and merits, and their prices, were merely withdrawn from public
scrutiny and made informal. In current times, for example, entrepreneurs may be lured into making a donation to political parties in
exchange for an honour, or may be denied a contract if, solicited to
make a donation, they refuse to do so.

Among the examples of transactional corruption, those illustrating
not simply the interface but the complete overlapping of politics and
business should be mentioned. I am alluding to the custom whereby
politicians who resign from their careers as public representatives are
offered prestigious positions in private companies. These politicians
support, in Parliament or government, the interests of those private
firms which, at the end of their mandate, receive them into their ranks.
The privatization of some essential services and the deregulation of
others take place by courtesy of individual or collective political initiative, in a transaction which is somewhat postponed. A contract or the
franchising of a service is bartered with the future commitment to open
the company board of directors to those who have favoured it. In this

respect, it is legitimate to suggest that electoral campaigns of those who support this or the other company are funded by the very companies which offer them future employment. In 1989 the official registry of financial interests of House of Commons members revealed that one-third of ministers were advisers, consultants, and directors of public relations agencies, a euphemism clumsily hiding their direct relationships with the private sector.

This type of transactional corruption, as the examples mentioned above would appear to indicate, tends to increase with the privatization of services formerly delivered by the state. This tendency intensifies as a consequence of financial devolution occurring in the public sector, which implies the growing autonomy of 'quasi-governmental agencies' (quangos).

The quangos administer around a fifth of the public budget, and include schools, colleges, public health agencies, regional development agencies, and so on. Most appointments to their boards of directors are made by members of government, and are therefore not open to public competition between applicants. The quangos are encouraged to operate according to market logic and, in the name of efficiency, end up fostering clientelism. Manifestations of this include the appointment of experts, advisers, and managers who rapidly join and leave the agency while pursuing large sums of severance money or generous pension treatment. In exchange, such advisers and managers guarantee substantial returns to those employing them by constantly moving between the agencies themselves and the political decision-making arena. This mixture of professional, private, and public interest takes shape in a virtual legislative void which leaves regulation entrusted to vague codes of conduct. The effects of this devolution are particularly visible in education, where the appointment of unjustifiably highly salaried managers is accompanied by arbitrary payments made to consultants and external collaborators and, at times, by financial irregularities.

Within this brief phenomenology, some well-known cases need mentioning. One concerns Robert Maxwell, who was born in Czechoslovakia and settled in England in the late 1930s. After joining the British army, he fought with heroism and was awarded a Military Cross, an award which was destined to help his future career in the business world. He set up a large publishing company, Pergamon Press, which received a Queen's Prize for exemplary entrepreneurial merits. His business career seemed as successful as his political career was undistinguished: having become an MP in the Labour Party, his mandate was unremarkable (Punch, 1996). The founder of the *Daily Mirror*, he also acquired a number of financial companies and institutions. The collapse of his empire brought to light a variety of irregularities in his business dealings: tax evasion, insider dealing, fraud, false accountancy, and theft. Among his victims were international banks, the shareholders of some of his own companies, and the pensioners who had entrusted him with their savings through the Mirror Group Pension Fund. The Maxwell case illustrates the tolerance of the London financial world for adventurers and the flexible nature of controls undertaken within the City, which 'continued to support him right up to the end' (ibid.: 7).

Finally, some episodes which occurred at the local level will complete this short overview. In 1993 the chair of the London Borough of Lambeth, a member of the Labour Party, was charged with diverting public funds into his personal account, awarding contracts without observing the established procedure, offering 'golden hand-shakes' to his favourites, and giving contracts to companies belonging to friends or former collaborators. In the Borough of Westminster, local administrators of the Conservative Party were accused of having sold council flats and houses, at suspiciously reasonable prices, to distinguished supporters of the party, in order to saturate the area with reliable voters and to keep the prestigious urban zone under firm Conservative control.

Secrecy and the Market

It has been suggested that virtuous political classes are those whose allegiance falls into the domain of the Protestant ethic and its traditional values: responsibility, honesty, transparency, integrity, and trust (Davigo, 1998). The English case is not easily interpretable with these categories, especially when such categories are regarded as synonyms. In particular, transparency, integrity, and trust do not appear to be consequentially related. The trust enjoyed by the English political class does not always generate transparency and integrity. On the contrary, it is exactly the excessive trust placed in politicians which jeopardizes their probity. This excessive trust makes institutional action far from transparent, and offers politicians, administrators, and entrepreneurs a variety of illicit opportunities, while simultaneously granting them protection from those who could potentially expose them.

We have seen how in England it has always been hard neatly to distinguish public from private interests. Traditionally, reliance was placed on the sense of honour and propriety which was assumed to be innate in the conduct of gentlemen (Doig, 1996). This assumption included all sectors of the elite as well as public servants in general. In the past, 'public' servants were in fact servants of a monarchy, of an empire, of a social order which was, and still remains, profoundly marked by social divisions. Public servants and administrators were expected to, and indeed did, derive gratification from their being part of the state, from *being* the state. If among these 'servants' one bad apple was discovered the apparatus did react, but the need to review procedures was hardly acknowledged nor was the system based on trust questioned. Structural reform aimed at preventing malpractice through increased opportunities for external control and independent monitoring found obstacles erected by centuries of undisturbed social isolation.

Paradoxically, over the last two decades, the appointment of personal secretaries, assistants, and collaborators by Members of Parliament has in a sense filled a social lacuna: those who are appointed act as important mediators between an elitist and distant political system and a restless business world. The growing emphasis on market freedom has exposed a crucial contradiction: how can an adventurous economy be reconciled with such stifling political apparatus? The 'money for questions' practice can be judged as an almost acceptable way, in a static social environment, to make English society more mobile, and certainly more consistent with the deregulation of the economy.

It is in this climate that the term *sleaze* appeared in English political jargon. In my view the word, which refers to a mixture of sloppiness, inconsistency, moral slovenliness, and sexual untidiness, conveys with its vagueness the desperation of observers who are unable to identify what the behaviour of the elite actually is and what it should be. Inspired by distance and invisibility, the term 'sleaze' combines everything which one commonly attributes to one's political rival: cupidity, arrogance, insatiability, and disloyalty; in sum, everything one imputes to the inaccessible inhabitants of another world. A political world which is so secretive, separate, so accustomed to reproducing itself through socio-cultural forms of incest, cannot be precisely deciphered, hence the use of a word which sounds as much inconclusive as suggestive. Such a political system may, on the one hand, elicit the bewilderment of those who, having always given it their trust, suddenly begin to feel they have been defrauded. On the other hand, such a system may generate the mute resentment of those who feel that they will never gain access to it. Hence, I believe, the persistence in England of political discourses and some organizations which, while opposing the 'system', display such a low degree of analytical sophistication, expressed in such a rigid political vocabulary, that to their Continental counterparts they appear irretrievably archaic.

The setting up, in October 1994, of the Nolan Committee was the result of a similar form of bewilderment and desperation. The committee took its impetus from public anxiety about the moral standard of the political class and tried to establish what exactly was going on. There was a general feeling that too many cases of bad sexual conduct had come to light, public administration was too untidy, too many indulged in rule-bending, there was too much uncertainty over what was appropriate and what inappropriate in public life, and, finally, private and public interests were too worryingly intertwined:

It was plain that political relationships once founded on personality, the hallmark of a constitution designed to be worked by sound chaps who, up to a point, knew and trusted each other, had suffered serious erosion (Colls, 1998: 118).

The Nolan Committee, however, could not establish whether standards in public life had actually declined, though admitting that a degree of confusion existed over what was and what was not acceptable behaviour. The Committee identified a number of principles, all borrowed from tradition (what else?), in order to rectify the behaviour of administrators and politicians: altruism, integrity, objectivity, transparency, reliability, and self-control, all qualities regarded as innate to the elite, which only temporarily appeared to have inexplicably declined. A 'new' code of conduct for public figures was deemed the ideal solution to the general concerns, with the word 'new' alluding to that which was deemed to belong to 'old' times, when honesty allegedly prevailed.

In observing the English political system, it may be suggested that the degree of corruption characterizing specific elites depends upon their capacity to neutralize the imputations of corrupt behaviour levelled against them. The larger the distance between social groups, the lower the transparency and legibility of the groups' respective conduct. In a society in which classes experience a very limited prospect of mobility, opportunities to observe and learn from each other's behaviour are equally limited. Many cases of corruption, in England, cannot come to light, owing to the discretionary curtain which hides the elite. Only recently have TV cameras gained access to Parliament, and they are still struggling to be granted access to courts. Parliament, in turn, still retains the old, paternalistic prerogative to impose news embargoes on issues which are deemed likely to arouse public apprehension. In 1999 discussions about whether the procedures for the release of government documents should be reformed were still deadlocked over whether 'all government information should be released to the press and the public unless it can be shown to cause substantial hardship', or whether 'information could only be released provided it did not prejudice the government' (*The Independent*, 22 April 1999).

We can now turn to the other myth, that the expansion of market freedom contributes to the decline of corruption (Davigo, 1998). This myth hides the conviction that markets incorporate self-regulatory mechanisms which make external monitoring and control redundant. In this view, fewer restraints on market forces translate into higher economic propriety and greater efficiency in the mobilization and distribution of resources. In contrast, it could be suggested that the progressive liberalization of the economy in England produced a clientelist polarization of markets, which tended to become more turbid rather than more transparent. An idyllic situation of competitiveness encouraged the resort to protective devices, to cautionary tools, in brief to extra-economic artifices utilized with a view to tempering the effects of competition itself. In a context in which, traditionally, the elites bred within closed networks of affiliation, these extra-economic artifices became available only to those who had easy access to the political class. More market freedom, therefore, turned into a more pronounced tendency towards public–private consortia. Expectations that public officials and contractors should be completely separate became increasingly low. For example, if it had been 'natural' for representatives of building companies to sit on local or national development agencies, with the growing emphasis on market forces the overlap between private developers and general community interests in urban redevelopment became a necessity. The exploitation of this overlap was

the reason why government . . . in Britain has introduced legislation granting an important place (even majority control) on local development boards to private companies (Eve, 1996: 42).

This overlap occurred outside the market, namely in the dark areas in which exchange and mutual promotion between the public and the private sectors take place. Here is a paradox: the growing emphasis on market freedom produced a displacement of economic dynamics outside the market itself; while assuming that exchange would increasingly display an impersonal character, in reality it took on a particularistic and personalistic nature.

Radiant Unity

The argument presented so far may lead to the conclusion that English society, being characterized by such marked divisions, is consequently an extremely conflictual society. This conclusion overlooks the role of what I would define as a 'restraint-producing mechanism' in generating consensus despite the growing discredit of the elite. As Miliband (1982: 2) argued, the most remarkable feature of British history since the Industrial Revolution is how successful the elites have been in containing pressure from below. If the British record is in this respect not unique, 'in no other major capitalist country has this been achieved quite so smoothly and effectively'. In comparison with other major capitalist countries, 'power and privilege in Britain have been enjoyed by some, and accepted by the majority, in conditions of relative but quite remarkable social peace'. Anglophilia, in this respect, describes not only indefinable admiration from without, but also a similar form of admiration produced within the country. Abroad, this stemmed, and to a degree still stems, from the capacity of the English system to avoid extremism and to find compromise between normally irreconcilable opposites. Anglomaniacs, in sum, express a fascination for the English upper classes. On the other hand, similar feelings are expressed within the country itself, where even sections of the underprivileged have been persuaded that the privileges of the upper classes are the best safeguard of their freedom (Buruma, 1999). 'Where else in the world could a blue blood find a social bargain like that?' (Ascherson, 1999: 14).

Surely, also in England, very often the choice of political representatives is not undertaken on the basis of candidates' merits and their genuine capacity to implement policies (Pizzorno, 1998). In sum, in England, too, the power of symbols, images, and communicative skills largely overshadows the old alternatives of political contest. And yet, notwithstanding the general awareness that careers have replaced principles, there remains a strong feeling of unity among the different social

groups which is due to a residual, but powerful, 'national' identification. In the past, this strong national identity allowed the elites to
remain 'compact and homogeneous', and 'helped them to sustain the
challenge of war, empire, revolution, social change and political dissent' (Colley, 1992: 155). I would like to argue that England displays
the persistence of one of those forms of 'radiant unity' which Braudel
(1966: 455) identifies with shared feelings and a common understanding allowing all to take pride in the achievements of a few. This radiant
unity marks the country with a 'fraternal atmosphere', 'as if one common beam of light brightened the whole'. Such powerful collective
identification allows for the dilution of citizens' resentment against
their own political and entrepreneurial class, which in a vicious circle
reproduces their secrecy and their social separateness, altering the way
in which the behaviour of the elite is perceived. Let us see how this
manifests itself.

True, the English privileged classes enjoy greater trust than their
counterparts in most European countries, both within the establishment and among citizens (Nelken, 1994). See, for example, how rarely
the criminal justice system intervenes to penalize the illicit practices of
politicians and entrepreneurs. As we have seen, this trust is also exemplified by the way in which the conduct of the elite is self-regulated by
club-like bodies with informal, flexible rules (Eve, 1996). It is true, in
brief, that in England public interest means the interest of the elite (Levi
and Nelken, 1996). However, this peculiar hierarchical ethos is intertwined with a sense of national belonging which all too often transcends social divisions. In sum, trust possesses explicative power only
when connected with the context in which it is embedded, one characterized by strong national identification. It is not surprising, for example, that under some circumstances even individuals belonging to the
underprivileged groups may enjoy forms of trust similar to that granted
to the elite. Of course, this only happens when their conduct, which in
the domestic context would be stigmatized and penalized, produces
effects abroad. English girls arrested in Thailand in possession of quantities of heroin, lorry drivers caught at the French border with loads of
cannabis, babysitters charged with infanticide in the USA, and nurses
sentenced for murder in Saudi Arabia are all cases in point. The trust
enjoyed by these ordinary citizens takes the shape of solidarity and
mobilization, at times expressed through campaigns in which their
compatriots seem to claim that only the English can judge other
English. The only occasion when English public opinion, in recent

times, was mobilized against the death penalty in the USA was, after all, when the man sentenced to death was a British citizen.

All nationalisms are based on imagined communities and, despite the actual inequality and exploitation prevailing in them, the nation is always conceived of as a deep, horizontal comradeship:

Ultimately it is this fraternity that makes it possible, over the past two centuries, for so many millions of people, not so much to kill, as to be willing to die for such limited imaginings (B. Anderson, 1996: 7).

However, national communities echo within them the way in which they relate to other national communities (Cole, 1998). Internal national relations, in other words, are affected by relationships with the 'other': colonial history, for example, shapes the 'inside' as well as the attitudes towards the 'outside'. As Nairn (1981: 42–3) argues, British nationalism was periodically and successfully mobilized for external wars, and each time internal unity was strengthened:

The result was a particularly powerful inter-class nationalism—a sense of underlying insular identity and common fate, which both recognised and yet easily transcended marked class and regional divisions.

An overseas-oriented system managed to remove the need for change and dynamism, and to maintain its patrician structure and conservatism. 'Hierarchy and deference became the inner face of its outward adventure' (ibid.: 69).

In official rhetoric, in part also supported by popular conviction, English integrity is naturally juxtaposed with foreign corruption, an argument which is used by some to remain outside Europe (Adonis, 1995). A departure from this conviction translates into a certain tolerance accorded to businessmen operating abroad, where, it is assumed, even the English are forced to adapt. To be involved in corrupt exchange outside the national territory may, after all, be beneficial to the wealth of the nation.

A lot has been written about this cohesion, both imposed and genuinely felt, among social groups. It has been suggested, for example, that the outward-looking nature of English capitalism made conservatives, liberals, and Fabians alike all 'militantly imperialist in aims', that the 'nascent socialist movement shared in the general jingoism', and that the working class 'was, undeniably, deflected *from* confrontation with the class exploiting it' (P. Anderson, 1966: 24). In forging the nation a crucial role was played by the very morphology of the country, an island vulnerable to invasions of conquerors and their fanaticism (Colley, 1992). Hence an obsessive attitude constructed around the need to defend the shore against the enemy, an obsession which played an important part in forging a collective bellicose identity. The statue of Boadicea, which towers a few metres from the Houses of Parliament, reminds everyone of heroic resistance to the Roman invasion. It is part of a foundational myth, like the 'guardian spirit of London', Gog, the first recorded patriot in British history, who shows how 'by unity things grow great'. Gog was the Cornish giant who, according to the Albion legend, challenged the Trojans when they landed at Totnes, Devon, and after 'a titanic struggle was dashed to pieces on the rocks' (Samuel, 1998: 12). Judging by the lack of substantial opposition (when compared with other European countries) to the wars in which Britain has been involved in the last two decades or so, the spirit of Gog appears to persist in the pride and bellicose haughtiness of his compatriots. 'Gentle' traces of Gog, in my personal experience, survive in English colleagues and some friends who regularly spend their holidays in Provence or Umbria: they avoid mixing with peers and equals, preferring to interact with those who serve them; the sole purpose of their visits abroad, it would appear, is to re-experience, back in England, a sense of 'superiority' and to appreciate the fortunate circumstances that made them British citizens.

At the receiving end of this bellicosity has long been France, whose negative example is utilized to highlight English virtues. The portraits of the Duke of Wellington and Napoleon Bonaparte are a vivid fabrication of this rhetorical rivalry, and of this identity constructed through juxtaposition. While Napoleon looks cruel and impulsive, Wellington appears reliable, steady, serene, blessed with that British 'bottom' which leads to historical achievement. As ordinary as a working man, Wellingtonian ordinariness constitutes the trait most beloved by his compatriots, who cherish continuity and measure. 'Preoccupied with continuity, the English love facial likenesses because they are the elevation of genealogy and pedigree into visual art' (Porter, 1992: 16). For several hundred years the English had, against all contrary evidence, asserted their superiority over all, a necessary claim aimed at making their economic and military dominance acceptable. 'It was disconcerting when Waterloo suggested this boasting might be true after all' (Pears, 1992: 218).

Those who witnessed the celebration of the fiftieth anniversary of the end of the Second World War may have tasted some residues of this bellicosity, which perhaps in a less pompous fashion still cements the national identity. Most Europeans are not aware that with VE Day the British do not celebrate, like everybody else, the defeat of Nazism and Fascism, but the victory of Britain in Europe: even the homeless, while sadly begging, were waving the Union Jack.

It is legitimate to wonder whether all of this may have an effect on the way in which corrupt exchange is perceived in England. The high degree of homogeneity among the members of the dominant class makes it a closed and inaccessible enclave, one marked by similarity of social background, education, and life-style. Concealment, a characteristic of English gentlemen, naturally turns 'reservedness' into 'secrecy' when gentlemen join the state apparatus. 'State secrecy joined with the constitutional precepts of "convention" and "prerogative" to provide British governments with almost uncheckable power' (Colls, 1998: 100). The dramatic widening of the gap between high and low earners and the visibly increasing distantiation between classes over the last two decades or so have added to the invisibility of the elites (Sennett, 1998). Undetectable because of the rigid isolation and divisions, undecipherable because of the limited mixing of social groups between them, corruption also receives little attention from the judiciary or the police. As Hennessy (1996) laments, if in other countries jurists interpret the constitution and politicians put it into practice, in the UK politicians do both. As for the police, only 1 per cent of the force belongs to designated fraud squads aimed at business crime, though the financial damage caused by such crime is nearly half the total damage caused by criminal activity (Doig, 1995). A winner-take-all parliamentary system, in turn, compounds such invisibility and, while phasing out dissent, increases reliance on trust and self-regulation. Finally, in a deformed perception of insularity, corruption may find limited chances to emerge. As in Conan Doyle's novels, where the most callous criminals are normally from abroad, the corrupt do not find space in the imagination of the country, which sees itself wholesome in all its components. In this way, too, as Moretti (1997) argues, England became an island.

We are faced with the same dilemma which runs through every page of this book. In this specific case, is it the lack of the sense of the state and civic consciousness, or is it the excess of both, which determines corrupt exchange and affects its collective perception? How can a strong sense of belonging and its opposite play a similar role in different contexts? We have returned to an important aspect of anti-criminological research, on which a few final words must be spent. But before doing so, let us relax for a while with a second Intermezzo.

11

Second Intermezzo:
Daniel Defoe and Business Crime

Crime and social control in eighteenth-century England have been the object of numerous studies. Some authors remark that the ideology and practice of the law embodied the supreme value placed upon property by the ruling oligarchy (Hay, 1977; Porter, 1982). Others focus on the 'appropriation by the poor of the means of living (resulting in "urban crime")' (Linebaugh, 1991: p. xxi), or on the way in which collective outbursts and hostile mobs were handled (Rudé, 1964). The prevailing definitions of crime and the ideology and practice of law enforcement have often been said to mirror the uncertainties of a society in transition towards industrialism. In the atmosphere of 'tentative morality' generated by this transition, the underprivileged allegedly resorted to criminal activity both as a means of survival and because such activity was not customarily regarded as criminal. Smuggling, poaching, logging, but also simply growing crops and fishing are cases in point. All of these activities, which came to be seen as attacks upon royal and private property, were perceived as legitimate activities by perpetrators (Thompson, 1977). Industrialization and privatization required the drawing of new boundaries between legitimate and illegitimate behaviour and the adoption by social groups of new specific occupational ethics.

Mercy and terror, pardon and punishment, firmness and delicacy, were responses to these uncertainties, a mixture of majesty and patronage which allowed the authorities 'to maintain order without anything resembling the political police used by the French' (Hay, 1977: 49). However, in the absence of formal policing, a system of rewards and punishments was used to encourage people to inform on one another (Hay and Snyder, 1989). On the other hand, the frequency of executions in England was notorious in other European countries, though in the opinion of some commentators 'this was the price the English cheerfully paid for liberty and prosperity . . . and a few hangings were better than the ubiquitous police controls of a despotic state' (Gatrell, 1994: 8). Almost half of those sentenced to death were reprieved, a practice which enhanced the majestic features of the law, and exemplified the paternalistic overtones of the legal system. This majestic, almost spiritualistic, aura emanating from the law has been interpreted as a sign of how the origins of English Enlightenment are indeed 'very dim' (Tarello, 1975). This patronizing aura has also been analysed as a tool used by ruling groups to negotiate the character of crime and identify criminals in a society undergoing dramatic economic and moral change (Rock, 1985).

In a way that is reminiscent of contemporary criminological research, most of the historical work available on the subject revolves around the definition and perception of criminal activity conducted by powerless individuals. It is the argument of this chapter that in eighteenth-century England the crimes of the powerful were the object of similar negotiation and redefinition to those of the powerless, and that the ruling groups were concerned not only with drawing the boundaries between acceptable and unacceptable behaviour of those they ruled but also with the identification of the ethics of their own economic behaviour. What constituted business crime? How could the new commercial and productive activities find moral legitimation? Where was the border between acceptable and unacceptable economic practices to be placed?

Students of these issues have focused on the ambiguity arising from the need to raise the standards of honesty among merchants, whose ultimate interest was the protection of their commodities and transactions (Hall, 1935). In a similar vein, this chapter analyses the ambiguities inherent in some of Daniel Defoe's writings, in particular his novels and essays on trade, honest or dishonest economic ventures, and business conduct. In these writings, answers to the preceding questions are as tentative and contradictory as the responses of the ruling groups to conventional crime. As an ironical confirmation of the anticipatory sensibility commonly attributed to him, Defoe's ethical uncertainties echo the difficulties and moral dilemmas that one encounters in respectively defining and rationalizing today's business crime.

Defoe (1660?–1731), the son of a butcher named James Foe, changed his name to the more distinguished-sounding De Foe or Defoe in 1703. He was a soldier, a traveller in Spain, Italy, Germany, and France, and a hosiery merchant before becoming a controversial journalist

(Burgess, 1979). He was a Dissenter who initially opposed the Church of England, and suffered for his radicalism in prison and in the pillory. His reports and novels are so realistic (Praz, 1983) that when he invents, 'he somehow persuades the reader that he is merely reporting what actually happened' (Burgess, 1979: 178). For example, Defoe was only five years old when the Great Plague broke out in London—the last epidemic of bubonic plague to hit an English city—but he persuades us that he is actually there, an adult reporter, from beginning to end of the disaster. His shifting from the Tories to the Whigs and vice versa earned him the reputation of a political opportunist, an accusation that could be levelled at many of his contemporaries searching for institutional compromises and engaged in justifying the new economic order, along with their own existence as economic actors.

Why Defoe? First, because his writings were and are read more than those of Locke, whose apparent lack of uncertainty was partly due to a theory of property riddled with theological undertones. Secondly, because he expresses an ordinary people's version of preoccupations afflicting the elite, including law professionals. I am thinking of the conflict between a notion of freedom and law 'based upon a logic of universal individualism, and the need to protect a particular social order' (Norrie, 1993: 27). Thirdly, because Defoe was a trader and a political activist, and his concerns gave rise to experimentation with commercial practices and political ideas. Finally, because his moral confusion and entrepreneurial uncertainty, which he shares with his time, brought him to prosecution and to the pillory.

This chapter briefly describes Defoe's England and the conflicts and institutional compromises characterizing it. It then focuses on a number of variables which are mobilized by Defoe to identify the boundary separating legitimate from illegitimate business practices. These variables hinge on notions of self-restraint and in many of his writings they appear in the form of 'penitence', the control of greed, the limitation of luxury, and relative honesty. We shall see how these variables are used by Defoe in his unsuccessful search for an ethical foundation of business.

Defoe's England

Defoe hailed the advent of an era of prosperity, but at the same time his moral misgivings in the face of business practices are redolent of Cobbett's nostalgia for the rural past (Trevelyan, 1967; Hobsbawm,

1969). On the one hand, he depicts England as healthy and harmonious, while on the other he is concerned that a backward administrative machinery may hamper business development and cause disharmony.

Defoe's England is characterized by both conflict and compromise between rural squires and traders, with the former accusing the latter of economic parasitism and war-profiteering. However, as Trevelyan (1967: 310) argues, the activities of the emerging bourgeoisie doubled the rent of many a squire, as profits made in trade were frequently invested in land, while landlords themselves enlarged their fortunes by turning into mercantile investors:

This interplay of the activity of town and country, not yet subversive of the old social order, gave to Queen Anne's England a fundamental harmony and strength, below the surface of the fierce distracting antagonisms of sect and faction.

Defoe writes after the Restoration of 1660 and the constitutional settlement of 1688 have fundamentally altered the features of the country, and his novels and economic writings accompany a process of property concentration which, by the eighteenth century, sees 'nearly half of the cultivated land owned by some five thousand families' (R. Williams, 1985: 60). In Defoe's England, land enclosure is not so much the result of Parliamentary Acts as of common law and agreement, be this forced or otherwise. The development of trade is intertwined with, and to a degree caused by, the favourable conditions enjoyed by agriculture. In England, by contrast with many other countries, a tax regulating transactions over crops is non-existent, a circumstance by which Defoe himself is delighted, though he fails to note that this encourages the growth of mediators and traders who, by exporting corn overseas, contribute to the increase in its price on the domestic market.

During Queen Anne's reign riots over the price of corn do erupt, but the confrontation between landlords and the rural proletariat is tempered by the existence of an intermediate social class formed by 'an increasingly stratified hierarchy of smaller landowners, large tenants, surviving small freeholders and copyholders, middle and small tenants, and cottagers and craftsmen with residual common rights' (R. Williams, 1985: 60). This intermediate group provides the backbone to the rising class of manufacturers and merchants whose activity is soon to revolve, though not exclusively, around the cloth industry. The compromise between this ascending class and the large landowners belonging to the aristocracy derives from their joint interest in developing intensive productive processes in agriculture.

An ideology of improvement slowly took shape, whereby land came to be viewed less as an inheritance than as an opportunity for investment carrying unprecedented returns. Social relations standing in the way of this kind of modernization were broken down, while the bounty on corn export and the enclosure of commons were praised for their beneficial effect on work discipline (Thompson, 1963; Hill, 1969). The extinction of common rights marks the decline of small farms and the transition of commoners from some degree of independence to complete dependence on a wage.

In London the contrast of wealth and poverty was more intense than in the rural areas. The visibility of prosperous markets and merchants made deprivation all the more evident, and triggered unpredictable and sometimes violent movements of social protest. Among other markets, London also had a marriage market, to which wealthy families brought their daughters, who were deemed undeserving of education. The want of education in women was discussed,

one side defending it as necessary in order to keep wives in due subjection, while the other side . . . ascribed the frivolity and the gambling habits of ladies of fashion to an upbringing which debarred them from more serious interests (Trevelyan, 1967: 327).

Pressure for better education for women started around 1675, and was led by groups of women supported by John Locke and Jonathan Swift addressing the gentry, and John Dunton and Daniel Defoe addressing the bourgeoisie (Stone, 1979: 228).

The Tolerance Act of 1689 sealed, at the ideological level, the compromise between the different groups within the ruling elite. Radical Puritanism was deemed unlikely to capture the Church of England, and protestants of all kinds were trusted to combine, if necessary, against the resurgence of Catholicism. 'Tolerated dissent lost its missionary zeal, grew respectable and prosperous' (Hill, 1969: 76).

Daniel Defoe mirrors the compromise and the duplicity of his time, for example when his views regarding competition between small and large landowners are examined. He shares the hatred of the small gentry for the 'great lords', among whom are large merchants who buy land for social prestige and political power. But he is also against the excessive fragmentation of the land and industry. In this, he shares the ambiguous attitudes of many of his contemporaries, who waver between celebration of the new rural productive virtues and animosity against the new landowners: that 'pitiless crew' whose entitlement to property has been achieved 'in the long process of conquest, theft, political intrigue, courtiership, extortion and the power of money' (R. Williams, 1985: 50).

In the period of emerging mercantile capitalism when Defoe was writing, attitudes towards the separation of banking from government varied substantially. The Bank of England, which gained independence from the Crown in 1694, epitomizes the victory of merchants but also their subjugation. However, complaints about the excessive financial load imposed on 'merchant bankers' to meet the costs of wars over-looked the fact that such wars were indispensable for merchants them-selves to monopolize world trade (Polanyi, 1944). Opposition to spending too much on wars (Arrighi, 1994) clashed with the perception that 'men and women of trade played a vital part in preserving the nation from invasion from without and in supporting its world-wide aggression' (Colley, 1992: 71).

Defoe mirrors the contradictions and ambiguities of his time with respect to the moral acceptability of business and its unprecedented expansion. In 1720, in an issue of the *Commentator*, he notes the 'little visible Difference between the lawful Applications of Industry and Business, and the unlawful Desires after exorbitant Wealth'. Gaining money, he bemoans, is so general a duty that it seems the only goal of life: 'How then shall we distinguish the Virtue from the Extreme? And where are the Bounds between the Duty and the Crime?' If the most common rationalization accredited to street criminals revolved around their condition of poverty and their sudden loss of customary rights, what techniques of neutralization are mobilized in order for some busi-ness practices to be perceived as acceptable and others to be labelled as criminal?

Redemption through Penitence

One of the rationalizations used by a number of Defoe's characters hinges on individual reformation and repentance, a device which allows them to erect a barrier between their past enterprises and their present feelings. Defoe's heroes and heroines adopt this temporal device in the form of moral or didactic soliloquism, which often con-sists of a 'diary of the conscience' the conclusion of which is already known from the prologue. In the full title of *Moll Flanders*, for example, readers cannot but perceive a moral happy ending which engenders benevolence in the face of what they are set to read: 'The Fortunes and Misfortunes of the famous Moll Flanders, who was born in Newgate, and during a Life of continued Variety, for three score years beside her childhood, was Twelve Years a Whore, Five Times a Wife (whereof once to her own Brother), Twelve Years a Thief, Eight Years a Transported Felon in Virginia, at last grew Rich, lived Honest and died a Penitent'. Moll's diary is riddled with self-castigation conducted in hindsight; it is written by a repenting woman whose dignified present annuls the crimes committed in the past. Instead, a synchronic diary, with the character's morality mirroring the acts performed step by step, would have alienated readers and, perhaps, embarrassingly exposed the writer's 'duplicitous' attitude towards crime. Defoe is well aware that Moll cannot be given the opportunity to write 'in a language more like one still in Newgate than one grown penitent and humble'. For this reason, he feels obliged to 'clean' the text and to warn readers that 'there is not a wicked action in any part of it, but is first or last rendered unhappy or unfortunate, there is not a superlative villain brought upon the stage, but either he is brought to an unhappy end, or brought to be a penitent'. The exploits and depredations of this 'lady of fame', he claims, are a warning to honest people about how to avoid them.

However, despite the temporal device and moral declaration, the views of Defoe on crime can hardly fail to emerge. As a conventional criminal, Moll exemplifies Defoe's fascination for the art of surviving in a hostile or indifferent world, for people who get ahead, whether on a desert island or in London, and who manage to rise to a prosperous state. Moll acquires social status through conventional crime and fraud, but once she has achieved status and wealth, these are profitably used in the commercial and business domain. Providence, which plays a crucial role in Defoe's biographical fiction, appears in Moll's life and determines her successful career (Hazlitt, 1840). Two major episodes in the heroine's life describe significant encounters she has with the business world. In both it is possible to detect how and where Defoe draws, albeit tentatively, the boundary between acceptable and unacceptable commercial practices, and how he tries to come to terms with the 'general scandal upon trade' bemoaned by his contemporaries.

Moll Flanders continues to commit acquisitive crime even when she is no longer compelled by poverty or necessity. Her first encounter with the world of trading sees her wrongful arrest for shoplifting. She is dragged to the shop where the theft took place and badly treated, especially by the assistants of the shopkeeper. When she is taken to court, a crowd accompanies her, wondering 'which is the rogue and which is the mercer'. Those who identify the latter pelt him with stones and dirt. In this scene, it is easy to read a manifestation of the popular feeling that traders are as dishonest as those who rob them, a feeling that Defoe himself unsuccessfully tries to conceal. He is aware that, with the increase of commerce, a degree of 'moral confusion' will inevitably follow. However, there are crucial hints in this episode which seem to convey Defoe's confusion within this very confusion. The author here anticipates some of the contents of his writings on commerce and economics, where traders are required both to lie and to be aware of their peers or customers who lie. He personifies the 'lie' of commerce in the 'man that stands behind the counter', who is expected to hide his feelings and opinions and be led by mere economic achievement. Moll's integrity as a wealthy thief appears to be superior to that of the shopkeeper, whose business requires the suppression of good and generous instincts (Faller, 1993). As already remarked, the support that Moll enjoys from the crowd signals the widespread cynicism generated by commerce and the prevailing confusion between ethical and unethical practices. In pelting the trader with stones and dirt, bystanders 'offer a more direct and even somewhat romantic response to the general scandal upon trade' (ibid.: 165). Moreover, readers are bound to sympathize with Moll, who proves better at her trade than the shopkeeper at his: she is at least the better 'hypocrite'. Hence the confusion into which, whether inadvertently or otherwise, Defoe falls in the very moment when he condemns the moral confusion engendered by commerce. Ultimately, one is led to wonder whether Defoe is asserting that Moll is a truer merchant.

That Defoe's intention is to generate some sort of sympathy for Moll is also shown in the final part of the novel, when the heroine is transported across the Atlantic as a felon. She is a convict holding criminal proceeds which she intends to invest, and persuades her husband that the voyage will not kill him and that he will not have to work as a slave. As soon as they arrive, they buy a certificate stating that, having served their term, they can now move freely and establish their plantation wherever they wish. They buy land and additional property and 'with the aid of a slave and two servants they clear their land and begin to live the life of the colonial gentry' (Novak, 1962: 153). In brief, Moll creates wealth, increases employment, imports products from England to use in her plantation: she is the perfect colonist. Her repentance for the crimes of the past ideally completes her rehabilitation and determines her successful moral trajectory. Most importantly, Moll has shown her awareness of where to stop, that is to say where to curb her greed and compulsion to accumulate wealth. Her last years are spent 'in peace and modesty' back in England, where 'notwithstanding the fatigues and all the miseries' she has gone through, Providence grants her good heart and health.

The capacity of his characters to adopt some form of self-regulation, and to establish self-control of greed, along with an *ex post* ability to repent, helps Defoe to draw the boundaries between their legitimate and illegitimate economic behaviour. These aspects constantly recur in his other celebrated novels.

The Vagueness of the Variable 'Greed'

Colonel Jack's inconsistencies are deemed to prove that Defoe was writing at high speed, the novel being riddled with repetitions and conflicting claims. Such inconsistencies, however, may also be attributed to the equally high speed with which the social changes described by Defoe were occurring. After a career as a thief, Jack becomes a merchant, an occupation which leads him to engage in novel crimes. In other words, his ascent to the business world enhances rather than halts his criminal career. The crimes of his boyhood are caused by necessity and ignorance of the criminal nature of his activity (Holt Monk, 1970). As we have seen, Defoe condones these types of crime, provided they are not the result of a licentious life and do not victimize individuals who are as needy as the perpetrators. 'The Man is not Rich because he is Honest, but he is Honest because he is Rich. . . . Give me not Poverty Lest I steal' (*The Review*, 15 September 1711). However, when Jack engages in business crime, Defoe implicitly contrasts the behaviour of his hero with that of his 'ideal tradesman'.

Transported to Virginia by a gang of kidnappers, Jack manages to escape slavery and, following a familiar Defoean pattern of release from dependence, becomes a planter (Richetti, 1975; Earle, 1976). He then moves to Europe and back, and instead of settling down he seizes a variety of commercial opportunities. His restlessness, which in itself may be regarded as a positive feature within Defoe's view of commercial entrepreneurship, is in this case ominous, prompted as it is both by his pursuit of the status of gentleman which does not belong to him by birth and by his being persecuted for his Jacobite sympathies. Let us focus on the specific episode in which Jack becomes a business criminal.

Jack and his crew are struck by a violent storm which drives them near the coast of Cuba, a territory subject to the commercial monopoly of Spain. 'However in the Morning we were surrounded with five Spanish Barks, or Boats, such as they call Barco Longos, full of Men; who instantly boarded us, took us, and carry'd us into the Havana, the most considerable Port belonging to the Spaniards in that Part of the World.' During the course of long negotiations for his release, Jack manages to persuade the local Corregidor to accept a present as a form of ransom. He then strikes a deal with 'three considerable Merchants Spaniards, Two of them not Inhabitants of the Place'. He sells his goods to them, and they resell 'at a prodigious Advantage; so that they got above a Hundred per Cent after I had gain'd very sufficiently before'. Jack's smuggling network is thus established. These and other merchants will become his agents or partners in the illegal trade he sets up between England and Spanish-governed colonies.

From crime to business, and back to crime: this oscillatory movement makes Jack a different character from Moll Flanders. Both continue to steal when no longer 'pushed' by necessity, but while Moll evolves into a respectable businesswoman and redeems herself through repentance, Jack is unrepentant, and pursues immoderate wealth by circumventing the established rules of trade (Novak, 1962). 'Jack doesn't need the money, he risks a great deal to get it, and the illicit nature of the enterprise damages the good standing he has begun to win back as a character' (Faller, 1993: 182). Led by his excessive avarice, he also damages commerce in general, by violating the principles of mercantilist economics. However, Defoe's condemnation of Jack does not appear to be as complete as one would expect. In the final reflection on his own 'unhappy life', Jack claims that 'in recollecting the various Changes, and Turns of my Affairs, I saw clearer than ever I had done before how an invisible over-ruling Power, a Hand influenced from above, Governs all our Actions of every Kind, limits all our Designs, and orders the Events of every Thing relating to us'. In this passage readers are entitled to suspect that such a hand consists of the rules of the free market and that its invisibility is akin to that theorized by supporters of laissez-faire. One is driven to see the moral tangle in which Defoe has again put himself: is he trying to say that 'business ethics' is an oxymoron? If this is the case, unlike Moll, Jack does not have to repent of his immoral practices to be forgiven, because a force which underlies the market is the sole source responsible for his undertakings. That hand, Providence, seems to annihilate Jack's will, placing him beyond moral condemnation. Unlike Moll, Jack appears to be guilty of not 'knowing where to stop' his greed. But on the other hand, he is only a powerless manifestation of a force which guides all events, and 'makes causes and consequences', independently of or against the hero's free will. That Hand is invoked by Jack as a final rationalization of his crimes: that Hand belongs 'to the first Mover, and Maker of all Things'. But is Jack referring to God or to the market?

The Civilized Treatment of Slaves

Both Moll and Jack use the work of slaves to become entrepreneurs and establish themselves as business people. It is interesting to examine to what extent slavery, like greed, allows Defoe to identify what constitutes unethical business conduct. As Said (1993: p. xiii) suggests, cultural forms such as the novel are extremely important in the formation of imperial attitudes, and Defoe's *Robinson Crusoe* is a prototypical modern realist novel that 'not accidentally is about a European who creates a fiefdom for himself on a distant, non-European island'. Some of Defoe's novels are unthinkable without the 'colonizing mission' that the author shares with his contemporaries. However, it is not the use of slaves in itself, which he finds acceptable and necessary, that helps identify the immorality of some businesses and the morality of others. Defoe places his view on slavery within his own political framework, in which a crucial role is played by the concept of governance. Whether he applies this concept to the monarchy and its subjects, to masters and their servants, to planters and their slaves, Defoe believes that 'managing' and governing should be based on what he deems two basic instincts in human nature: fear and gratitude. Morley (1889) and H. H. Anderson (1941) claim that Defoe held contradictory opinions about the justifiability of the slave trade, condemning it from a religious point of view while justifying it for economic reasons. However, it is again the identification of a limit beyond which slaves should not be exploited that informs Defoe's argument.

Although within a moral biography different from Moll's, Jack follows in the heroine's footsteps with respect to 'managing' slaves with kindness and courtesy rather than 'with a Rod of Iron'. In doing so, he establishes a limit beyond which the productive use of slaves would be at risk, and resentment and ultimately rebellion would ensue. This limit resembles the limit business people should establish to restrain their own greed, which, as we have seen, is an important variable for Defoe in order to establish, albeit tentatively and contradictorily, the degree of morality of specific businesses. The identification of this limit is invoked by Defoe time and again in his discussion, and condemnation, of luxury. Nobody, he stresses, has the right to live in complete idleness and luxury. His proposal in this regard is a 'good sumptuary law' which reduces the national debt by taxing luxuries. Although he is later to express doubts regarding both the wisdom and the feasibility of such a law, he strongly believes in some form of regulation as a means of restraining the excesses of luxury (Novak, 1962). Similarly, he is against the excesses of power, whether personified by politicians or planters, and, according to him, the way in which the latter treat slaves designates the morality or immorality of their enterprise.

Defoe is said to use fiction as colonial propaganda. 'Almost all Defoe's novels and many of his fictionalized biographies are concerned with parts of the world he believed might be profitably colonized' (ibid.: 140). However, the propaganda stemming from his novels should be located against the background of what seems to be Defoe's genuine search for moral justifications of commerce and business. Although often unclear in his judgement, Defoe reflects the uncertainties of the ruling groups of eighteenth-century England, who are in the process of making their economic conduct acceptable to others as well as to themselves. Also with respect to slavery, Defoe vaguely identifies the excessive greed which would endanger this process. The variable 'greed' makes yet another return in *Captain Singleton*, in which once again readers searching for precise, axiomatic moral principles in business will invariably be disappointed. Is Defoe unclear about where to place the boundaries between business and crime, or is he just claiming that such boundaries are impossible to place?

The Limits of Repentance

Singleton is an orphan and a pirate by the time he is 17, and his ability and willingness to exploit slaves are described as signs of his entrepreneurial talents. His business partner is William the Quaker, who is presumably used by Defoe to satirize the business abilities of this religious sect. 'William's main purpose is to remind the crew that their sole reason for being pirates is to earn money' (Novak, 1962: 118). When Singleton, rather than limit himself to plundering other ships, seems pushed by a romantic desire to fight their crews, William dissuades him and leads him back to their real pursuit. This business partnership comes to an end when both feel that they are 'rich enough' and start planning a way to secure their wealth and enjoy retirement. After travelling to Venice with a cargo of 'goods, money and jewels', they finally reach England, and by settling there they demonstrate that repentance can also come in the guise of moderation. William converts him in the following fashion: 'Now that you're rich, have you not had enough of this wicked life, which will certainly lead you to eternal damnation?' Singleton too knows 'where to stop', and for this reason he is rewarded with wealth and a happy marriage that he himself regards as undeserved.

But are repentance and control of greed used by Defoe as universal indicators of acceptable commercial practices? As the case of *Colonel Jack* shows, those who do not repent may also be absolved by appealing to a higher omnipotent force. Moreover, what is the limit beyond which greed must be controlled? In *Lady Roxana*, Defoe's answers to these questions are again inconsistent, and mirror the moral confusion of his time in establishing clear boundaries between legitimate and illegitimate business.

Roxana regards 'Vanity and Great Things' as irresistible, and consequently joins the world of riches and high finance. Originally from France, Roxana finds a perfect financial adviser in Sir Robert Clayton, who epitomizes the avarice which Defoe also condemns in his writings on trade and economics. As Roxana is a clever courtesan in getting money from her victims, so her adviser is covetous and 'Will sell his Wife, his Master, or his Friend'. Roxana's mysterious end is the retribution exacted by Defoe for her business ruthlessness as well as her sin of luxury. Defoe encounters some difficulties in explaining exactly why his heroine is not to be redeemed. Roxana does repent, although, as she admits, her repentance is only the consequence of her misery, as her misery is of her crimes. 'One would like to add that a much-travelled, much-troubled and penitent Roxana lived happily ever after. But this time Defoe has no intention of protecting his heroine from Nemesis as he protected Moll. Perhaps he never really liked Roxana' (Freeman, 1950: 261). The author may in his condemnation reflect the general attitude towards the 'frivolity' of women which prevails in his time, an attitude depicting women as failures when involved either in business or in crime. But why did this attitude not emerge in his treatment of Moll Flanders? Perhaps Defoe detests how Roxana dresses in foreign clothes and dances a lascivious Turkish dance: her behaviour encourages the extravagance and the excesses of the nobility. The fact remains that repentance is not sufficient in Roxana's case to make her business undertakings ethically acceptable.

Most of Defoe's criminal biographies could also be read as biographies of traders, in which the writer is intrigued by the conflicts among business, expediency, and ethics. Defoe writes his fiction during the rise and fall of the South Sea Company, 'and it is not surprising that he found the resemblance between his successful criminals and their more respectable, if far less honest, counterparts a source of humour and irony' (Novak, 1962: 103). It seems, however, that his resort to fiction permits him to assert with vehemence that which his non-fictional writings can only whisper. In other words, Defoe uses his novels as a more direct way of addressing the public, and by employing accessible language he communicates those feelings and ideas that only very patient readers could detect in his non-fictional writings (Boulton, 1965; Shugrue, 1968; Praz, 1983). If, as we have seen, Defoe's novels display the difficulties of the author in identifying criminal practices in business, how do his non-fictional essays fare in this respect?

Speculators and Frenchmen

Difficulties in identifying the nature and characteristics of business crime emerge in a number of Defoe's pamphlets on the evils of stock speculation (Curtis, 1979). Here, by contrast with his novels, such difficulties are compounded by the fact that the author cannot resort to allegories in order to put characters in a bad or good light. He cannot charge characters with the weight of emotions, and is therefore forced to rationalize his moral invectives. *The Freeholder's Plea* (1701), *The Villainy of Stock-jobbers* (1701), and *The Anatomy of Exchange Alley* (1719) deal with different aspects of stock speculation. The first is an invective against corrupt electoral practices in which stock manipulators engage. The second draws attention to the disastrous effects of stock speculation on the credit and trade of England as a whole. The third describes the specific methods by which speculators manipulate the stock market.

It should be noted that Defoe's phrase 'stock-jobbing', which denotes any activity in the market, has clear overtones of self-interest and corruption (Dickson, 1967). However, Defoe is not alone in his opposition to this specific feature of the new financial system, nor is he alone in placing stock-jobbers lower than Singleton and Jack in his moral scale (J. Sutherland, 1971). Speculators are worse than thieves because they victimize entire nations; stock-jobbing 'is neither less or more than high treason in its very nature, and its consequences'. Defoe goes as far as likening them to conspirators who lead rebellions and organize invasions from abroad. They are 'traytors to King George, and to his Government, family and interest, and to their country'. Finally, 'some, and not a few, of our stock-jobbing brokers, are Frenchmen'. As in the case of Roxana, greed is to be imputed to some foreign elements: and is Jack not a Jacobite, after all?

Defoe here provides an example of how national identities are contingent and relational, and how, as Colley (1992: 6) puts it, the English came to define themselves as a people 'not because of any political or cultural consensus at home, but rather in reaction to the Other beyond their shores'. However, Defoe transcends the customary use by his contemporaries of negative images of France for the identification of positive values. He is concerned with the identification of the most viable economic model for his country (Healey, 1946). In this he shows some naivety, as he underestimates the future of England as among the most important financial markets. For example, the plea of a humble freeholder, in plain, semi-literate speech, is used by Defoe to contrast with the obscure dealings of those 'who understand nothing but their own petty trade interests, and who lack sense, not to mention honesty' (Curtis, 1979: 245). His condemnation is addressed to the practice of bribery in parliamentary elections, which is favoured by an electoral system granting over-representation to municipal corporations and economically declining towns at the expense of propertied county voters and flourishing new towns. The competing Old and New East India Companies seize on this system to gain representation in Parliament and monopolize the lucrative trade with the East Indies. While Defoe pinpoints the moral ambiguities of such practices, he undervalues how such ambiguities are destined to become crucial for the future development of Britain as well as other industrialized countries.

Defoe also identifies forms of 'insider dealing', whereby the false circulation of rumours or news alters the price of stocks to the advantage of those who circulate them (Secord, 1938). However, he is incapable of distinguishing what exactly makes stock-jobbing immoral or under what circumstances stock-jobbers are to be regarded as criminals. His condemnation seems to encompass all financial activities, and remains instinctive rather than rationally explicable. In other words, his detestation of financial misbehaviour reveals only a generic antagonism against powerful individuals (Moore, 1939, 1958). Instinctively, he seems to be opposed to the transformation of England 'into a stock exchange, a mere piece of property, owned by government ministers and populated by automatons' (Curtis, 1979: 248). However, by resenting financial entrepreneurs and presumably favouring productive entrepreneurs, he fails to understand the connections between the two. He cannot see the political and economic importance of the securities market which was developing in London, and manifests a nostalgic opposition to the financial revolution which would have changed the features of the country. Limiting greed is yet again the central variable through which Defoe conducts his search for an ethical foundation of business, a search which leaves the distinction between acceptable and unacceptable practices blurred.

Retirement as Honesty

In his most important writing on commerce, Defoe reaches extreme clarity of exposition, although his suggestions regarding the boundaries between business and crime are not endowed with equal clarity. *The Compleat English Tradesman* has been described as a pompous analysis of every detail, every little trick and 'sneaking address' that is necessary for tradesmen to get along in their occupation (Bülbring 1890; Rogers, 1972). Enthusiasts and detractors alike agree that the hundreds of anecdotes and dialogues, told in his usual lively style, make the book among the most amusing ever written by Defoe. Charles Lamb defines it as Defoe's best novel, though he senses that the ironical tone of the writing conveys a dubious satire of the business world as a whole, a satire which is highly damaging for its 'vile and debasing tendency' (Rogers, 1972; Praz, 1981). However, *The Compleat English Tradesman* can be interpreted less as a satire than as yet another example of Defoe's precarious argument *vis-à-vis* business ethics. It consists of a detailed list of advice addressed to beginners lest they be cheated by customers or competitors. In other words, this economic writing warns traders against their own occupation, and describes the business world as typically inhabited by dubious characters. In his description Defoe reveals both repulsion from and enthusiasm for business, though the former takes the shape of a romantic attitude towards the past, presumably characterized by a just economic community where general welfare is shared. On the other hand, the negotiable character of business malpractice also emerges in this writing, as can be seen in the following examples.

Tradesmen have a duty to train their apprentices, but must refrain from teaching them too well, lest they become their future rivals (Faller, 1993). Defoe castigates the exaggerations of shopkeepers in praising their merchandise, and feels uneasy in the face of those forms of self-promotion which we now call advertisement. Similarly, he warns tradesmen against their suppliers, who will inevitably try to deceive them. Traders must show competence: they must know 'what they are about . . . and cannot easily be imposed upon'. Fraud is a constant possibility. The trader must bear this in mind, so that the supplier 'treats you like a man that is not to be cheated, comes close to the point, and does not crowd you with words, and rattling talk, to set out his wares, and to cover their defects'. For example, when buying a horse, tradesmen must show confidence and expertise, while if they act awkwardly the jockey or 'horse-courser' will immediately sense that they cannot tell a horse from a donkey. Consequently, 'he falls upon you with his flourishes, and with a flux of horse rhetorik, imposes upon you with oaths and asseverations, and in a word, conquers you with the meer clamour of his trade'. Defoe advises florists to learn the name, colour, shape, and scent of their merchandise, and tells the story of a gardener 'who sold another person a root of white painted thyme for the right *Marum Syriacum*, and thus they do every day'. Surely, one has also to use some forms of self-promotion, though these may often border on hypocrisy. Defoe tells of a man who rented a workshop, and the hustle and bustle, the noise made by employees in pounding and beating 'some very needless thing', were just part of a set-up to persuade the neighbourhood that 'he must be a man of vast business . . . for the neighbours, believing he had business, brought business to him; and the reputation of having a trade, made a trade for him'.

Defoe feels uncomfortable in the face of business expansion, because he fears that this would damage smaller businesses. We have already seen how he morally favours small traders as opposed to large ones. Over-trading, he warns, is for tradesmen what over-lifting is for strong men. In another metaphor: 'For a young tradesman to over-trade himself, is like a young swimmer going out of his depth; when, if help does not come immediately, 'tis a thousand to one but he sinks, and is drowned.' Here, one should note Defoe's contradiction in the face of competition; he appears to be both for and against it. He teaches traders the tricks of market competition, but is unaware that while traders compete they may cause the expulsion of competitors from the market. Does Defoe really abhor commercial monopolies? The flaws in his economic argument mirror the precariousness of his moral reasoning. Excessive competition, he dreads, would result in factories springing up in every parish, and this would impede the general circulation of trade (J. Sutherland, 1938). For example, wool would be manufactured where it was sheared, and towns and even parishes would become self-supporting and independent of each other. The hectic activity of competing entrepreneurs would become uncontrollable. 'The whole economic balance of the nation would be upset' (ibid.: 129).

Traders should not invest profits in the stock market for the immorality inherent in this market. At the same time, traders may use subterfuge, for example by quoting a price higher than appropriate with the intention of reducing it during the course of bargaining. They may also promise payments even though their commitment to pay is based on potential, rather than existing, funds. However, traders should restrain themselves, they should refrain from pleasures and diversions that demand too many of their working hours, and finally should avoid a luxurious life-style. The most common reasons for the ruin of traders include: expensive living, marrying too early, innocent diversions, giving and taking too much credit, entering into dangerous partnerships.

In this work also the moral foundation of business lies in the restraint of greed. In the case of traders, this is translated into the decision to retire in good time, after a certain amount of profit has been accumulated. Retirement, therefore, replaces repentance as if, by abandoning the market and its tricks, self-restrained traders could atone for the money earned. Similarly, in the closing paragraph of *Robinson Crusoe*, Defoe remarks that the adventures of his hero are a 'memorable example', that 'he is happiest who confines his Wants to natural Necessities; and he that goes further in his Desires, increases his Wants in Proportion to his Acquisitions'.

Relative Honesty

Cynicism and morality intermingle in other essays by Defoe, who seems attracted to the very things he deplores. But is the elusiveness of his

moral argument one of his individual characteristics or rather a characteristic of his time? *On Bankrupts* consists of advice and polemic around
the elements of 'barbarity' that Defoe detects in the law on bankruptcy.
This law 'gives a loose to the malice and revenge of the creditor, as well
as a power to right himself, while it leaves the debtor no way to show
himself honest'. While tending to the destruction of the debtor, the law
is deemed to do very little to the advantage of the creditor (Morley
1889). The former may escape the forfeiture of his merchandise by concealing or transferring it abroad, as 'no statute can reach his effects
beyond the seas'. Bankrupt shopkeepers can hire firms specializing in
the removal and warehousing of goods, and find sanctuary in 'the Mint
and Friars'. In advocating the reform of the law, and the suppression of
sanctuaries and 'refuges of thieves, the Mint, Friars, Savoy, Rules, and
the like', Defoe also describes those 'masterpieces of plot and intrigue'
consisting of individuals setting up businesses with the deliberate intention of falling into debt and defrauding their creditors: 'a man coming
in good credit and with a proffer of ready money in the middle of the
day, and buy £500 of goods, and carry them directly from my ware-
house into the Mint, and the next day laugh at me'.

Defoe looks at the many 'commissions of bankrupt' every week in
the *Gazette*, and notes their constant increase in numbers. He attributes this to 'the age of pleasure' in which he lives, 'an age of drunkness
and extravagance, of luxurious and expensive living, and thousands
ruin themselves by that'.

The cynicism of Defoe in describing the world of traders and commerce is matched by his annoyance at the technical difficulties with
which even lawyers are met when it comes to defining commercial
irregularities and detecting illegal practices. Defoe's lament is
addressed to the whirlwind of obscure terms which are heard in court,
where arguments erupt about 'exchanges, discounts, protests, demur-
rages, charter-parties, freights, portcharges, assurances, barratries,
accounts current, accounts in commission, and accounts in company'.
Juries, in their turn, find it impossible to understand and follow court
cases, if 'the very lawyer and judge can hardly understand them'. *On a
Court Merchant* is an essay specifically devoted to this issue, which
echoes similar difficulties in today's detection and prosecution of business crime, and is aimed to encourage the establishment of forms of
self-regulation in the business world.

Defoe, who is constantly escaping from creditors, except on Sundays,
when one cannot be arrested for debt, writes widely on honesty

(Chadwick, 1859). In *Serious Reflections* he develops a concept of 'relative honesty', and likens it to a plant which varies 'according to the soil or climate in which it grows'. He also sees differences among social groups in their respective perception of honest behaviour. 'Some call that honesty which others say is not. . . . In New England, I have heard they have a kind of honesty which is worse than the Scottish, and little better than the wild honesty, called cunning.'

Conclusion

All too often Defoe is commended because he allegedly anticipates the future rather than mirrors his own time (Schonhorn, 1991). The writings I have examined convey a different image of Defoe, one of an eighteenth-century intellectual striving to find moral orientation amid a revolutionary economic era. His endeavour mirrors the analogous striving of the social groups spearheading dramatic changes in commerce and industry, who, while sensing the revolutionary nature of the era in which they were living, are also concerned with finding legitimation for their practices and their very *raison d'être*. In a sense, Defoe represents the popular counterpart of the moral philosophers of his time, who engage in the elaboration of a theory of property with a view to making the new economic system acceptable to themselves and others. John Locke is also engaged in such an endeavour, his effort revolving around the identification of the ethical basis of property and of the restriction, if any, to place upon property holders (Reeve, 1991).

While de-mythologizing the anticipatory qualities of Defoe's writings, one cannot deny that his reflections on business ethics do contain a contemporary flavour. But whether this is due to Defoe's intellectual and political far-sightedness or whether it is the result of the perennial dilemma surrounding the notion of 'business ethics' is hard to establish. It could be argued that even Edwin Sutherland (1983) managed only partially to resolve this dilemma. This is illustrated by his unsuccessful attempt to draw a clear distinction between corporate criminals and professional thieves, an attempt which is as unconvincing as Defoe's recourse to the variables 'repentance' and 'greed' to justify both. To appreciate Defoe's modernity one had better not look to criminologists who followed in Edwin Sutherland's footsteps, many of whom in a sense crystallized that distinction which in Sutherland was only embryonic. One perhaps has to resort to some theories of the firm and aspects of the sociology of organizations, where concepts and explanations seem tailored to guide both licit and illicit enterprises (Ruggiero, 1996*d*).

Defoe's essays and novels, like his life, are said to be riddled with inconsistencies and violent contradictions (Freeman, 1950). As a trader, Defoe does not even follow his own advice not to marry too early. His disastrous career as a businessman does not stop him lecturing on how to become a successful trader. 'Young Beginners who purchased his book were buying the wisdom of repeated failure. . . . one hesitates to take lessons in the art of self-defence from one whose face is disfigured with innumerable scars' (J. Sutherland, 1938: 253). However, Defoe the spy, the ambiguous, the opportunistic, the evasive, the duplicitous, the successful writer, and the disastrous trader is but a reflection of the moral dilemmas of his time. This is a time when the 'law of theft' becomes necessary with the development of property interests. However, as Porter (1982) remarks, to say that eighteenth-century institutions favour the propertied and privileged is truistic. This is a time, like today, when the nature and definition of not only street crime but also business crime are uncertain and negotiable.

12

Conclusion

After examining a number of 'crimes in the street' and 'crimes of the elite', one is tempted to conclude that the excess of resources and opportunities, rather than the lack of both, is the major cause of criminal activity. This conclusion may derive from subjective evaluation of the overall social damage caused by the two types of criminal behaviour. In this book, however, illegitimate activities conducted by a range of individuals and social groups, endowed with different resources and status, have been described. Against the backdrop of what I have termed the causality of contraries, I have noted that both the deficiency and the abundance of legitimate opportunities may lead to criminal activity. It should be added that selective processes are in place whereby only some who are involved in such activity are also exposed to social stigma and institutional penalization. I have also noted that even within the domain of conventional crime the division of roles results in powerless people tending to perform acts of 'self-victimization' and powerful people acts of 'self-valorization'.

Often, individuals who are engaged in the same criminal economy owe the choice of their activity to opposing motivations. In the economy of illicit drugs, as we have seen, those who have no resources may seek a vicarious occupation which is likely to be poorly paid, while those who do possess them may aim for the added value that their resources can generate. The activities presented above have been described as 'essays in anti-criminology', not only for the uncertainty surrounding their respective social impact, but also because each activity presented appears to be determined by specific causes which do not lend themselves to generalizations. In this sense, some phenomena and their dynamics have been described irrespective of their legitimacy or degree of morality. I am willing to leave to readers the task of establishing why, and according to which social and institutional procedure, the acts described above should be defined as criminal.

Throughout the book it is easy to detect an implicit rejection of any general theory of crime. Both the 'crimes in the street' and the 'crimes of the elite' have been located within the current economic situation, which is characterized by entrepreneurial freedom and constraint of labour, the latter being exemplified by flexibility and insecurity. There is nothing new in this joint observation of powerless and powerful groups and in the simultaneous description of their respective criminal conduct. Traditional popular culture offers numerous examples of how difficult it is to distinguish between those who accumulate wealth legitimately and those who do so illegitimately. Cervantes is never sure whether his characters epitomize entrepreneurship or fraud. The heroes of many popular songs possess such fuzzy features that one is never certain whether theirs is a form of criminal honesty or law-abiding criminality. In the poems and songs of Raffaele Viviani (1977), for example, the laments of thieves, pickpockets, and *guappi* are interspersed with those of the entrepreneur, who offers a causality of his behaviour diametrically opposed to that of his counterparts operating in the street. While thieves humbly ascribe their behaviour to a social system denying them a role and any sort of responsibility, the entrepreneur begs for understanding in the name of the important role he plays and the many responsibilities he bears.

In examining these two symmetrical forms of criminal activity, the use of explanatory variables has been parsimonious and at times contradictory. When such variables have been mobilized, I have tried to emphasize that the causes of criminal behaviour in one context may find their complete reversal in different contexts.

In conclusion, it is worth returning to the false dilemma whether the major determinant of criminal behaviour is the abundance of opportunities and resources or the lack of both. In this respect, while rejecting any claim of 'neutrality', which in the social sciences always retains a glib undertone, a few words should be said on the differentiated opportunities which are offered to social groups.

Social inequalities determine varied degrees of freedom, whereby individuals are granted a specific number of choices and a specific range of potential actions they can carry out. Each degree of freedom offers an ability to act, to choose the objectives of one's action, and the means to make choices realistic. The greater the degree of freedom enjoyed, the wider the range of choices available, along with the potential decisions to be made and the possibility of realistically predicting their outcomes. This formulation echoes aspects of Simmel's (1978) writings on the philosophy of money, where those who enjoy less freedom are also those who, having less money at their disposal, are led to invest it in initiatives whose outcome they are unable to control. Attracted by the stock exchange, which Simmel defines as 'the financial god', they are then led to unrealistic calculation in respect of what they can achieve. This asymmetric distribution of freedom makes some turn the acts performed by others into means for their own goals (Bauman, 1990). This may be realized through coercion or legitimacy, which award those endowed with more resources the prerogative to establish which means and which ends are to be considered acceptable. We have seen in the analysis of 'crimes in the street' how criminal labour, namely the set of actions performed by individuals with little freedom, is translated into means for the achievement of other people's ends, normally people with more freedom. We have also seen, in the analysis of the 'crimes of the elite', how criminal designations are controversial and highly problematic, due to the higher degree of freedom enjoyed by the elite. The capacity to control the effects of their actions allows those who have more freedom to conceal the criminal nature of those actions.

If we translate the notion of freedom into that of resources, we can argue that those possessing a larger quantity and variety of them also have greater possibilities of attributing criminal definitions to others and repelling those that others attribute to them. They also have greater ability to control the effects of their criminal activity, and usually do not allow this to appear and be designated as such.

The inhabitants of Lilliput regard as 'true crime' the offences committed by individuals who enjoy public trust. They are convinced that one can always find defences against thieves, perhaps by being vigilant and using some common sense (Swift, 1982). By contrast, there is little defence against the crimes of the powerful, who are capable of turning their greater legitimate opportunities into greater criminal ones. When Gulliver takes a lenient stance with a fraudulent official, finding extenuating circumstances in the fact that his is only an act of abuse of trust, 'the Emperor found it monstrous that someone saw as extenuating the circumstances which in his culture were aggravating'.

Bibliography

ADONIS, A. (1995), 'Grande-Bretagne: la vertu civique à l'épreuve' in Della Porta, D., and Mény, Y. (eds.), *Démocratie et corruption en Europe* (Paris: La Découverte).

ÅKERSTRÖM, M. (1993), *Crooks and Squares* (New Brunswick, NJ: Transaction).

ALBINI, J. (1971), *The American Mafia: Genesis of a Legend* (New York: Appleton-Crofts).

ALGAR, M. (1973), *Ripping and Running* (New York: Seminar Press).

ALPHEIS, H. (1996), 'Hamburg: Handling an Open Drug Scene' in Dorn, N., Jepsen, J., and Savona, E. (eds.), *European Drug Policies and Enforcement* (Basingstoke: Macmillan).

AMNESTY INTERNATIONAL (1997), *Made in Britain: How the UK Makes Torture and Death Its Business* (London: Amnesty International).

ANDERSON, B. (1993), *Britain's Secret Slaves* (London: Anti-Slavery International).

—— (1996), *Imagined Communities* (London: Verso).

ANDERSON, H. H. (1941), 'The Paradox of Trade and Morality in Defoe', *Modern Philosophy* XXXIX: 23–46.

ANDERSON, P. (1966), 'Origins of the Present Crisis' in Anderson, P., and Blackburn, R. (eds.), *Towards Socialism* (New York: Cornell University Press).

ANTI-SLAVERY INTERNATIONAL (1978), *Child Labour in Morocco's Carpet Industry* (London: Anti-Slavery International).

—— (1990), *Report to the United Nations Working Group on Contemporary Forms of Slavery* (London: Anti-Slavery International).

—— (1997), *Redefining Prostitution on the International Agenda*, Briefing, June (London: Anti-Slavery International).

ARLACCHI, P. (1983), *La mafia imprenditrice* (Bologna: Il Mulino).

—— (1992), *Gli uomini del disonore* (Milan: Mondadori).

—— (1998), 'Some Observations on Illegal Markets' in Ruggiero, V., South, N., and Taylor, I. (eds.), *The New European Criminology* (London: Routledge).

—— (1999), *Schiavi. Il nuovo traffico di esseri umani* (Milan: Rizzoli).

ARNAO, G. (1991), 'Perché legalizzare la droga significa ridurre la pericolosità' in Manconi, L. (ed.), *Legalizzare la droga* (Milan: Feltrinelli).

ARRIGHI, G. (1994), *The Long Twentieth Century* (London: Verso).

ASCHERSON, N. (1999), 'Put Out More Flags', *The New York Review of Books*, 20 May.

AULD, J., DORN, N., and SOUTH, N. (1986), 'Irregular Work, Irregular Pleasures: Heroin in the 1980s' in Matthews, R., and Young, J. (eds.), *Confronting Crime* (London: Sage).

BAILEY, D. (1966), 'The Effects of Corruption in a Developing Nation', *Western Political Quarterly* 19: 719–32.

BARBAGLI, M. (1998), *Immigrazione e criminalità in Italia* (Bologna: Il Mulimo).

BARCA, L., and TRENTO, S. (eds.) (1994), *L'economia della corruzione* (Rome/Bari: Laterza).

BAUMAN, Z. (1990), *Thinking Sociologically* (Oxford: Blackwell).

BEAN, P., and PEARSON, Y. (1992), 'Cocaine and Crack in Nottingham' in Mott, J. (ed.), *Crack and Cocaine in England and Wales* (London: HMSO).

BECCHI, A., and REY, G. (1994), *L'economia criminale* (Rome/Bari: Laterza).

BECKER, G. (1968), 'Crime and Punishment: An Economic Approach', *Journal of Political Economy* 76: 169–217.

BENJAMIN, W. (1983), *Charles Baudelaire. A Lyric Poet in the Era of High Capitalism* (London: Verso).

BINDER, A., and POLAN, S. (1991), 'The Kennedy–Johnson Years, Social Theory, and Federal Policy in the Control of Juvenile Delinquency', *Crime and Delinquency* 37(2): 242–61.

BOUHDIBA, A. (1982), *Exploitation of Child Labour* (Strasburg: United Nations).

BOULTON, J. T. (ed.) (1965), *Daniel Defoe* (London: Batsford).

BOURGOIS, P. (1989), 'In Search of Horation Alger: Culture and Ideology in the Crack Economy', *Contemporary Drug Problems* 4: 619–49.

—— (1996), *In Search of Respect. Selling Crack in El Barrio* (Cambridge: Cambridge University Press).

—— LETTIERE, M., and QUESADA, J. (1997), 'Social Misery and the Sanctions of Substance Abuse: Confronting HIV Risk among Homeless Heroin Addicts in San Francisco', *Social Problems* 44(2): 155–73.

BRAUDEL, F. (1966), *Il mondo attuale* (Turin: Einaudi).

BRAVERMAN, H. (1974), *Labor and Monopoly Capital* (New York: Monthly Review Press).

BRODY, S. L. (1990), 'Violence Associated with Acute Cocaine Use in Patients Admitted to a Medical Emergency Department' in De La Rosa, M., Lambert, E. Y., and Gropper, B. (eds.) (1990), *Drugs, and Violence* (Rockville, Md.: National Institute on Drug Abuse).

BROWN, R. (1995), *The Nature and Extent of Heavy Goods Vehicle Theft* (London: Police Research Group).

BÜLBRING, K. (ed.) (1890), *The Compleat English Gentleman* (London: David Nutt).

BUONAVOGLIA, R. (1999), 'Guerra contrabbandieri-scafisti, diminuiscono gli sbarchi puglia'. *Il Corriere della Sera*, 11 January.

BURGESS, A. (1979), *They Wrote in English* (Milan: Tramontana).

BURR, A. (1984), 'The Illicit Non-Pharmaceutical Heroin Market', *British Journal of Addiction* 79: 337–43.

BURUMA, I. (1999), *Anglomania. A European Love Affair* (London/New York: Random House).

CABALLERO, F. (1989), *Droit de la drogue* (Paris: Précis Dalloz).

CAFERRA, V. M. (1992), *Il sistema della corruzione* (Rome/Bari: Laterza).

CAMPBELL, D. (1990), *That Was Business. This Is Personal* (London: Secker & Warburg).

—— (1994), *The Underworld* (London: BBC Books).

CAMPORESI, P. (1995), *Il governo del corpo* (Milan: Garzanti).

CANETTI, E. (1962), *Crowds and Power* (London: Victor Gollancz).

CATANZARO, R. (1988), *Il delitto come impresa* (Padua: Liviana).

—— (1994), 'Violent Social Regulation: Organised Crime in the Italian South', *Social & Legal Studies* 3(2): 267–70.

CAZZOLA, F. (1988), *Della corruzione* (Bologna: Il Mulino).

—— (1992), *L'Italia del pizzo* (Torin: Einaudi).

CENTORRINO, M., and SIGNORINO, G. (1994), 'Criminalità e modelli di economia locale' in Zamagni, S. (ed.), *Mercati illegali e mafie* (Bologna: Il Mulino).

CHADWICK, W. (1859), *Life and Times of Daniel Defoe* (London: John Russell Smith).

CHRISTIE, N. (1996), 'Four Blocks against Insight. Notes on the Over-socialisation of Criminologists', *Theoretical Criminology* 1(1): 13–23.

CLARKE, M. (1990), *Business Crime. Its Nature and Control* (Cambridge: Polity).

COHEN, S. (1985), *Visions of Social Control* (Cambridge: Polity).

—— (1988), *Against Criminology* (New Brunswick, NJ: Transaction Books).

COLE, P. (1998), 'The Limits of Inclusion: Western Political Theory and Immigration', *Soundings* 10: 134–44.

COLLEY, L. (1992), *Britons. Forging the Nation 1707–1837* (London: Pimlico).

COLLS, R. (1998), 'The Constitution of the English', *History Workshop Journal* 46: 97–127.

COLOMBO, A. (1998), *Etnografia di un'economia clandestina* (Bologna: Il Mulino).

COLUSSI, G. (1998), 'Lamerica', *Narcomafie* vi(7/8): 4–7.

COMMISSIONE ANTIMAFIA (1976), *Relazione sul traffico mafioso di tabacchi e stupefacenti* (Rome: Poligrafico dello Stato).

CONNOR, J. (1990), 'Women, Drug Control and the Law', *Bulletin on Narcotics* 42(1): 41–7.

CORNICK, M. (1993), 'From the Sublime to the Ridiculous: Scandals in France', *Modern and Contemporary France* 3: 301–17.

CRESSEY, D. (1969), *Theft of the Nation* (New York: Harper & Row).

CROALL, H. (1992), *White Collar Crime* (Buckingham: Open University Press).

CROMWELL, P. (1996), *In Their Own Words. Criminals on Crime* (Los Angeles, Calif.: Roxbury).

CROSS, P. (1991), *Cashmiri Carpet Children* (London: Anti-Slavery International).

CURTIS, L. A. (1979), *The Versatile Defoe* (London: George Prior).

CUSTOMS & EXCISE (1998), *Smuggling in Tobacco and Alcohol* (London: HMSO).

DAI, B. (1937), *Opium Addiction in Chicago* (Montclair, Calif.: Patterson Smith).

DAL LAGO, A. (1995), *I nostri riti quotidiani* (Genoa: Costa & Nolan).

—— (1999), *Non-persone. L'esclusione dei migranti in una società globale* (Milan: Feltrinelli).

DAVIGO, P. (1998), *La giubba del re. Intervista sulla corruzione* (Rome/Bari: Laterza).

DAVIS, M. (1992), *City of Quartz* (New York: Vintage Books).

—— (1994), *Beyond Blade Runner: Urban Control—The Ecology of Fear* (New York: The New Press).

—— (1998), *Ecology of Fear. Los Angeles and the Imagination of Disaster* (New York: Metropolitan Books).

—— and RUDDICK, S. (1988), 'Los Angeles: Civil Liberties between the Hammer and the Rock', *New Left Review* 170: 37–60.

DE LA ROSA, M., LAMBERT, E. Y., and GROPPER, B. (eds.) (1990), *Drugs and Violence* (Rockville, Md.: National Institute on Drug Abuse).

DELLA PORTA, D., and MÉNY, Y. (eds.) (1995), *Démocratie et corruption en Europe* (Paris: La Découverte).

DERRIDA, J. (1989), *Rhétorique de la drogue* (Paris: Autrement).

DE TOCQUEVILLE, A. (1956), *Democracy in America* (New York: Mentor).

DEVINAT, F. (1996), 'Drogues: deal et combines dans Paris', *Metro. L'actualité de la Région Parisienne*, 21 January.

DICKSON, P. G. M. (1967), *The Financial Revolution in England* (London: Macmillan).

DOIG, A. (1995), 'A Fragmented Organisational Approach to Fraud in a European Context: The Case of the United Kingdom Public Sector', *European Journal on Criminal Policy and Research* 3(2): 48–64.

—— (1996), 'From Lynskey to Nolan: The Corruption of British Politics and Public Service?' in Levi, M., and Nelken, D. (eds.), *The Corruption of Politics and the Politics of Corruption* (Oxford: Blackwell).

DORN, N., and SOUTH, N. (eds.) (1987), *A Land Fit for Heroin?* (London: Macmillan).

—— —— (1990), 'Drug Markets and Law Enforcement', *British Journal of Criminology* 30: 171–88.

DOUGLAS, M. (1966), *Purity and Danger* (London: Routledge & Kegan Paul).

DOWNES, D., and ROCK, P. (1988), *Understanding Deviance* (Oxford: Oxford University Press).

DUPREZ, D., and KOKOREFF, M. (1997), 'Drug Trafficking and Deprived

Neighbourhoods' in Korf, D., and Ripe, H. (eds.), *Illicit Drugs in Europe* (Amsterdam: Bonger Institute of Criminology).

DWORKIN, R. (1989), 'Liberal Community', *California Law Review* 77: 479–87.

EARLE, P. (1976), *The World of Daniel Defoe* (London: Weidenfeld).

ELLERO, P. (1978), *La tirannide borghese* (Milan: Feltrinelli).

EMCDDA (EUROPEAN MONITORING CENTRE FOR DRUGS AND DRUG ADDICTION) (1998), *Annual Report on the State of the Drugs Problem in the European Union* (Lisbon: EMCDDA).

ETCHEGOYEN, A. (1995), *Le corrupteur et le corrompu* (Paris: Julliard).

EVE, M. (1996), 'Comparing Italy: The Case of Corruption' in Forgacs, D., and Lumley, R. (eds.), *Italian Cultural Studies* (Oxford: Oxford University Press).

FAGAN, J. (1989), 'The Social Organization of Drug Use and Drug Dealing among Urban Gangs', *Criminology* 27: 633–67.

—— and CHIN, K. (1990), 'Violence as Regulation and Social Control in the Distribution of Crack' in De La Rosa, M., Lambert, E. Y., and Gropper, B. (eds.), *Drugs and Violence* (Rockville, Md.: National Institute on Drug Abuse).

FALCONE, G. (1991), *Cose di cosa nostra* (Milan: Rizzoli).

FALLER, L. B. (1993), *Crime & Defoe* (Cambridge: Cambridge University Press).

FEINBERG, J. (1986), *Harm to Self* (New York: Oxford University Press).

—— (1988), *Harmless Wrongdoing* (New York: Oxford University Press).

FELDMAN, H. (1968), 'Ideological Supports to Becoming and Remaining a Heroin Addict', *Journal of Health and Social Behaviour* 9: 131–9.

FEO, F. (1989), *Persone e luoghi della droga a Napoli* (Naples: Fondazione Colasanto).

FERRAJOLI, L. (1989), *Diritto e ragione* (Rome/Bari: Laterza).

—— (1991), 'Proibizionismo e diritto' in Manconi, L. (ed.), *Legalizzare la droga* (Milan: Feltrinelli).

FINESTONE, H. (1957), 'Cats, Kicks and Color', *Social Problems* 5(1): 15–24.

FLEISHER, M. S. (1995), *Beggars & Thieves. Lives of Urban Street Criminals* (Milton, Wis.: University of Wisconsin Press).

FREARS, J. (1988), 'No Sex, the Abuse of Power: Political Scandal in France', *Corruption and Reform* 3: 307–24.

FREEMAN, W. (1950), *The Incredible De Foe* (London: Herbert Jenkins).

FRENCH, R., and POWER, R. (1998), 'A Qualitative Study of Social Contextual Use of Alkyl Nitrites (Poppers) among Targeted Groups', *Journal of Drug Issues* 28(1): 56–76.

GAETNER, G. (1992), *L'argent facile. Dictionnaire de la corruption en France* (Paris: Stock).

GALLO, E. (1995), 'The Penal System in France', in Ruggiero, V., Ryan, M. and Sim, J. (eds.), *Western European Penal Systems* (London: Sage).

GAMBETTA, D. (1992), *La mafia siciliana* (Turin: Einaudi).

GATRELL, V. A. C. (1994), *The Hanging Tree* (Oxford: Oxford University Press).

GATTI, U., MALFATTI, D., and VERDE, A. (1997), 'Minorities, Crime, and Criminal Justice in Italy' in Marshall, I. H. (ed.), *Minorities, Migrants and Crime* (London: Sage).

GEERTZ, C. (1988), *Works and Lives* (Cambridge: Polity).

GEERTZ, C., GEERTZ, H., and ROSEN, L. (1979), *Meaning and Order in Moroccan Society* (Cambridge: Cambridge University Press).

GERTH, H., and MILLS, C. W. (eds.) (1991), *From Max Weber: Essays in Sociology* (London: Routledge).

GÉRY, Y. (1999), 'Les filières bulgare et albanaise', *Le Monde Diplomatique*, 10 February.

GIGGS, J. (1991), 'The Epidemiology of Contemporary Drug Abuse' in Whynes, D., and Bean, P. (eds.), *Policing and Prescribing* (London: Macmillan).

GILMAN, M., and PEARSON, G. (1991), 'Lifestyles and Law Enforcement' in Whynes, D., and Bean, P. (eds.), *Policing and Prescribing* (London: Macmillan).

GIRARD, R. (1980), *La violenza e il sacro* (Milan: Adelphi).

—— (1987), *Il capro espiatorio* (Milan: Adelphi).

GOLDSTEIN, P. J. (1985), 'The Drugs–Violence Nexus: A Tripartite Conceptual Framework', *Journal of Drug Issues* 15: 493–506.

—— (1986), 'Homicide Related to Drug Traffic', *Bulletin of the New York Academy of Medicine* 62: 509–16.

GORDON, D. R. (1994), *The Return of the Dangerous Classes* (New York: W. W. Norton & Co.).

GRAHAM, G. (1991), 'Criminalisation and Control' in Whynes, D., and Bean, P. (eds.), *Policing and Prescribing* (London: Macmillan).

GRAMSCI, A. (1951), *Lettere dal carcere* (Turin: Einaudi).

GRAPENDAAL, M., LEUW, E., and NELEN, H. (1995), *A World of Opportunities: Lifestyles and Economic Behaviour of Heroin Addicts in Amsterdam* (Albany, NY: SUNY Press).

GREEN, G. (1990), *Occupational Crime* (Chicago, Ill.: Nelson-Hall).

GREEN, P. (1991), *Drug Couriers* (London: Howard League).

GREENE, G. (1982), *J'accuse. The Dark Side of Nice* (London: The Bodley Head).

GUNST, L. (1995), *Born Fi' Dead. A Journey Through the Jamaican Posse Underworld* (Edinburgh: Payback Press).

HABERMAS, J. (1988), *Tanner Lectures on Human Values* (Salt Lake City, Utah: University of Utah Press).

—— (1992), *Morale. Diritto. Politica* (Turin: Einaudi).

HALIMI, S. (1995), 'Un journalisme de révérence', *Le Monde Diplomatique*, 13 February.

HALL, J. (1935), *Theft, Law and Society* (Indianapolis, Ind.: Bobbs-Merrill).

HALLER, M. (1992), 'Bureaucracy and the Mafia: An Alternative View', *Journal of Contemporary Criminal Justice* 8: 1–10.

HAMID, A. (1990), 'The Political Economy of Crack-Related Violence', *Contemporary Drug Problems* 5: 31–78.

HANSON, B., BESHNER, G., WALTERS, J. M., and BOVELLE, E. (1985), *Living with Heroin. Voices from the Inner City* (Lexington, Mass.: Lexington Books).

HAY, D. (ed.) (1977), *Albion's Fatal Tree* (Harmondsworth: Penguin).

—— and SNYDER, F. (1989), *Policing and Prosecution in Britain 1750–1850* (Oxford: Clarendon Press).

HAYWARD, K. (1990), *The West German Aerospace Industry and Its Contribution to Western Security* (London: Royal United Services Institute for Defence Studies).

HAZLITT, W. (ed.) (1840), *The Works of Daniel Defoe* (London: John Clements).

HEALEY, G. H. (1946), *The Meditations of Daniel Defoe* (Cummington, Mass.: Cummington Press).

HEBBERECHT, P. (1997), 'Minorities, Crime and Criminal Justice in Belgium' in Marshall, I. H. (ed.), *Minorities, Migrants and Crime* (London: Sage).

HELMER, J. (1975), *Drugs and Minority Oppression* (New York: Seabury Press).

HENNESSY, P. (1996), *The Hidden Wiring: Unearthing the British Constitution* (London: Gollancz).

HENRY, S. (1978), *The Hidden Economy* (Oxford: Martin Robertson).

HILL, C. (1969), *Reformation to Industrial Revolution* (Harmondsworth: Pelican).

HIRST, P. (ed.) (1989), *Reversing Industrial Decline* (London: Berg).

—— and THOMPSON, G. (1996), *Globalisation in Question* (Cambridge: Polity).

HOBBS, D. (1988), *Doing the Business* (Oxford: Clarendon Press).

—— (1995), *Bad Business* (Oxford: Oxford University Press).

HOBSBAWM, E. (1969), *Industry and Empire* (Harmondsworth: Pelican).

HOLT MONK, S. (1970), 'Introduction' to Defoe, D., *Colonel Jack* (Oxford: Oxford University Press).

HUNTINGTON, S. (1968), *Modernization and Corruption* (New Haven, Conn.: Yale University Press).

IMERGLIK, H. (1994), 'Corruzione in Francia: il ruolo della magistratura', *Questione Giustizia* XIII: 646–58.

INCIARDI, J. (1992), *The War on Drugs II* (Mountain View, Calif.: Mayfield).

—— and McBRIDE, D. C. (1991), 'The Case against Legalization' in Inciardi, J. (ed.), *The Drug Legalization Debate* (Newbury Park, Calif.: Sage).

INGLIS, B. (1976), *The Opium War* (London: Coronet).

IOM (INTERNATIONAL ORGANIZATION FOR MIGRATION) (1996), *Trafficking in Women from the Dominican Republic for Sexual Exploitation* (Brussels: IOM).

IOM (International Organization for Migration) (1998), *Trafficking in Migrants* (Brussels: IOM).

ISTAT (Istituto Nazionale di Statistica) (1992), *Statistiche Giudiziarie* (Rome: Poligrafico dello Stato).

—— (1999), *Il traffico delle donne immigrate per sfruttamento sessuale: aspetti e problemi* (Rome: ISTAT).

Jacobs, J. (1961), *Death and Life of the Great American Cities* (New York: Random House).

Jarvis, G., and Parker, H. (1989), 'Young Heroin Users and Crime. How Do the "New Users" Finance Their Habit?', *British Journal of Criminology* 29: 123–35.

Jenkins, B., and Morris, P. (1993), 'Political Scandal in France', *Modern and Contemporary France* 2: 127–31.

Johnson, B., Williams, T., Dei, K., and Sanabria, N. (1990), 'Drug Abuse in the Inner City' in Tonry, M., and Wilson, J. Q. (eds.), *Drugs and Crime* (Chicago, Ill.: University of Chicago Press).

Johnston, M. (1986), 'The Political Consequence of Corruption: A Reassessment', *Comparative Politics* 18: 459–77.

Kaminski, D. (1997), 'The Transformation of Social Control in Europe: The Case of Drug Addiction and Its Socio-Penal Management', *European Journal of Crime, Criminal Law and Criminal Justice* 5: 123–33.

Kaplan, J. (1983), *The Hardest Drug: Heroin and Public Policy* (Chicago, Ill.: University of Chicago Press).

Karel, R. B. (1991), 'A Model Legalisation Proposal', in Inciardi, J. A. (ed.), *The Drug Legalization Debate* (Newbury Park, Calif.: Sage).

Katz, J. (1988), *Seductions of Crime* (New York: Basic Books).

Kelsen, H. (1975), *La dottrina pura del diritto* (Turin: Einaudi).

Kelly, R. J. (1997), 'Trapped in the Folds of Discourse: Theorizing about the Underworld' in Ryan, P. J., and Rush, G. E. (eds.), *Understanding Organised Crime in Global Perspective. A Reader* (London: Sage).

Kempadoo, K., and Doezema, J. (eds.) (1998), *Global Sex Workers* (London: Routledge).

Khan, K. (1997), *Race, Drugs, Europe* (London: City University).

Kohn, M. (1987), *Narcomania. On Heroin* (London: Faber & Faber).

—— (1992), *Dope Girls: The Birth of the British Drug Underground* (London: Lawrence & Wishart).

Kornblum, W., and Williams, T. (1985), *Growing Up Poor* (Lexington, Mass.: Lexington Books).

Labrousse, A. (1991), *La drogue, l'argent et les armes* (Paris: Fayard).

Laguerre, M. (1994), *The Informal City* (London: Macmillan).

Lap, M. (1995), 'Dealers, Dice and Dope', *International Journal of Drug Policy* 6(4): 258–67.

Leiken, R. (1997), 'Controlling the Global Corruption Epidemic', *Foreign Policy* 105: 37–54.

Le Nouvel Observateur (1994), 'Le dossier noir de la corruption', 6–12 October.

LETKENMAN, P. (1973), *Crime as Work* (Englewood Cliffs, NJ: Prentice Hall).

LEUKEFELD, C. G., and TIMS, F. M. (eds.) (1988), *Compulsory Treatment of Drug Abuse* (Rockville, Md.: National Institute on Drug Abuse).

LEVI, M. (1991), 'The Victims of Fraud', paper presented at the Second Conference on Fraud, Corruption and Business Crime, University of Liverpool, 14–19 March.

—— (1994), 'Violent Crime' in Maguire, M., Morgan, R., and Reiner, R. (eds.), *The Oxford Handbook of Criminology* (Oxford: Clarendon Press).

—— (1997), 'Evaluating the "New Policing": Attacking the Money Trail of Organised Crime', *The Australian and New Zealand Journal of Criminology* 30: 1–21.

—— and NELKEN, D. (eds.) (1996), *The Corruption of Politics and the Politics of Corruption* (Oxford: Blackwell).

LEWIS, R. (1998), 'Drugs, War and Crime in the Post-Soviet Balkans' in Ruggiero, V., South, N., and Taylor, I. (eds.), *The New European Criminology* (London: Routledge).

LINDESMITH, A. (1965), *The Addict and the Law* (New York: Vintage Books).

LINEBAUGH, P. (1991), *The London Hanged* (London: Allen Lane).

LOMBROSO, C. (1902), *Delitti vecchi e delitti nuovi* (Turin: Bocca).

LORENZI, P.-A. (1995), *Corruption et imposture* (Paris: Balland).

LOVERING, J. (1997), 'Labour and the Defence Industry: Allies in Globalisation', *Capital & Class* 65: 9–20.

LUHMANN, N. (1991), *Soziologie des Risikos* (Berlin: Walter de Gruyter).

McCORMACK, R. (1996), 'International Corruption: A Global Concern', *Criminal Justice International* 12(4): 13–20.

McCOY, A. W. (1991), *The Politics of Heroin* (New York: Lawrence Hill).

McINTOSH, M. (1975), *The Organization of Crime* (London: Macmillan).

MACK, J. (1964), 'Full-Time Miscreants', *British Journal of Sociology* XV(1): 38–53.

MACLEAN, M. (1993), 'Dirty Dealing: Business and Scandal in Contemporary France', *Modern and Contemporary France* 2: 161–73.

MAGRIS, C. (1999), *Utopia e disincanto. Storie speranze illusioni* (Milan: Garzanti).

MANDEVILLE, B. (1970 [1723]), *The Fable of the Bees* (Harmondsworth: Penguin).

MAROTTA, G. (1995), *Immigrati: devianza e controllo sociale* (Padua: Cedam).

MARSHALL, I. H. (ed.) (1997), *Minorities, Migrants and Crime* (London: Sage).

MATTERA, O. (1997), 'Adriatico, il mare delle mafie', *Limes* 1: 95–100.

MELOSSI, D. (1998), *Multiculturalismo e sicurezza* (Bologna: Regione Emilia Romagna).

MÉNY, Y. (1992), *La corruption de la République* (Paris: Fayard).

—— (1995), 'France: la fin de l'éthique républicaine?' in Della Porta, D., and Mény, Y. (eds.), *Démocratie et corruption en Europe* (Paris: La Découverte).

MERCKLING, O. (1998), *Immigration et marché du travail. Le développement de la flexibilité en France* (Paris: L'Harmattan).

MERTON, R. (1968), *Social Theory and Social Structure* (New York: Free Press).

MICHELET, J. (1981), *Storia della rivoluzione francese* (Milan: Rizzoli).

MILIBAND, R. (1982), *Capitalist Democracy in Britain* (Oxford: Oxford University Press).

MILL, J. S. (1910 [1859]), 'On Liberty', in *Utilitarianism, Liberty and Representative Government* (New York: Dutton).

MILLER, G. (1996), *Search and Destroy. African-American Males in the Criminal Justice System* (Cambridge: Cambridge University Press).

MILLS, C. W. (1956), *The Power Elite* (Oxford: Oxford University Press).

MINC, A. (1995), *L'ivresse démocratique* (Paris: Fayard).

MIRZA, H., PEARSON, G., and PHILLIPS, S. (1991), *Drugs, People and Services in Lewisham* (London: Goldsmiths College).

MITCHELL, A., SIKKA, P., and WILLMOTT, H. (1998), *The Accountants' Laundromat* (Basildon: Association for Accountancy & Business Affairs).

MONZINI, P. (1999), *Gruppi criminali a Napoli e a Marsiglia* (Catanzaro: Meridiana).

MOORE, J. R. (1939), *Defoe in the Pillory and Other Studies* (Bloomington, Ind.: Indiana University Press).

—— (1958), *Daniel Defoe: Citizen of the Modern World* (Chicago, Ill.: University of Chicago Press).

MORETTI, F. (1997), *Atlante del romanzo europeo* (Turin: Einaudi).

MORLEY, H. (1889), *The Earlier Life and the Chief Earlier Works of Daniel Defoe* (London: Routledge & Kegan Paul).

MORRISON, J. (1998), *The Cause of Survival. The Trafficking of Refugees to the UK* (London: The Refugee Council).

MURJI, K. (1998), *Policing Drugs* (Aldershot: Avebury).

—— (1999), 'White Lines: Culture, "Race" and Drugs' in South, N. (ed.), *Drugs. Cultures, Controls & Everyday Life* (London: Sage).

MYERS, W. H. (1996), 'The Emerging Threat of Transnational Organised Crime from the East', *Crime, Law and Social Change* 24: 181–222.

NADELMANN, E. A. (1991), 'The Case for Legalization' in Inciardi, J. (ed.), *The Drug Legalization Debate* (Newbury Park, Calif.: Sage).

NAFFINE, N. (1997), *Feminism & Criminology* (Cambridge: Polity).

NAGEL, T. (1987), 'Moral Conflict and Political Legitimacy', *Philosophy and Public Affairs Journal* 16(3): 215–34.

NAIRN, T. (1981), *The Break-Up of Britain* (London: Verso).

NELKEN, D. (ed.) (1994), *The Futures of Criminology* (London: Sage).

NELSON, D. (1999), 'Slave Oil Rig Workers To Be Sacked', *The Observer*, 21 February.

NORRIE, A. (1993), *Crime, Reason and History* (London: Weidenfeld).

NOVAK, M. E. (1962), *Economics and the Fiction of Daniel Defoe* (Berkeley, Calif.: University of California Press).

NOVE, P. (1991), 'Underground Banking Systems', *International Criminal Police Review* 431: 5–9.

NYE, J. (1967), 'Corruption and Political Development: A Cost-Benefit Analysis', *American Political Science Review* 61: 417–27.

O'CONNOR, J. (1973), *The Fiscal Crisis of the State* (New York: St. Martin's Press).

OFDT (OBSERVATOIRE FRANÇAIS DES DROGUES ET DES TOXICOMANIES) (1996), *Drogues et toxicomanies. Indicateurs et tendances* (Paris: OFDT).

OFFE, C., and PREUSS, U. (1991), 'Democratic Institutions and Moral Resources' in Held, D. (ed.), *Political Theory Today* (Cambridge: Polity).

OHNO, T. (1993), *Lo spirito Toyota* (Turin: Einaudi).

OXFAM (1998), *Out of Control. The Loopholes in UK Controls of the Arms Trade* (London: Oxfam).

PACI, M. (1992), *Il mutamento della struttura sociale in Italia* (Bologna: Il Mulino).

PADILLA, F. M. (1992), *The Gang as an American Enterprise* (New Brunswick, NJ: Rutgers University Press).

PALIDDA, S. (1997), *Immigrant Delinquency* (Brussels: European Commission).

PANSA, G. (1987), *Lo sfascio. Politici, politicanti, portaborse e malfattori* (Milan: Rizzoli).

—— (1989), *Il malloppo* (Milan: Rizzoli).

PANTALEONE, M. (1976), *Mafia e droga* (Turin: Einaudi).

PARETO, V. (1966), *Sociological Writings* (London: Pall Mall Press).

PARKER, H., BAKX, K., and NEWCOMBE, R. (1987), *Living with Heroin* (Milton Keynes: Open University Press).

PARKER H., MEASHAM, F. and ALDRIDGE, J. (1995), *Drug Futures* (London: Institute for the Study of Drug Dependance).

PARSSINEN, T. (1983), *Secret Passions, Secret Remedies: Narcotic Drugs in British Society* (Manchester: Manchester University Press).

PASSAVANT, P. A. (1996), 'A Moral Geography of Liberty: John Stuart Mill and American Free Speech Discourse', *Social & Legal Studies* 5: 301–20.

PAZ, O. (1990), *Alternating Current* (New York: Arcade).

PEARCE, F., and WOODIWISS, M. (eds.) (1993), *Global Crime Connections* (London: Macmillan).

PEARS, I. (1992), 'The Gentleman and the Hero: Wellington and Napoleon in the Nineteenth Century' in Porter, R. (ed.), *Myths of the English* (Cambridge: Polity).

PEARSON, G. (1987), *The New Heroin Users* (Oxford: Blackwell).

—— (1991), 'Drug Control Policies in Britain' in Tonry, M., and Morris, N. (eds.), *Crime and Justice* (Chicago, Ill.: University of Chicago Press).

—— GILMAN, M., and McIVER, S. (1987), *Young People and Heroin* (Aldershot: Avebury).

PEPINO, L. (1991), *Droga e legge. Tossicodipendenza, prevenzione e repressione* (Milan: Franco Angeli).

PÉRALDI, M., FOUGHALI, N., and SPINPUSA, N. (1995), 'Le marché des pauvres, espace commercial et espace public', *Revue Européenne des Migrations Internationales* 11(1): 77–98.

PHYTHIAN, M. (1997a), 'The Arms Trade', *Parliamentary Affairs* 50(1): 41–54.

—— (1997b), *Arming Iraq* (Boston, Mass.: Northeastern University Press).

PIZZORNO, A. (1992), 'La corruzione nel sistema politico' in Dalla Porta, D., *Lo scambio corrotto* (Bologna: Il Mulino).

—— (1998), *Il potere dei giudici. Stato democratico e controllo della virtù* (Rome/Bari: Laterza).

PLANT, M. (1975), *Drug Takers in an English Town* (London: Tavistock).

POLANYI, K. (1944), *The Great Transformation* (New York: Holt).

POLSKY, N. (1971), *Hustlers, Beats and Others* (Harmondsworth: Penguin).

PORTER, R. (1982), *English Society in the Eighteenth Century* (Harmondsworth: Penguin).

—— (ed.) (1992), *Myths of the English* (Cambridge: Polity).

POWER, R. (1998), 'Contemporary Issues Concerning Illicit Drug Use in the British Isles', *Journal of Drug Issues* 28(1): 1–8.

PRAZ, M. (1981), 'Introduzione' in Lamb, C., *Saggi di Elia* (Milan: Rizzoli).

—— (1983), *Studi e svaghi inglesi* (Milan: Garzanti).

PREBLE, E., and CASEY, J. (1969), 'Taking Care of Business', *International Journal of Addictions* 4(1): 1–24.

PRYCE, K. (1986), *Endless Pressure: A Study of West-Indian Lifestyles in Bristol* (Harmondsworth: Penguin).

PUNCH, M. (1996), *Dirty Business* (London: Sage).

PUTTERMAN, L. (ed.) (1986), *The Economic Nature of the Firm* (Cambridge: Cambridge University Press).

RAINNIE, A. (1991), 'Just-in-Time, Subcontracting and the Small Firm', *Work, Employment and Society* 5(3): 13–25.

—— (1993), 'The Reorganisation of Large Firm Subcontracting', *Capital & Class* 49: 53–76.

REDLINGER, L. (1975), 'Marketing and Distributing Heroin: Some Sociological Observations', *Journal of Psychedelic Drugs* 7(4): 331–53.

REEVE, A. (1991), 'A Theory of Property' in Held, D. (ed.), *Political Theory Today* (Cambridge: Polity).

RESTA, E. (1992), *La certezza e la speranza* (Rome/Bari: Laterza).

REUTER, P. (1983), *Disorganized Crime* (Cambridge, Mass.: MIT Press).

—— MacCOUN, R., and MURPHY, P. (1990), *Money from Crime* (Santa Barbara, Calif.: Rand Corporation).

REVELLI, M. (1996), *Le due destre* (Turin: Bollati Boringhieri).

RICHARDSON, C. (1991), *My Manor* (London: Sidgwick & Jackson).

RICHETTI, J. (1975), *Defoe's Narratives: Situations and Structures* (Oxford: Oxford University Press).

RICŒUR, P. (1995), *Le Juste* (Paris: Esprit).

RITZER, G. (1993), *The McDonaldization of Society* (Newbury Park, Calif.: Pine Forge Press).

ROCK, P. (1985), 'Law, Order and Power in Late Seventeenth and Early Eighteenth-Century England' in Cohen, S., and Scull, A. (eds.), *Social Control and the State* (Oxford: Blackwell).

ROGERS, P. (ed.) (1972), *Defoe: The Critical Heritage* (London: Routledge & Kegan Paul).

ROSE-ACKERMAN, S. (1978), *Corruption: A Study in Political Economy* (New York: Academic Press).

ROSENBAUM, M., and MURPHY, S. (1990), 'Women and Addiction: Process, Treatment and Outcome' in NIDA (National Institute on Drug Abuse), *The Collection and Interpretation of Data from Hidden Populations* (Rockville, Md.: US Department of Health and Human Services).

RUDÉ, G. (1964), *The Crowd in History* (New York: Wiley).

RUGGIERO, V. (1987), 'Turin Today: Premodern Society or Post-Industrial Bazaar?', *Capital & Class* 31: 25–38.

—— (1992*a*), *La roba. Economie e culture dell'eroina* (Parma: Pratiche).

—— (1992*b*), 'Heroin Use and the Formal Economy', *British Journal of Criminology* 32: 273–91.

—— (1993*a*), 'Organised Crime in Italy. Testing Alternative Definitions', *Social & Legal Studies* 2: 131–48.

—— (1993*b*), 'Brixton, London: A Drug Culture without a Drug Economy?', *International Journal of Drug Policy* 4(2): 83–90.

—— (1996*a*), *Economie sporche* (Turin: Bollati Boringhieri).

—— (1996*b*), 'Falling Revenues of Violence', *Science as Culture* 5: 627–47.

—— (1996*c*), 'War Markets: Corporate and Organised Criminals in Europe', *Social & Legal Sudies* 5: 5–20.

—— (1996*d*), *Organized and Corporate Crime in Europe* (Aldershot: Dartmouth).

—— (1998), 'The Country of Cesare Beccaria: The Myth of Rehabilitation in Italy' in Weiss, R. P., and South, N. (eds.), *Comparing Prison Systems* (Amsterdam: Gordon & Breach).

—— (1999), *Delitti dei deboli e dei potenti* (Turin: Bollati Boringhieri).

—— (2000), 'Criminal Franchising. Albanians and Illicit Drugs in Italy', in Natarajan, M. and Hough, M. (eds.), *Illegal Drug Markets* (New York: Criminal Justice Press).

—— and SOUTH, N. (1995), *Eurodrugs. Drug Use, Markets and Trafficking in Europe* (London: UCL Press).

—— and SOUTH, N. (1997), 'The Late-Modern City as a Bazaar', *British Journal of Sociology*, 48: 54–70.

RUGGIERO, V., South, N. and TAYLOR, I. (1998) (eds.), *The New European Criminology* (London: Routledge).

RYAN, M., and SIM, J. (1995), 'The Penal System in England and Wales: Round Up the Usual Suspects' in Ruggiero, V., Ryan, M., and Sim, J. (eds.), *European Penal Systems. A Critical Anatomy* (London: Sage).

SAID, E. (1985), *Orientalism: Western Concepts of the Orient* (Harmondsworth: Penguin).

—— (1993), *Culture and Imperialism* (London: Chatto & Windus).

SAMUEL, R. (1998), *Island Stories. Unravelling Britain* (London: Verso).

SANTINO, U., and LA FIURA, G. (1993), *Dietro la droga* (Turin: Gruppo Abele).

SATTAUR, O. (1993), *Child Labour in Nepal* (London: Anti-Slavery International).

SCHONHORN, M. (1991), *Defoe's Politics. Parliament, Power, Kinship, and Robinson Crusoe* (Cambridge: Cambridge University Press).

SCOTT, J. (1969), 'Corruption, Machine Politics and Social Change', *American Political Science Review* 63: 1142–59.

SECORD, A. W. (ed.) (1938), *Defoe's Review* (New York: Facsimile Text Society).

SENNETT, R. (1976), *The Fall of the Public Man* (New York: Alfred A. Knopf).

—— (1993), *The Conscience of the Eye* (London: Faber & Faber).

—— (1998), *The Corrosion of Character* (New York: Norton).

SHAW, C. (1930), *The Jack-Roller. A Delinquent Boy's Own Story* (Chicago, Ill.: University of Chicago Press).

SHINER, M., and NEWBURN, T. (1999), 'Taking Tea with Noel: The Place and Meaning of Drug Use in Everyday Life' in South, N. (ed.), *Drugs. Cultures, Controls and Everyday Life* (London: Sage).

SHUGRUE, M. F. (ed.) (1968), *Selected Poetry and Prose of Daniel Defoe* (New York: Holt).

SIBLEY, D. (1995), *Geographies of Exclusion* (London: Routledge).

SIGNORELLI, A. (1990), 'I santi in paradiso', *Micromega* 4: 127–35.

SILVESTRI, F. (1996), 'Le società nere di Corso Sempione', *Narcomafie* iv: 3–6.

SIMMEL, G. (1971 [1903]), *Individuality and Social Forms* (Chicago, Ill.: University of Chicago Press).

—— (1978 [1907]), *The Philosophy of Money* (London: Routledge).

SMART, C. (1984), 'Social Policy and Drug Addiction: A Critical Study of Policy Development', *British Journal of Addiction* 79: 31–9.

SOLIVETTI, L. (1994), 'Drug Diffusion and Social Change: The Illusion about a Formal Social Control', *The Howard Journal of Criminal Justice* 33: 41–61.

SOUTH, N. (1992), 'Moving Murky Money' in Farrington, D., and Walklate, S. (eds.), *Offenders and Victims: Theory and Practice* (London: British Society of Criminology).

—— (1994a), 'Voices from the Past: Drugs and Social History', *International Journal of Drug Policy* 5(4): 254–6.

—— (1994b), 'Drugs: Control, Crime and Criminological Studies' in Maguire,

M., Morgan, R., and Reiner, R. (eds.), *The Oxford Handbook of Criminology* (Oxford: Oxford University Press).

—— (ed.) (1995), *Drugs, Crime and Criminal Justice* (Aldershot: Dartmouth).

SPEAR, B. (1969), 'The Growth of Heroin Addiction in the United Kingdom', *British Journal of Addiction* 64: 245–55.

STANLEY, C. (1996), *Urban Excess and the Law* (London: Cavendish).

Statewatch (1999), 'The Cycle of UK Racism', *Statewatch* 9(1): 1–4.

STIGLER, G. (1970), 'The Optimum Enforcement of Law', *Journal of Political Economy* 78: 526–36.

STIMSON, G. (1987), 'The War on Heroin' in Dorn, N., and South, N. (eds.), *A Land Fit for Heroin?* (London: Macmillan).

STONE, L. (1979), *The Family, Sex and Marriage in England 1500–1800* (Harmondsworth: Penguin).

STRONG, N., and WATERSON, M. (1987), 'Principals, Agents and Information' in Clarke, R., and McGuinness, T. (eds.), *The Economics of the Firm* (Oxford: Blackwell).

SUTHERLAND, E. (1949), *White Collar Crime* (New York: Holt, Rinehart and Winston).

—— (1983), *White-Collar Crime: The Uncut Version* (New Haven, Conn.: Yale University Press).

SUTHERLAND, J. (1938), *Defoe* (Philadelphia, Penn.: Lippincott).

—— (1971), *Daniel Defoe: A Critical Study* (Cambridge: Cambridge University Press).

SUTTER, A. (1966), 'The World of the Righteous Dope-Fiend', *Issues in Criminology* 2(2): 177–222.

SUTTON, M. (1993), 'From Receiving to Thieving', *Home Office Research Bulletin* 34: 3–8.

SWIFT, J. (1982), *Gulliver's Travels* (Harmondsworth: Penguin).

SYKES, G., and MATZA, D. (1957), 'Techniques of Neutralization: A Theory of Delinquency', *American Sociological Review* 22: 664–73.

TARELLO, G. (1975), 'Le poco luminose origini dell'Illuminismo dell'area inglese' in Tarello, G. (ed.), *Idee e atteggiamenti sulla repressione penale* (Bologna: Il Mulino).

TARRIUS, A. (1995), 'Naissance d'un dispositif commercial international arabe de type colonial dans la France contemporaine' in Péraldi, M., and Perrin, E. (eds.), *Réseaux productifs et territoires urbains* (Toulouse: Presse Universitaire du Mirail).

—— (1996), *Arabes de France. Dans l'économie mondiale souterraine* (Paris: L'Aube).

—— (1999), *Fin de siècle incertaine à Perpignan* (Canet Catalunya): Llibres del Trabucaire).

TAYLOR, A. (1993), *Women Drug Users* (Oxford: Clarendon Press).

TAYLOR, I. (1992), 'The International Drug Trade and Money Laundering', *European Sociological Review* 8(2): 168–82.

—— (1999), *Crime in Context. A Critical Criminology of Market Societies* (Cambridge: Polity).

THOMPSON, E. P. (1963), *The Making of the English Working Class* (Harmondsworth: Penguin).

—— (1977), *Wigs and Hunters* (Harmondsworth: Penguin).

THRASHER, F. (1927), *The Gang* (Chicago, Ill.: University of Chicago Press).

TORRÈS, D. (1996), *Esclaves. 200 millions d'esclaves aujourd'hui* (Paris: Phébus).

TOTTERDILL, P. (1989), 'Local Economic Strategies as Economic Policy', *Economy and Society* 58(4): 47–58.

TREVELYAN, G. M. (1967), *English Social History* (Harmondsworth: Pelican).

TRIGILIA, C. (1992), *Sviluppo senza autonomia* (Bologna: Il Mulino).

TRIMBLE, J. E., BOLEK, S. C., and NIEMCZYK, S. J. (eds.) (1992), *Ethnic and Multicultural Drug Abuse* (New York: Haworth Press).

TROUILLE, H. (1994), 'The Juge d'Instruction: A Figure under Threat or Supremely Untouchable?', *Modern and Contemporary France* 2: 11–29.

TURONE, S. (1984), *Corrotti e corruttori dall'unità d'Italia alla P2* (Rome/Bari: Laterza).

TUTELEERS, P., and HEBBERECHT, P. (1997), 'Drug Tourism and Drugs Smuggling in Rotterdam', paper presented at the seminar 'The Informal Economy: Threat and Opportunity in the City', Max Planck Institute, Freiburg, 13–15 November.

UNITED NATIONS (1987), *The UN and Drug Abuse Control* (New York: United Nations).

—— (1996), *Report on the Mission of the Special Rapporteur to Poland on the Issue of Trafficking and Forced Prostitution in Women* (Vienna: UN).

—— (1997), *World Drug Report* (Oxford: Oxford University Press).

VAN HOOREBEEK, B. (1997), 'Prospects for Reconstructing Aetiology', *Theoretical Criminology* 1(4): 501–18.

VIET, V. (1998), *La France immigrée. Construction d'une politique* (Paris: Fayard).

VIVIANI, R. (1977), *Poesie* (Naples: Guida).

VOGELWEITH, A., and VAUDANO, M. (1995), *Mains propres. Mains liées* (Paris: Austral).

WALLERSTEIN, I. (1995), *After Liberalism* (New York: The New Press).

WALTON, P., and YOUNG, J. (1998) (eds.), *The New Criminology Revisited* (London: Macmillan).

WHYNES, D., and BEAN, P. (eds.) (1991), *Policing and Prescribing. The British System of Drug Control* (London: Macmillan).

WHYTE, F. W. (1943), *Street Corner Society* (Chicago, Ill.: University of Chicago Press).

WILLIAMS, P. (ed.) (1997), 'Illegal Immigration and Commercial Sex: The New Slave Trade', special issue of *Trends in Organized Crime* 3(4).

WILLIAMS, R. (1985), *The Country and the City* (London: Hogarth).

WILLIAMS, T. (1989), *The Cocaine Kids* (Reading: Addison-Wesley).

WILSON, J. Q. (1990), 'Corruption: The Shame of the State' in Heidenheimer, A., Johnson, M., and LeVine, V. (eds.), *Political Corruption: A Handbook* (New Brunswick, NJ: Transactions).

—— and KELLING, G. (1982), 'Broken Windows', *Atlantic Review*, March: 29–38.

WINER, J. M. (1996), 'Alien Smuggling: Transnational Crime Versus National Borders', paper presented at *Working Group on Organized Crime*, National Strategy Information Center, Washington, 8 October.

WORLD DEVELOPMENT MOVEMENT (1994), *Inquiry into the Pergau Hydro-Electric Project, the Aid and Trade Provision and the Implications of Overseas Aid Expenditure* (London: World Development Movement).

—— (1995), *Gunrunners' Gold. How the Public's Money Finances Arms Sales* (London: World Development Movement).

YOUNG, J. (1988), 'Radical Criminology in Britain: The Emergence of a Competing Paradigm', *British Journal of Criminology* 28: 159–83.

—— (1998), 'From Inclusive to Exclusive Society: Nightmares in the European Dream' in Ruggiero, V., South, N., and Taylor, I. (eds.), *The New European Criminology* (London: Routledge).

—— (1999), *The Exclusive Society* (London: Sage).

ZAMAGNI, S. (1990), *Dalla periferia al centro* (Bologna: Il Mulino).

ZIMRING, F. E., and HAWKINS, G. (1992), *The Search for Rational Drug Control* (Cambridge: Cambridge University Press).

Index